THE ACTIVE READER
FOR WRITERS

SANDRA PANMAN, M.A., M.P.S.
STATE UNIVERSITY OF NEW YORK AT NEW PALTZ

RICHARD PANMAN, PH.D.
STATE UNIVERSITY OF NEW YORK AT NEW PALTZ

ACTIVE LEARNING CORPORATION
NEW PALTZ, NEW YORK
(845) 255-0844

THE ACTIVE READER FOR WRITERS

Address all inquiries to:

Active Learning Corporation
P.O. Box 254
New Paltz, New York 12561

Phone/Fax: (845) 255-0844
Email: info@activelearningcorp.com
www.activelearningcorp.com

Cover Art: Cami Fischer
Cover Typestyles: Albertus Capitals, Script MT, New Berline (logo)
Text Design: Linda Gluck
Typestyles: Palatino and Helvetica Black
Typesetting: AB Typesetting
Printed in the United States of America/Victor Graphics 2007

ISBN-13: 978-0-912813-37-0
ISBN-10: 0-912813-37-7

Dedication

This book is dedicated to my mother, Jean Garson, an immigrant, single parent, and woman of little means who steadfastly and wholeheartedly encouraged my passion for reading and writing. She knew then, as many parents struggling at the poverty level today also know — education is the way out.

Sandra Panman

ACKNOWLEDGMENTS

Every reasonable effort has been made to trace the owners of copyrighted materials in this book, but in some instances this has proven impossible. The publishers will be glad to receive information leading to more complete acknowledgments in subsequent printings of the book, and in the meantime extend their apologies for any omissions.

BRUCE BALDWIN "Stand Up for Yourself" © 1987 by Bruce A. Baldwin. Reprinted by permission of *PACE* magazine (Piedmont Airlines), February 1987, Greensboro, N.C.

BRUNO BETTELHEIM "About Discipline" from *A Good Enough Parent* by Bruno Bettelheim. Copyright ©1987 by Bruno Bettelheim. Reprinted by permission of Alfred A. Knopf Inc.

TADEUSZ BOROWSKI "This Way For The Gas, Ladies and Gentlemen" from *This Way For The Gas, Ladies and Gentlemen* by Tadeusz Borowski. Copyright © 1959 by Maria Borowski. English Translation copyright ©1967 by Penguin Books Ltd. All rights reserved. Reprinted by permission of Viking Penguin, a division of Penguin Books USA, Inc.

RAY BRADBURY "Tricks! Treats! Gangway!" from *Reader's Digest*, October 1975. Copyright ©1975 by Ray Bradbury. Reprinted by permission of Don Congdon Associates, Inc.

JANE BRODY "Exercise: A New Dietary Requirement" from *Jane Brody's Good Food Book, Living the High-Carbohydrate Way,* by Jane E. Brody. Reprinted by permission of W. W. Norton & Company, Inc. Copyright ©1985 by Jane E. Brody.

ETHAN CANIN "Emperor of the Air" from *Emperor of the Air* by Ethan Canin. Copyright ©1988 by Ethan Canin. Reprinted by permission of Houghton Mifflin Company.

RACHEL CARSON "The Birth and Death of Islands" from *The Sea Around Us*, Revised Edition, by Rachel L. Carson. Copyright ©1950, 1951, 1961 by Rachel L. Carson; renewed 1979 by Roger Christie. Reprinted by permission of Oxford University Press, Inc.

EUGENIA COLLIER "Sweet Potato Pie" Reprinted by permission of *Black World* Magazine and Eugenia Collier, ©1972 Johnson Publishing Company, Inc.

NORMAN COUSINS "Why Johnny Can't Write" from *Present Tense: An American Editor's Odyssey.* Copyright ©1967 by McGraw-Hill Book Company. Reprinted with permission.

JOAN DIDION "The Santa Ana" excerpt from "Los Angeles Notebook" from *Slouching Towards Bethlehem* by Joan Didion. Copyright ©1967, 1968 by Joan Didion. Reprinted with permission of Farrar, Straus and Giroux, Inc.

M. F. K. FISHER "Young Hunger" from *As They Were* by M. F. K. Fisher. Copyright ©1982 by M.K. Fisher. Reprinted by permission of Alfred A. Knopf, Inc.

DAVID P. GARDNER "A Nation at Risk." Essay excerpted from the 1982 *United States Commission on Excellence in Education Report* also entitled "A Nation at Risk."

WILLIAM GOLDING "Painted Faces and Long Hair" from *The Lord of the Flies* by William Golding. Copyright ©1954 by William Golding. Reprinted by permission of the Putnam Publishing Group.

MARTIN LUTHER KING, JR. "Letter From Birmingham Jail" from *Why We Can't Wait* by Martin Luther King, Jr. Copyright ©1963, 1964 by Martin Luther King, Jr. Reprinted by permission of Harper & Row, Publishers, Inc.

MICHAEL KRAMER "Free to Fly Inside the Cage" by Michael Kramer. Copyright ©1989 The Time Inc. Magazine Company. Reprinted by permission.

JAMES A. MICHENER from *Return to Paradise* by James A. Michener. Copyright ©1951 by James A. Michener. Reprinted by permission of Random House, Inc.

N. SCOTT MOMADAY "The Way to Rainy Mountain" first published in *The Reporter*, 26 January 1967. Reprinted from *The Way to Rainy Mountain*, ©1969, The University of New Mexico Press.

WILLIAM OUCHI "Japanese and American Workers: Two Casts of Mind" from *Theory Z*, ©1981, Addison-Wesley Publishing Co., Inc., Reading, Massachusetts. Reprinted by permission of the publisher.

H. ALLEN SMITH "How to Kill a Wasp" from *The Best of H. Allen Smith*, copyright ©1972 by H. Allen Smith. Reprinted by permission of the Harold Matson Company, Inc.

JOHN STEINBECK from *Cannery Row* by John Steinbeck. Copyright ©1945 by John Steinbeck. Copyright renewed © 1973 by Elaine Steinbeck, John Steinbeck IV and Thom Steinbeck. All rights reserved. Reprinted by permission of Viking Penguin, a division of Penguin Books USA, Inc.

GEORGE STEWART "Junk" from *Not So Rich as You Think* by George R. Stewart. Copyright ©1967 by George R. Stewart. Reprinted by permission of Houghton Mifflin Company.

JAMES THURBER "University Days" from *My Life and Hard Times*, published by Harper & Row. Copyright © 1933, 1961 by James Thurber.

JOHN UPDIKE "Spirituality" by John Updike. From "Making the Spiritual Connection," first published in *Lear's*, December 1989. Copyright ©1989 by John Updike. Reprinted by permission of the author.

MARGARET WALKER excerpt from "On Being Female, Black, and Free" by Margaret Walker is reprinted from *The Writer on Her Work*, edited by Janet Sternburg, by permission of W. W. Norton & Company, Inc. Copyright ©1980 by Janet Sternburg.

E. B. WHITE "The Three New Yorks" from "Here is New York," in *Essays of E. B. White*. Copyright ©1949 by E. B. White. Reprinted by permission of Harper & Row, Publishers, Inc.

RANDALL WILLIAMS "Daddy Tucked The Blanket" from *The New York Times*, July 10, 1975. Copyright ©1975 by The New York Times Company. Reprinted by permission.

MARIE WINN from *The Plug-In Drug* by Marie Winn. Copyright ©Marie Winn Miller, 1977. All rights reserved. Reprinted by permission of Viking Penguin, a division of Penguin Books USA, Inc.

WILLIAM ZINSSER "The Transaction" from *On Writing Well*, Second Edition, published by Harper & Row. Copyright ©1980 by William K. Zinsser. Reprinted by permission of the author.

CONTENTS

INTRODUCTION

HOW TO USE THIS BOOK

The ACTIVE READER for Writers is a collection of readings that illustrate effective writing. Model paragraphs and essays present excellent examples of the type of writing students will learn to master. The text has many interesting readings that will provoke much thought and discussion. The writing instruction based on these readings is straightforward and effective. Students will find this text to be both enjoyable and challenging to use.

TEXT PURPOSE

The ACTIVE READER for Writers is a reader with two major purposes. The first is to present model reading selections by professional writers on a variety of subjects that may serve to stimulate student writing. The Active Reading exercise following each selection explicates the passage and gives students practice in critical analysis. Specific questions about form and content encourage rereading of the model and help students comprehend the author's meaning.

The second purpose of this reader is to teach the techniques of professional writers, their styles and the way they present information. By studying the works of accomplished writers, students learn how to organize an essay: how to begin, how to develop paragraphs, how to make transitions, and how to conclude. Through this process students learn how to write, to make their own meaning comprehensible to others.

TEXT ORGANIZATION

The ACTIVE READER for Writers classifies reading selections by writing strategies. This offers several advantages. First, students see how writers handle different subjects using the same strategy. Second, students get to practice different patterns of writing and learn to use these "mental maps" to organize and convey information. Third, these strategies offer an excellent way to integrate reading and writing. Learning how to recognize and use these patterns will help students to become more efficient readers and more effective writers. Finally, this learning can be immediately applied by the student in all academic courses.

This book contains ten chapters, each of which has three reading selections of varying length and complexity: one paragraph, a short essay of three to five paragraphs, and an extended essay. The diverse topics are interesting and often provocative. Written by well known authors, each passage will capture the attention of readers and stir thoughts and feelings. The first chapter, "Paragraph and Essay Development," provides a general introduction. The remaining nine chapters each illustrate a specific pattern or strategy for reading and writing paragraphs and essays.

Narration, telling a story, is presented first because it is the earliest form of communication both historically and developmentally. The first strategy used by cave dwellers was to tell their stories in pictures on cave walls. The first strategy young children learn is story telling.

Description is presented next because a good narrative is improved by adding descriptive details that make the characters and events more vivid for the reader. Descriptive writing appeals to the five senses: sight, sound, taste, touch, and smell.

Illustration through the use of examples aims to make the writing more exciting for the reader. Examples can be used in any of the writing strategies, including all forms of exposition and persuasion.

Exposition is writing that informs the reader by explaining facts and ideas so that they are easily understood. The subject of an explanation might be a person, place, event, or idea. The key patterns of exposition are process analysis, comparison and contrast, classification, definition, and cause and effect.

Process Analysis explains how to do something, how to get somewhere, or why something is the way it is. This pattern presents a sequence of steps or events and shows how they are related to each other. **Comparison and Contrast** is used to explain the similarities and differences between subjects. **Classification** sorts information into groups or categories on the basis of shared characteristics. **Definition** is a way of identifying or making clear the meaning of a word, an object, or an abstract concept.

Cause and Effect writing is a form of exposition that explains relationships—how one thing leads to another—and tells why something is the way it is.

The last writing strategy in the text is **Persuasion and Argument**. Every day readers encounter messages that try to convince them to take an action, consider an idea, or accept an opinion. The writers of these messages support their main point with appeals to reason and emotion. The goal is to convince the reader to see things in a particular way.

The final chapter is followed by **Transitions**, a list of words and phrases for students to use in writing compositions. Transitions are links or connections made between sentences, paragraphs, or groups of paragraphs. By using transitions, a writer achieves coherence and unity. A **Glossary** of literary and rhetorical terms, many of which have been used and defined in context, follows the list of transitions. When these terms appear in chapter lessons, they are presented in bold type for emphasis.

A separate *Answer Key* booklet contains answers for all of the Active Reading exercises, a grading grid, and two progress charts. The Active Reading exercise can be scored using the answer key and grading grid. By entering grades in the progress charts, students create a visual record of their accomplishments. The "To The Teacher" section below has a detailed explanation of how this booklet may be used in conjunction with the text.

The reading selections presented in this text are separately bound in a booklet titled *Reading Models*. This valuable reference helps students to answer questions in the Active Reading exercise without having to turn back and forth from model to questions.

CHAPTER FORMAT

The introduction to each chapter defines the writing strategy to be learned and explains how the pattern is used. Brief, yet thorough, the introduction gives students an overview which prepares them for the reading selections and the activities that follow.

Each selection begins with biographical information about the author and background material that frames the context for the passage. The **Word Alert** list defines words from the reading model that students may need to know in order to comprehend the selection. Students can build vocabulary by previewing definitions and having them at hand as the words appear in context. These words are presented in alphabetical order which makes them easy to find. The student may want to use a dictionary to learn the meaning of other unfamiliar words.

Each chapter presents a different writing strategy. Readings for each chapter begin with a paragraph and include two essays, one moderate in length and the other longer and more complex. Paragraphs in each essay are identified by number in the margin. Selections are followed by **Active Reading** exercises that guide the student, paragraph by paragraph, through rereading with specific questions about the form and content of the passage. Questions in the Active Reading exercise are grouped to correspond with paragraphs in the reading model where answers can be found. Literary and rhetorical terms are introduced and defined in context.

This detailed analysis of the model helps to extend and sharpen students' understanding of each selection. Further discussion in class might examine alternative interpretations to the ones presented and consider other aspects of the author's topic. Active reading makes students more efficient readers by training them to identify important aspects of the model passage. This analytic approach to reading also helps students to become more effective writers.

Active reading analysis reveals the author's writing plan which students can then apply to their own writing. **Guided Writing** assignments at the end of each chapter help the student in planning, organizing, and expressing ideas in writing. Writing topics are followed by a prewriting exercise for generating ideas, detailed plans for writing paragraphs and essays, and a checklist to help students revise, edit and proofread their work.

The process of writing a paper can be divided into three stages: prewriting or planning, writing a first draft, and revising. The first step in writing anything is to gather the information. The prewriting exercises will help the student with this part of the process. Depending on the topic, students may rely on their own experience and creativity, conduct interviews, or do library research and use reference works to generate ideas and information.

The writing plan helps the student to organize and utilize the information collected. The plan guides the student through drafting of a paragraph or essay in steps parallel to the active reading analysis of model passages. This plan, specific to each strategy, presents an organizational sequence, suggests introductions, elicits the thesis statement, promotes the development of main points, and offers a variety of conclusions.

The checklist for revision in the Guided Writing section of each chapter will help the student to evaluate a composition in three areas: content, form, and mechanics. Students review content to make sure that main ideas are clearly stated and supported throughout the paper. They look at form to determine whether the draft is unified and coherent. Ideas must be logically connected to one another and to the main idea of the paragraph or essay. Proofreading is the final step in the revision process and involves reading to correct errors in mechanics: punctuation, capitalization, spelling, grammar, and usage.

CLASSROOM APPLICATION

The ACTIVE READER for Writers is designed to accommodate the needs of students and teachers in a variety of classroom settings: the writing workshop approach, the traditonal lecture format, and the individualized writing program. The text is flexible enough to be used with any of these structures separately, or in combination.

Active Reading

In a discussion group/writing workshop approach, the Active Reading section can be completed individually or as a group exercise. If students complete the Active Reading exercise individually, the teacher may choose to distribute the *Answer Key* booklets and have students grade their own work. As a group exercise, the Active Reading questions are answered in class as part of the discussion. To foster the active participation of students, have them read the selections in advance of class readings and discussions. Every student should have progress charts, so that they can enter grades and have a visual record of their accomplishments.

In a classroom with a traditional lecture format, the Active Reading exercise for each chapter may be used as a test of student comprehension. The teacher can grade these tests or have students grade them by exchanging papers. **Answer Key** booklets would be distributed for this purpose. Students enter grades on the progress chart, creating a vivid record of their accomplishments. Teachers who use the lecture format may require students to do the bulk of their reading and writing assignments as homework.

In an individualized writing program, each student works at his or her own pace consistent with goals established by student and teacher. These goals are often stated in a work contract that identifies the amount of work required of the student, per unit of time, to achieve a specific grade.

In this setting the student reads each selection, answers questions in the Active Reading exercise, and evaluates responses using the **Answer Key** booklet. This booklet makes it easy for the teacher to structure an individualized, self-paced program.

Guided Writing

The Guided Writing exercise is completed in much the same way regardless of how the course is structured. When the student drafts a composition, it is submitted for evaluation and either graded or returned for revision. All students should have the opportunity to incorporate instructor suggestions by revising a composition at least once before it is graded.

In a workshop environment feedback may be given publicly, both by the teacher and peers. Errors are often used as the basis for a discussion of correct grammar, usage, punctuation, and spelling. In the traditional classroom, feedback about written work is usually indicated by the teacher on the student's paper. Corrective work may be included in lectures and homework assignments. In an individualized program feedback is given one-to-one. The teacher recommends corrective exercises which students complete and grade on their own.

Upon completion of the lessons in this text, each student will have created thirty original pieces of writing (ten paragraphs and twenty essays) using all of the major writing strategies. An optional ancillary for this program, the *Writing Portfolio Organizer*, will help students organize and keep track of written work. This booklet works well in all classroom settings.

TO THE TEACHER

Personal recognition by the teacher can have a very powerful and positive effect in motivating the student to learn. Regardless of the setting in which feedback is given, we offer these guidelines for evaluating written work:

1. Instructors have different methods of correcting and grading papers. Whatever your method, be sure students understand how it works. We recommend that you take the time to explain your system and symbols to students.

2. To gain students' trust and confidence, the instructor must be patient and reward what is positive about student writing. Be tolerant of poor handwriting, spelling, and mechanics, especially at the beginning of the course. Be aware of each student's level of ability. Identify and praise the student for one positive quality: ideas, enthusiasm, choice of subject, willingness to work, etc.

3. Write neatly on the student's paper and keep your comments brief. Do not write over the student's work; use the top of the page or margins. If you like, have students double space drafts so you can write in between the lines. When there are many errors in a paper, focus on the three or four most frequent ones. As these are eliminated you can point out others. It is not a good idea to overwhelm students with criticism before they develop confidence in their ability to write.

4. Evaluate drafts and grade only the final copy. Most students will not read your comments, much less revise work, if their paper has already been graded. Indicate revisions needed to improve the student's paper, making your comments specific enough for the student to act on.

5. Sometimes, written comments will be adequate. At other times, you may wish to offer additional feedback in a one-to-one conference. Give the student the good news first. Recognition and praise will help the student to accept your constructive criticism.

6. Make certain students know that criticism of their work is not criticism of them. When conferring with a student, always try to ask a question or two that indicates personal interest in what the student has written. This is often a good way to end a conference because it reassures the student that you recognize him or her for being, as well as for doing.

THE
ACTIVE
READER
FOR WRITERS

Chapter 1

PARAGRAPH
AND
ESSAY
DEVELOPMENT

This introductory chapter explains the format of the textbook and shows you how to write organized paragraphs and essays. Learning about the structure of the paragraph will prepare you for writing essays. A paragraph is a group of related sentences that develop one main idea. The paragraph consists of a topic sentence, supporting details, and a concluding sentence.

A paragraph should begin with an interesting opener that attracts the reader's attention. You might start with an unusual fact, an amusing anecdote, a famous quote, a vivid description, or a provocative question. Every paragraph has a topic sentence that states the main idea and points the direction for the other sentences that follow. While the topic sentence is usually at the beginning, it may also appear in the middle or at the end of a paragraph. A topic sentence can be a generalization about or a summary of the content of a paragraph.

A good paragraph should be unified and coherent. A paragraph is unified when all of the sentences in it relate to a single topic. A paragraph is coherent when all sentences are logically related to one another. Each sentence should be linked, by word or thought, to the sentences that come before and after it. Transitional words and phrases help to connect ideas. As you read models of paragraphs and essays, awareness of transitions will help you to understand the author's ideas. As you write your own paragraphs and essays, use transitions to help connect your ideas. Refer to the list of transitional words and phrases that begins on page 259 of this book.

To adequately develop your paragraph use supporting details such as examples, facts, reasons, descriptions, explanations, and opinions. Include enough details so that the reader understands the topic and the point you are making. To be effective, a paragraph needs a good closing sentence that restates the main idea, draws a conclusion, reaches a decision, or offers a personal opinion.

All writing has a point of view. Whoever is telling a story, describing, explaining something, or trying to persuade has a position as either a first or third-person narrator. The first-person narrator is talking as a participant in the action while the third-person narrator, speaking from a position outside of the action, is an observer of events.

Once you have learned to write an effective paragraph, you are capable of writing effective essays. Like a paragraph, an essay has an introduction, a development section, and a conclusion. An essay is defined as a composition with a thesis statement. This statement usually appears in the first paragraph and does the following: states the main idea, reflects the author's purpose to inform, to persuade, or to entertain (amuse), and asserts a point of view. The thesis statement may also include a plan for the essay.

Paragraphs following the introduction develop the topic through supporting details: examples, facts, reasons, descriptions, explanations, opinions, etc. The concluding paragraph(s) of an essay restates the topic and summarizes main points. Several of the selections in this text are excerpts from short stories. These passages, like essays, have a central theme, a purpose, a point of view, and above all something important to say to the reader.

While chapters in this text focus on different writing strategies, they are similar in structure: each contains three reading selections of various lengths (see box below). A short introduction to the author is followed by vocabulary with terms defined, to help you better understand the reading model. Active Reading exercises help to extend and sharpen your understanding of the selection and the writing strategy emphasized. The Guided Writing section at the end of each chapter takes you step-by-step through the writing process, and helps you to write original compositions. The work can be fun, even exhilarating as you realize that you, like the famous authors in this text, can create art with words.

Chapter Selections

The Way to Rainy Mountain *by N. Scott Momaday*

Painted Faces and Long Hair *by William Golding*

Young Hunger *by M. F. K. Fisher*

THE WAY TO RAINY MOUNTAIN

by N. Scott Momaday

N. Scott Momaday was born in 1934 in Lawton, Oklahoma, and was educated in the ways of the Kiowa Indians by his grandmother. His formal education was at the University of New Mexico and at Stanford University. He teaches English at the University of Arizona and has strong interests in American Indian art, history, and culture. Mr. Momaday's book, House Made of Dawn (1968), won the Pulitzer Prize for fiction. In The Way to Rainy Mountain (1969), a collection of Kiowa Indian folk tales, he retells the Kiowa myths that he learned from his grandmother and describes the Indian life he knew as a child. In the first paragraph of introduction to this autobiographical narrative, Momaday describes how the seasons shape the landscape of Rainy Mountain.

Word Alert

anvil	a heavy iron or steel block with a flat, smooth top on which metals are shaped by hammering
foliage	a cluster of leaves, flowers, and branches
grove	a small wood or group of trees without underbrush
Kiowa	member of an American Indian people of Colorado, Kansas, New Mexico, Oklahoma, and Texas
knoll	a small rounded hill or mound
isolate	solitary; alone
linear	of, pertaining to, or resembling a straight line
willow	a deciduous tree or shrub with narrow leaves, flowers, and strong lightweight wood
witch hazel	a shrub of eastern North America bearing yellow flowers that bloom in late autumn or winter
writhe	to move with a twisting or contorted motion

A single knoll rises out of the plain in Oklahoma, north and west of the Wichita Range. For my people, the Kiowas, it is an old landmark, and they gave it the name Rainy Mountain. The hardest weather in the world is there. Winter brings blizzards, hot tornadic winds arise in the spring, and in summer the prairie is an anvil's edge. The grass turns brittle and brown, and it cracks beneath your feet. There are green belts along the rivers and creeks, linear groves of hickory and pecan, willow and witch hazel. At a distance in July or August the steaming foliage seems almost to writhe in fire. Great green and yellow grasshoppers are everywhere in the tall grass, popping up like corn to sting the flesh, and tortoises crawl about on the red earth, going nowhere in the plenty of time. Loneliness is an aspect of the land. All things in the plain are isolate; there is no confusion of objects in the eye, but *one* hill or *one* tree or *one* man. To look upon that landscape in the early morning, with the sun at your back, is to lose the sense of proportion. Your imagination comes to life, and this, you think, is where Creation was begun.

ACTIVE READING

The Active Reading exercise gives you an opportunity to reread the paragraph with a critical eye. By answering the questions that follow, you will extend and sharpen your understanding of the selection. This activity will help you become a more efficient reader and a more effective writer. The first sentence gets the reader's attention by telling about the geographical location of the subject, without naming it. This makes us curious and we want to know more.

1. Where is the knoll located?

2. The next sentence, the topic sentence, tells the reader the subject of the paragraph. What is the topic sentence of this paragraph?

The author develops his paragraph with supporting details by offering facts, descriptions and examples related to the topic. The narrator tells us that Rainy Mountain has the hardest weather in the world and gives examples. For each season, find and write the phrase that tells about the weather.

3. winter:

4. spring:

5. summer:

The narrator says that the prairie is an anvil's edge. This kind of comparison, where one object is said to be the other, is called a **metaphor**. While a prairie and an anvil's edge are two very different things, the author wants us to see the prairie as having the qualities of an anvil's edge: flat, smooth, and razor sharp. In a metaphor, the qualities of one object are attributed to the other.

6. What season does the author choose to describe in detail?

The summer season becomes the focus of the paragraph. The author gives details about the land and animals that live on it. Using phrases or sentences, answer the questions below.

7. How does the author describe the grass?
8. What can be found along the rivers and creeks?
9. How do the leaves, flowers, and branches appear in July or August?
10. What are the grasshoppers doing?

". . . grasshoppers . . . popping up like corn" is an example of a **simile,** using the words *like* or *as* to make a comparison between two basically unlike things. The author is saying that grasshoppers are like corn in that both pop up out of the ground.

11. What are the tortoises doing and where are they going?

The narrator concludes the paragraph by referring to the emotional impact this land has on people.

12. What emotion does the author associate with the land?
13. What contributes to this sense of loneliness?
14. What are some examples of this isolation?
15. What other effect does viewing the landscape have?
16. What does this change in perception lead to?

The concluding sentence summarizes the point of the paragraph and reminds the reader of the topic.

17. The narrator of this paragraph puts himself in the scene. What point of view, first or third-person, has the narrator adopted?

Transitions are words and phrases that are used to connect ideas in order to show time, place or position, and relationships between ideas. They are also used to restate main ideas, draw conclusions, or show comparison and contrast. The author uses the following transitional words and phrases in this paragraph: out of, for, and, beneath, along, at a distance, like, on, but, or, upon, with.

Find them in the model paragraph to see how they are used. A complete list of transitions for your reference can be found at the back of this book.

18. The author's primary purpose in this selection is to:
    a. inform
    b. persuade
    c. entertain (amuse)

The Active Reading exercise can be scored using the answer key and grading grid. Enter your grade in the progress chart.

GUIDED WRITING

The Guided Writing section at the end of this chapter (page 20) provides topics and plans for writing paragraphs and essays. Select a topic and write a paragraph by following the writing plan that begins on page 21.

Continue work in this chapter until you have finished all three Active Reading and Guided Writing activities. Upon completion, you will have written three new compositions for your portfolio (one paragraph and two essays). Record grades in your progress chart and, if available, on the Academic Credit Statement in your *Writing Portfolio Organizer*.

PAINTED FACES AND LONG HAIR
by William Golding

William Golding was born in 1911 in Cornwall, England and educated at Oxford University. A highly imaginative and original writer, Golding is basically concerned with the eternal nature of man. In his best known work, Lord of the Flies *(1954), he describes the nightmarish adventures of a group of English schoolboys stranded on an uninhabited island and traces their degeneration from a state of innocence to that of blood lust and savagery. In writing about the theme of evil, he exposes man stripped of all the sanctions of custom and civilization, man alone in his essence. The excerpt presented here, which takes place early in the novel, describes a day on the island from dawn to dusk.*

Word Alert

blatant	completely obvious, conspicuous, brazen
menaced	threatened
mirage	an optical illusion; something illusory and unattainable
opalescence	the quality or state of exhibiting a milky iridescence like that of an opal
perpendicular	a line at right angles to the horizon; vertical; exactly upright
stark	bare, desolate, barren; having few or no ornaments
whelming	to cover or engulf completely; overwhelm

The first rhythm that they became used to was the slow swing from dawn to quick dusk. They accepted the pleasures of morning, the bright sun, the whelming sea and sweet air, as a time when play was good and life so full that hope was not necessary and therefore forgotten. Toward noon, as the floods of light fell more nearly to the perpendicular, the stark colors of the morning were smoothed in pearl and opalescence; and the heat—as though the impending sun's height gave it momentum—became a blow that they ducked, running to the shade and lying there, perhaps even sleeping.

2   Strange things happened at midday. The glittering sea rose up, moved apart in planes of blatant impossibility; the coral reef and the few stunted palms that clung to the more elevated parts would float up into the sky, would quiver, be plucked apart, run like raindrops on a wire or be repeated as in an odd succession of mirrors. Sometimes land loomed where there was no land and flicked out like a bubble as the children watched. Piggy discounted all this learnedly as a "mirage"; and since no boy could reach even the reef over the stretch of water where the snapping sharks waited, they grew accustomed to these mysteries and ignored them, just as they ignored the miraculous, throbbing stars. At midday the illusions merged into the sky and there the sun gazed down like an angry eye.

3   Then, at the end of the afternoon, the mirage subsided and the horizon became level and blue and clipped as the sun declined. That was another time of comparative coolness but menaced by the coming of the dark. When the sun sank, darkness dropped on the island like an extinguisher and soon the shelters were full of restlessness, under the remote stars.

ACTIVE READING

The Active Reading exercise gives you an opportunity to reread the essay with a critical eye. By answering the questions that follow, you will extend and sharpen your understanding of the selection. This activity will help you become a more efficient reader and more effective writer.

INTRODUCTORY PARAGRAPH   (par. 1)

The first sentence introduces the topic and reveals the author's plan for the development of the essay.

1. What is the topic sentence of this paragraph?
2. What words in the topic sentence reveal the author's plan to tell us about a day on the island?
3. Name three pleasures of the morning that the author refers to as he begins to develop this paragraph.
4. Why is the hope of rescue forgotten in the morning?

The transition from morning to noon is made through a reference to light, color, and heat.

5. Toward noon, the sun moves higher in the sky. How does this affect the floods of light from the sun (the angle of the sun's rays)?

6. In what way does the light change the stark colors of the morning?

"Toward noon . . . the heat . . . .became a blow that they ducked . . ." This kind of comparison, where one object is said to be the other, is called a metaphor. While intense heat and a blow (a forceful stroke) are two very different things, they can both inflict pain and are to be avoided.

7. How did the boys react to the noonday heat?

DEVELOPMENT PARAGRAPH   *(par. 2)*

8. Which sentence clearly states the topic to be developed in this paragraph?

9-11. The author supports the topic with examples and descriptions of strange things that happened. List three of these using sentences or phrases.

12. With what word does Piggy discount each of these mysteries?

13. Why did the boys ignore these mysteries?

14. Which sentence concludes and reinforces the topic of this paragraph?

". . . the sun gazed down like an angry eye" is an example of a simile, using the words *like* or *as* to make a comparison between two basically unlike objects. The author is saying that the sun, like an angry eye, is penetrating and hurtful.

15. The writer not only likens the sun to an eye, but also suggests that the sun has emotions. What human emotion does the author attribute to the sun?

CONCLUDING PARAGRAPH *(par. 3)*

16. What is the topic of this paragraph?

17. What happened as the sun declined?

18-22. Write five phrases from this paragraph that describe what happened on the island by the end of the afternoon.

23. Write the phrase from this paragraph that is a simile.

24. What two things are being compared in the simile above?

25. What do darkness and an extinguisher have in common?

The concluding sentence of this paragraph reminds us of the topic with a reference to the end of the day.

26. The narrator is outside the action and an observer of events. What is the point of view of the narrator?

This essay uses transitional words to link ideas and show changes in time and position as the story moves from dawn to dusk. The first column below contains ten of these transitions, and the second a list of words or phrases. Match each transition with the word or phrase it is linked to in the text.

27. first
28. toward
29. as
30. at
31. sometimes
32. since
33. then
34. when
35. soon
36. under

a. no boy could reach
b. the remote stars
c. the floods of light fell
d. rhythm
e. at the end of the afternoon
f. the sun sank
g. the shelters were full of restlessness
h. land loomed
i. noon
j. midday

37. The author's primary purpose in this selection is to:
   a. inform
   b. persuade
   c. entertain (amuse)

The Active Reading exercise can be scored using the answer key and grading grid. Enter your grade in the progress chart.

GUIDED WRITING

The Guided Writing section at the end of this chapter (page 20) provides topics and plans for writing paragraphs and essays. Select a topic and write a short essay by following the writing plan that begins on page 22. Continue work in this chapter until you have finished all three Active Reading and Guided Writing activities.

YOUNG HUNGER

by M. F. K. Fisher

Born in Michigan in 1908, M(ary) F(rances) K(ennedy) Fisher was raised in Whittier, California. She was educated at the University of California, Los Angeles and at the University of Dijon in France. For many years she wrote a newspaper column about cooking for The New York Times, *and is well known for her books on food and wines. Her most recent book,* Two Towns in Provence *(1983), discusses her gastronomical and other experiences in post-war France. In "Young Hunger," an essay from this book, Fisher remembers what it was like to be young and to be hungry. Fisher wrote: "I continue to be interested in the problems of aging. I enjoy the practice and contemplation of adapting the need to eat to the need to be properly nourished." This autobiographical narrative tells a story about her visit with her elderly godparents.*

amply	plentiful, more than adequate
avidity	excessive desire, greed
concave	hollowed or rounded inward like the inside of a bowl; curved in
conceited	self-centered; concerned only with oneself
deftly	skillfully; competent with the hands; dexterous
indescribably	beyond description
literally	actual, obvious; adhering to the fact; the truth, exact
pièce de résistance	the chief dish of a meal; an outstanding item, a showpiece
sedentary	staying in one area; not migratory
solitude	isolation, seclusion, being alone
wince	to flinch, recoil, shrink back from pain

It is very hard for people who have passed the age of, say, fifty to remember with any charity the hunger of their own puberty and adolescence when they are dealing with the young human animals who may be frolicking about them. Too often I have seen good people helpless with exasperation and real anger upon finding in the morning that cupboards and iceboxes have been stripped of their supplies by two or three youths—or even one—who apparently could have eaten four times their planned share at the dinner table the night before.

2   Such avidity is revolting, once past. But I can recall its intensity still; I am not yet too far from it to understand its ferocious demands when I see a fifteen-year-old boy wince and whiten at the prospect of waiting politely a few more hours for food, when his guts are howling for meat—bread—candy—fruit—cheese—milkmilkmilk—ANYTHING IN THE WORLD TO EAT.

3   I can still remember my almost insane desperation when I was about eighteen and was staying overnight with my comparatively aged godparents. I had come home alone from France in a bad continuous storm and was literally concave with solitude and hunger. The one night on the train seemed even rougher than those on board ship, and by the time I reached my godparents' home I was almost lightheaded.

4   I got there just in time for lunch. It is clear as ice in my mind: a little cup of very weak chicken broth, one salted cracker, one-half piece of thinly sliced toast, and then, ah then, a whole waffle, crisp and brown and with a piece of beautiful butter melting in its middle—which the maid deftly cut into four sections! One section she put on my godmother's plate. The next *two*, after a nod of approval from her mistress, she put on mine. My godfather ate the fourth.

5   There was a tiny pot of honey, and I dutifully put a dab of it on my piggish portion, and we all nibbled away and drank one cup apiece of tea with lemon. Both my godparents left part of their waffles.

6   It was simply that they were old and sedentary and quite out of the habit of eating amply with younger people: a good thing for them, but pure hell for me. I did not have the sense to explain to them how starved I was—which I would not hesitate to do now. Instead I prowled around my bedroom while the house slumbered through its afternoon siesta, wondering if I dared to sneak to the strange kitchen for something, anything, to eat, and knowing I would rather die than meet the silent, stern maid or my nice, gentle little hostess.

7   Later we walked slowly down to the village, and I was thinking sensuously of double malted ice-cream sodas at the corner drugstore, but

there was no possibility of such heaven. When we got back to the quiet house, the maid brought my godfather a tall glass of exquisitely rich milk, with a handful of dried fruit on the saucer under it, because he had been ill; but as we sat and watched him unwillingly down it, his wife said softly that it was such a short time until dinner that she was sure I did not want to spoil my appetite, and I agreed with her because I was young and shy.

When I dressed, I noticed that the front of my pelvic basin jutted out like two bricks under my skirt: I looked like a scarecrow.   *8*

Dinner was very long, but all I can remember is that it had, as *pièce de résistance*, half of the tiny chicken previously boiled for broth at luncheon, which my godmother carved carefully so that we should each have a bit of the breast and I, as guest, should have the leg, after a snippet had been sliced from it for her husband, who liked dark meat too.   *9*

There were hot biscuits, yes, the smallest I have ever seen, two apiece under a napkin on a silver dish. Because of them we had no dessert: it would be too rich, my godmother said.   *10*

We drank little cups of decaffeinized coffee on the screened porch in the hot Midwestern night, and when I went up to my room I saw that the maid had left a large glass of rich malted milk beside my poor god-father's bed.   *11*

My train would leave before five in the morning, and I slept little and unhappily, dreaming of the breakfast I would order on it. Of course when I finally saw it all before me, twinkling on the Pullman silver dishes, I could eat very little, from too much hunger and a sense of outrage.   *12*

I felt that my hosts had been indescribably rude to me, and selfish and conceited and stupid. Now I know that they were none of these things. They had simply forgotten about any but their own dwindling and cautious needs for nourishment. They had forgotten about being hungry, being young, being . . .   *13*

ACTIVE READING

The Active Reading exercise gives you an opportunity to reread the essay with a critical eye. By answering the questions that follow, you will extend and sharpen your understanding of the selection. This activity will help you become a more efficient reader and a more effective writer.

INTRODUCTORY PARAGRAPHS   *(par. 1–2)*

While the author introduces the topic in the first paragraph, she uses the second one to illustrate the topic. Her story really begins in paragraph three. This is a longer essay with more development paragraphs than the previous model passage.

1. The **thesis statement** in the first paragraph presents the main idea, reflects the author's purpose, and asserts a point of view. This thesis is supported throughout the essay with details including facts, examples, and descriptions. What is the thesis statement of this essay?

2. How do older people respond to having their cupboards and ice boxes stripped of their supplies by youths?

3. Paragraph two offers an example of the hunger of a fifteen year old boy. What words illustrate his intense desire for food?

DEVELOPMENT PARAGRAPH   *(par. 3)*

Paragraph three provides a **setting** for the story by offering some background information.

4. How old is the narrator at the time of her visit?

5. With whom is she staying?

6. What two strong words does the author use in this paragraph to sum up her recollection of the overnight visit?

7. Where has she come from?

8. How does the narrator feel by the time she reaches her godparents' home?

DEVELOPMENT PARAGRAPHS   *(par. 4–5)*

Paragraphs four and five describe lunch in detail. The narrator tells about the skimpy offerings and, by her choice of words, lets us know that she is disappointed.

9-11. What three foods are offered first and how is each described?

12. What food does the maid serve that stirs the narrator's interest?

13. Here the description takes on a positive tone, showing a change in the narrator's attitude. What words let you know that the sight of the waffle excites the narrator?

An **inference** is a reasonable conclusion about the behavior of a character or the meaning of an event drawn from limited details supplied by the author.

14-19. What six statements lead the reader to infer that the narrator is unhappy with her share of the waffle and the size of the portions?

DEVELOPMENT PARAGRAPH   *(par. 6)*

In paragraph six, the narrator compares her behavior with that of her godparents and offers an explanation as to why each of them—she and her godparents— behaved as they did.

20. Why were the godparents unaware of her hunger?

21. Why did the narrator say nothing?

22. What did she do instead?

"The house slumbered" is an example of **personification**, a figure of speech in which human qualities are attributed to an animal, object, or idea. A house can't sleep, but people in it do. The narrator uses this figure of speech to emphasize how quiet the house is with everyone asleep.

23. Why didn't she go to the kitchen for something to eat?

DEVELOPMENT PARAGRAPHS   *(par. 7–8)*

Paragraphs seven and eight detail the narrator's fantasy about food, telling what happens and why she doesn't get what she wants.

24. What does the narrator think about during the walk to the village? .

25. Back at the house, the maid brought the godfather some food. What did she bring him?

26. Why didn't the godmother offer the girl any food?

27. Why wasn't the author able to satisfy her desire for food?

28. Noticing how thin she is, the narrator compares herself to:

DEVELOPMENT PARAGRAPHS   *(par. 9–11)*

In paragraphs nine, ten, and eleven the topic is dinner. The writer's **tone**, her attitude toward the subject, is evident in her frequent references to small portions. Through **repetition**, the reader is reminded of the topic and prepared for the contrast between what the narrator gets and what her godfather gets.

Almost every item of food is referred to as small in some way. In the exercise below, match the food with its appropriate description. For each numbered item, write the letter that is a match.

29. hot biscuits   a. half of the tiny

30. decaffeinized coffee   b. a bit of the

31. breast   c. a snippet from the

32. leg   d. the smallest

33. chicken   e. little cups of

Only one item of food is described as large and it is introduced last, for emphasis, because it is exactly what the young girl wants.

34. What is this food and who is it for?

35. Taking what you have read in these paragraphs into account, is the author's reference to the chicken as *pièce de résistance* straightforward or sarcastic?

CONCLUDING PARAGRAPHS   *(par. 12–13)*

In the last two paragraphs of this essay the narrator is still focused on food. The narrator shifts from past to present in closing sentences in order to compare her feelings about the experience, then and now.

36. How does the narrator describe her sleep the night before she departs by train?

37. What happens when the food she dreamt about is put in front of her?

38. How did the girl feel about her hosts at the time?

At the close of the essay the narrator, in present time, realizes that her godparents' behavior was a result of their own dwindling and cautious need for nourishment.

39. What do you think accounts for her changed attitude?

40. What had her godparents forgotten?

41. The author uses transitional words and phrases to link ideas in this essay. List at least five.

42. The author's primary purpose in this selection is to:
    a. inform
    b. persuade
    c. entertain (amuse)

As a first-person narrator, the young woman is a character in the story and directly involved in the action. Throughout the essay, we experience the author's exasperation at being hungry all of the time. Because the paragraphs are well developed and include many details and vivid descriptions, the reader can identify with the young woman and feel her frustration, her anger, and above all her hunger.

The Active Reading exercise can be scored using the answer key and grading grid. Enter your grade in the progress chart.

GUIDED WRITING

The Guided Writing section that begins on the next page provides topics and plans for writing paragraphs and essays. Select a topic and write an extended essay by following the writing plan that begins on page 22.

GUIDED WRITING

This part of the chapter will help you apply what you have learned about writing paragraphs and essays. All three of the model passages you read in this chapter use description, narration or a combination of the two. The paragraph from "The Way to Rainy Mountain" describes a place. The short essay entitled "Painted Faces and Long Hair" describes a day on a deserted island and uses the passage of time, from morning to night, to tell what is happening. The extended essay, "Young Hunger," is primarily a narrative that also uses description.

Choose one of the topics listed below for each writing assignment that you do. If you want to write about something else, ask your instructor if the topic is appropriate for writing narration or description. Using either of these strategies, follow the plan that applies to write your composition. Submit your completed composition to the instructor for evaluation. When you receive a grade for this work, enter it in the progress chart.

WRITING TOPICS

- Describe an unusual place that you have visited.
- Describe a person, place, or thing that symbolizes your ethnic roots as did N. Scott Momaday in "The Way To Rainy Mountain."
- Tell about a day in your life and describe the changes you experienced.
- Use one of the following sentences or phrases from "Painted Faces and Long Hair" to start your own paragraph or essay:

  The first rhythm that they became used to was the slow swing from dawn to quick dusk.

  Strange things happened at midday.

  At the end of the afternoon . . .

- Tell about a time when you felt one way but acted another because you were too shy to ask for what you wanted, or didn't want to hurt someone's feelings.
- Tell about a time when you experienced an emotion so strongly that it was all you could think about. Describe your feelings and offer examples, as did the narrator in "Young Hunger."

PREWRITING: GENERATING IDEAS

Now that you have selected a topic, you will need to gather information and generate ideas before you begin to write. If you choose to tell a story, first provide information about the setting, the time and place of the narrative. Identify the major character(s) and decide the narrator's point of view. Then make a list, in chronological order, of the events that occur. You will be using this sequence of events to build the plot of your story: what is happening, to whom, and why. Decide the main point of your narrative and how it will end. Use the information you gather and your list of events as you follow the plan for writing a narrative paragraph or essay.

If you choose to describe a person, place, thing, or idea, you will be creating vivid images for the reader by appealing to the five senses. List the ways in which your subject appeals to one or more of the following: sight, sound, taste, smell and touch. You may decide to focus on one, some, or all of the five senses to describe your subject. Use this list as you follow the plan for writing a descriptive paragraph or essay.

WRITING PLAN: THE PARAGRAPH

1. Decide the point of view of the narrator, first or third person. Create an introduction that gets the reader's attention. Introduce your topic in the beginning of the paragraph.

2. Develop the topic adequately by including enough supporting details so that the reader clearly understands the point you are making. Details include facts, examples, descriptions, and explanations.

3. In a narrative provide specific details about the characters, what is happening to them, and why. In a descriptive paragraph appeal to as many of the five senses as you can, so that your words paint a picture for the reader.

4. Write a conclusion to your paragraph that reminds the reader of the topic by summarizing, reaching a conclusion, or expressing an opinion.

5. To create unity in your writing, make sure that each sentence in the paragraph relates to the topic. Your writing will be coherent if ideas follow one another in a logical pattern and sentences flow smoothly from one to the other. Use transitions to link or connect ideas. The list of transitional words and phrases at the back of this book is for your use and reference when you write (see pages 259–264).

6. Use variety in your choice of words to maintain reader interest. Where appropriate, use **figurative language** to increase the impact of your words and to stimulate the reader's imagination. The most commonly used figures of speech are the simile, metaphor, personification, and hyperbole. Definitions of literary and rhetorical terms can be found in the Glossary on pages 265–270.

7. Create a title for your paragraph, a word or phrase that captures the reader's interest and tells what you are writing about.

8. Use the *Checklist for Revision* provided at the end of this section to help you review and revise your paragraph.

WRITING PLAN: SHORT AND EXTENDED ESSAYS

While short and extended essays are similar—both have introductory and concluding paragraphs—the extended essay has more development paragraphs. "Painted Faces and Long Hair," a short descriptive essay, has one development paragraph. "Young Hunger" is a thirteen-paragraph extended narrative. Note that "Young Hunger" also has two introductory and two concluding paragraphs. Development paragraphs in both essays use vivid details to create a feeling, while the latter essay also develops plot and characters.

Introductory Paragraph(s)

1. Decide the point of view of the narrator, first or third person. Begin with a strong statement or a question that appeals to the reader's interest.

2. Begin with a statement(s) that challenges the reader's imagination. Tell what the essay is about by introducing your topic and purpose. This is the thesis statement, the main idea to be supported throughout the essay.

3. If you are writing a narrative essay, introduce the setting, characters, and background information. If you are writing a descriptive essay, use vivid details to introduce the setting and create a mood.

4. State your plan for the development of this essay. In an extended essay, more than one paragraph may be used to introduce the setting and provide background information.

Development Paragraph(s)

1. In a narrative essay, use your development paragraphs to build the plot through the sequence of events that occur. Provide specific details about the characters and tell what is happening to them, and why. Use this information to support your thesis statement, build the plot, and lead to the climax of your story.

2. If you are writing an extended narrative, you can use the development paragraphs to include more details, more events, and build a more intricate plot.

3. In a descriptive essay, each development paragraph can be used to examine a different aspect of your subject. Appeal to as many of the five senses as you can and include enough details, so that your words paint a picture for the reader.

4. If you are writing an extended descriptive essay, you can use each development paragraph to focus on a different aspect of your subject.

5. All sentences in a paragraph should relate to the topic and to one another. All paragraphs in an essay should support the topic and follow some logical order. Use transitions to link ideas within paragraphs and to make connections between paragraphs. Refer to the list of transitional words and phrases on pages 259–264.

6. Use variety in your choice of words to maintain reader interest. Where appropriate, use figurative language to increase the impact of your words and to stimulate the reader's imagination. The most commonly used figures of speech are the simile, metaphor, personification, and hyperbole. Definitions of literary and rhetorical terms can be found in the Glossary on pages 265–270.

Concluding Paragraph(s)

1. In concluding a narrative essay let the reader know the point of your story, either directly or indirectly. Express your opinion about the outcome of the narrative.

2. In a descriptive essay, let the reader know how you feel about the subject you are describing. Provide details about the subject that account for your feelings previously described.

3. In both narration and description let the reader know the outcome of the essay by summarizing, offering an opinion, or drawing a conclusion that reinforces the point of the essay.

4. More than one paragraph may be used to conclude an extended essay, as is the case with "Young Hunger."

5. The checklist on the next page will help you to review and revise your essay.

note: The title of your essay should be a word or phrase that captures the reader's attention and tells what you are writing about. Create a title for your first draft and review it before making it final.

CHECKLIST FOR REVISION

1. My paragraph/essay has a first- or third-person point of view. I begin with a strong statement that gets the reader's attention and introduce my topic. If I am writing an essay, my thesis statement appears in the opening paragraph(s).

2. In writing narration I introduce the setting, characters, and provide background information. To build the plot, I offer details about what is happening, to whom, and why.

3. The development paragraphs of my narrative essay include details and events that help me to build a more intricate plot.

4. In concluding my narrative paragraph or essay, I restate the point of my story and express my opinion about the outcome.

5. In writing description, I use vivid details to introduce the setting and create a mood. I appeal to one or more of the five senses to paint a picture for the reader.

6. Each development paragraph of my descriptive essay focuses on a different aspect of the subject.

7. In concluding my descriptive paragraph or essay, I let the reader know how I feel by providing details about the subject that account for my feelings.

8. Sentences within each paragraph relate to the topic. In an essay, development paragraphs follow a logical order and support the thesis. I use transitions to link ideas within paragraphs and to make connections between paragraphs.

9. I use variety in my choice of words to maintain reader interest. Where appropriate, I use figurative language to increase the impact of my words and to stimulate the reader's imagination.

10. As I revise the form and content of my work, I correct errors in punctuation, capitalization, spelling, grammar, and usage.

11. The title of my paragraph or essay tells what I wrote about and captures the reader's interest.

Continue work in this chapter until you have finished all three Active Reading and Guided Writing activities.

Chapter 2

NARRATION

Narration, storytelling that makes a point, involves a sequence of related events leading to a conclusion. Narratives, both fiction and nonfiction, have the common elements of setting, plot, character, and point of view. What you tell about depends on your purpose, the meaning you are trying to convey.

A fictional narrative might have a theme which expresses the underlying meaning of the work. The theme is expressed through all of the elements of the narrative. A nonfiction narrative will likely have a thesis statement that indicates the topic, provides an overview, and may present an attitude or opinion. Most important is that your narrative have a point, a reason for being, and that you make the reason clear to your reader.

The **setting** provides information about the time and place in which the narrative occurs. Setting also tells us what is happening and to whom. The place in which the story is set could be anywhere: a room or a palace, an island or a mountain, a town or a city. The story may take place over a period of minutes, hours, weeks, years, or over a lifetime. The setting may refer to a past or future time, include information about the climate of a place, or describe the culture of the people who live there. The setting tells us who, what, where, and when.

The **plot** is the sequence of events in a story through which the author reveals what is happening, to whom, and why. Often at the center of a plot is a problem or conflict. As characters in a narrative try to solve the problem, the plot builds to a climax, the point of greatest tension. This is followed by the resolution or conclusion of the narrative.

Characterization is the technique a writer uses to create and reveal the personalities of characters in a written work. The character's name, physical appearance, actions, words, thoughts, and feelings all contribute to making a character believable. What others say and what they feel about a character gives us additional insight. Often the information presented through the use of dialogue is the basis for making inferences and drawing conclusions about the characters. Through conversation the author can establish the situation, develop characters, present actions and ideas, and express themes.

Point of view refers to the position of the narrator and what he or she sees (interprets) from that vantage point. Basically, there are two positions from which a story can be told: first person and third person. A first-person narrator is involved in the action and talks directly to the reader using words like *I, me, my, we, our,* and *us.* A third-person narrator is an observer of events and tells the reader about them using words like *he, she, his, her,* and *they.*

Through point of view, the author tells us what is seen from the narrator's position. The author employs the narrator to introduce the setting, create characters, present conflicts and solutions, and develop themes. The author expresses attitudes, values, and opinions indirectly through the narrator. A skillful author can make the reader experience what the narrator sees, feels, and believes. In effect, the author *talks* to the reader through the narrator. A narrator may tell about events in the past, the present, or the future.

This chapter contains three reading sections, all examples of narrative writing. The first is a paragraph, the second a short essay, and the third a longer piece. Each is followed by an Active Reading exercise that helps you to understand the form and content of the reading model. The Guided Writing section at the end of this chapter will help you to create three original pieces of writing using narration.

Chapter Selections

Emperor of the Air *by Ethan Canin*

University Days *by James Thurber*

Daddy Tucked the Blanket *by Randall Williams*

EMPEROR OF THE AIR
by Ethan Canin

Ethan Canin, born in 1960, published his first collection of short stories, Emperor of the Air, *in 1987. Canin received the Houghton Mifflin Literary Fellowship which recognized him as a new author of outstanding literary merit. His work has appeared in* The Atlantic *and* Ploughshares, *among other magazines, and also in* The Best American Short Stories 1985. *Canin presents characters trying to come to terms with death, old age, superficial relationships, ambition, or unfulfilled ideals. Canin's method of storytelling hinges on something unexpected happening to his characters. These simple and striking events lead to discoveries about the essential meaning of things. The one-paragraph selection presented here is an excerpt from the short story entitled, "Emperor of the Air."*

Word Alert

asphyxiate	to kill or make unconscious through lack of adequate oxygen, presence of noxious agents, or other obstruction to normal breathing
bellowed	to make a very loud utterance or roar
deciduous	shedding foliage at the end of the growing season; temporary
firebreak	a strip of cleared land used to stop the spread of a fire
sickled	to mow or reap with a sickle, an agricultural tool with a curved metal blade
wireless	a radio telegraph or telephone system with no wires

When I was a boy in this town, the summers were hot and the forest to the north and east often dried to the point where the undergrowth, not fit to compete with the deciduous trees for groundwater, turned crackling brown. The shrubbery became as fragile as straw, and the summer I was sixteen the forest ignited. A sheet of flame raced and bellowed day and night as loud as a fleet of propeller planes. Whole families gathered in the street and evacuation plans were made, street routes drawn out beneath the night sky, which, despite the ten miles' distance to the fire, shone with orange light. My father had a wireless with which he communicated to the fire lines. He stayed up all night and promised that he would wake the neighbors if the wind changed or the fire otherwise turned toward town. That night the wind held, and by morning a firebreak the width of a street had been cut. My father took me down to see it the next day, a ribbon of cleared land as bare as if it had been drawn with a razor. Trees had been felled, the underbrush sickled down and removed. We stood at the edge of the cleared land, the town behind us, and watched the fire. Then we got into my father's Plymouth and drove as close as we were allowed. A fireman near the flames had been asphyxiated, someone said, when the cone of fire had turned abruptly and sucked up all the oxygen in the air. My father explained to me how a flame breathed oxygen like a man. We got out of the car. The heat curled the hair on our arms and turned the ends of our eyelashes white.

ACTIVE READING

The Active Reading exercise gives you an opportunity to reread the paragraph with a critical eye. By answering the questions that follow, you will extend and sharpen your understanding of the selection. This activity will help you become a more efficient reader and a more effective writer.

The opening sentence of this paragraph gets the reader's attention and provides background information. By telling us something about "who, what, where, when, and why," the author creates a **setting** and atmosphere for the story. For each of the seven phrases below, decide which question is being answered: Who? What? Where? When? Why?

1. I was a boy

2. in this town

3. during the summers

4. the forest

5. to the north and east

6. the undergrowth

7. the undergrowth, not fit to compete with the deciduous trees for groundwater, turned crackling brown.

After setting the scene, the author introduces the topic.

8. What is the topic sentence of the paragraph?

You may remember from the first chapter that a simile is the literary term used to describe the comparison of two unlike objects using the words *like* or *as*.

9. Name the two things being compared in the topic sentence and the characteristic they share in this context.

10. The third sentence in the paragraph is also a simile. What two things are being compared in this sentence?

11. What two characteristics do these objects share?

The narrator tells us about the **plot** through the sequence of events that occur after the forest bursts into flame. He also provides details about the characters and what is happening to them. His vivid descriptions and urgent tone make us want to know what will happen next. The questions below refer to these events.

12. **Who** gathered in the streets?

13. **What** kind of plans were made?

14. **Where** were street routes drawn out?

15. How far away (**where**) is the fire from the town?

16. **What** was the color of the night sky?

17. **What** did the narrator's father use to communicate with the fire lines?

18. **Why** did the father stay up all night?

19. **What** happened during the night?

20. **What** is a firebreak?

21. **Why** did the firefighters create a firebreak?

22. **Why** did a fireman near the flames become asphyxiated?

The narrator concludes this paragraph with a dramatic statement that shows how the fire affected the boy and his father personally.

23. **What** effect did the fire have on the narrator and his father?

24. **Point of view** identifies the position of the storyteller. Is this story told by a first or third-person narrator? What evidence is there for your answer?

25. The author uses transitional words and phrases to link ideas in this paragraph. List at least five.

26. The author's primary purpose in this selection is to:

    a. inform

    b. persuade

    c. entertain

The Active Reading exercise can be scored using the answer key and grading grid. Enter your grade in the progress chart.

GUIDED WRITING

The Guided Writing section at the end of this chapter (page 45) provides topics and plans for writing narrative paragraphs and essays. Select a topic and write a paragraph by following the writing plan on page 46.

Continue work in this chapter until you have finished all three Active Reading and Guided Writing activities. Upon completion, you will have written three new compositions for your portfolio (one paragraph and two essays). Record grades in your progress chart and, if available, on the Academic Credit Statement in your *Writing Portfolio Organizer*.

UNIVERSITY DAYS

by James Thurber

James Thurber (1894–1961), one of America's finest humorists, was born in Columbus, Ohio. Thurber lost one eye in a childhood accident and was completely blind when he died. For more than thirty years he contributed hundreds of stories, essays, and articles to The New Yorker *magazine. He was also a talented cartoonist and illustrated many of his own works. He is the author of several books for children, among them* The Wonderful O. *Thurber used incidents from his childhood in writing his most famous collection of stories,* My Life and Hard Times. *Two of his stories are particularly well known. In "The Secret Life of Walter Mitty," he created his most memorable character, a man who lives a double life. In "University Days" he has described, with whimsical humor, his predicament in trying to use a microscope.*

Word Alert

botany	a branch of biology that studies plant life
constellation	a gathering or assemblage of similar or related persons or things
deferred	delayed or postponed
flars	the word *flowers* said with an accent
lacteal	relating to or resembling milk
Barrymore, Lionel	(1878–1954) a much admired character actor who appeared in films in the thirties and forties. He is best known for his role as a physician in the Dr. Kildare films.
maladjustment	poor or faulty adjustment
nebulous	misty, cloudy, or hazy
opacity	something opaque, obscure; cannot be seen through
phenomenon	a rare or unusual fact or event
variegated	having streaks, marks, or patches of a different color or colors

I passed all the other courses that I took at my University, but I could   1
never pass botany. This was because all botany students had to spend
several hours a week in a laboratory looking through a microscope at

plant cells, and I could never see through a microscope. I never once saw a cell through a microscope. This used to enrage my instructor. He would wander around the laboratory pleased with the progress all the students were making in drawing the involved and, so I am told, interesting structure of flower cells, until he came to me. I would just be standing there. "I can't see anything," I would say.

2   He would begin patiently enough, explaining how anybody can see through a microscope, but he would always end up in a fury; claiming that I could *too* see through a microscope but just pretended that I couldn't. "It takes away from the beauty of flowers anyway," I used to tell him. "We are not concerned with beauty in this course," he would say. "We are concerned solely with what I may call the *mechanics* of flars." "Well," I'd say, "I can't see anything." "Try it just once again," he'd say, and I would put my eye to the microscope and see nothing at all, except now and again a nebulous milky substance—a phenomenon of maladjustment. You were supposed to see a vivid, restless clockwork of sharply defined plant cells. "I see what looks like a lot of milk," I would tell him. This, he claimed, was the result of my not having adjusted the microscope properly, so he would readjust it for me, or rather, for himself. And I would look again and see milk.

3   I finally took a deferred pass, as they called it, and waited a year and tried again. (You had to pass one of the biological sciences or you couldn't graduate.) The professor had come back from vacation brown as a berry, bright-eyed, and eager to explain cell structure again to his classes. "Well," he said to me, cheerily, when we met in the first laboratory hour of the semester, "we're going to see cells this time, aren't we?" "Yes, sir," I said. Students to the right of me and left of me and in front of me were seeing cells; what's more, they were quietly drawing pictures of them in their notebooks. Of course, I didn't see anything.

4   "We'll try it," the professor said to me, grimly, "with every adjustment of the microscope known to man. As God is my witness, I'll arrange this glass so that you see cells through it or I'll give up teaching. In twenty-two years of botany, I—" He cut off abruptly for he was beginning to quiver all over, like Lionel Barrymore, and he genuinely wished to hold onto his temper; his scenes with me had taken a great deal out of him.

So we tried it with every adjustment of the microscope known to man. 5
With only one of them did I see anything but blackness or the familiar
lacteal opacity, and that time I saw, to my pleasure and amazement, a
variegated constellation of flecks, specks, and dots. These I hastily drew.
The instructor, noting my activity, came from an adjoining desk, a smile
on his lips and his eyebrows high in hope. He looked at my cell drawing.
"What's that?" he demanded, with a hint of squeal in his voice. "That's
what I saw," I said. "You didn't, you didn't, you *didn't*!" he screamed,
losing control of his temper instantly, and he bent over and squinted into
the microscope. His head snapped up. "That's your eye!" he shouted.
"You've fixed the lens so that it reflects! You've drawn your eye!"

ACTIVE READING

The Active Reading exercise gives you an opportunity to reread the essay with a
critical eye. By answering the questions that follow, you will extend and sharpen
your understanding of the selection. This activity will help you become a more
efficient reader and a more effective writer.

INTRODUCTORY PARAGRAPH   *(par. 1)*

The narrator begins his story by telling about a problem he is having, which gets
the reader's attention. He continues by telling the time and place of the story, and
what is happening to the characters. The main idea of this essay is stated in the
first two sentences.

1. **When** does the story take place: in the past, present, or future?

2. **Where** does the story take place?

3. **Who** is the story about?

4. **What** subject was the student having trouble passing?

5. **Why** does he have this problem?

6. **What** was the instructor's reaction to the student's problem?

7. **How** did the instructor feel about the other students in the laboratory,
   and why?

8. **Who** is telling the story, a first or third-person narrator?

DEVELOPMENT PARAGRAPH *(par. 2)*

Paragraph two uses examples to show, in greater depth, the conflict between the student and the professor. This struggle is illustrated by the argument between the two about the student's inability to see through a microscope. The first sentence of the paragraph defines the topic and sets the mood for the selection. **Mood** is the atmosphere and feeling a writer creates through setting, imagery, details, and description.

9. What two conflicting emotions does the professor experience when he attempts to get this student to see through a microscope?

10. How does the instructor explain the student's inability to see through the microscope?

11. What does the student say to rationalize his inability to see through the microscope?

12. What is the professor's response to this?

13. When the student looks through the microscope again, what does he see?

14. What was he supposed to see?

DEVELOPMENT PARAGRAPH *(par. 3)*

In paragraph three we learn that the student has taken a deferred pass in the course. This paragraph tells what happens when he tries the course again a year later.

15. Why is the student taking the class again?

16. Describe the professor's attitude at the beginning of the semester.

17. What did the student and professor agree on?

18. What were other students in the course doing?

19. What did the narrator see through the microscope?

DEVELOPMENT PARAGRAPH *(par. 4)*

In this fourth paragraph the author uses **hyperbole**, also known as exaggeration, to emphasize the point that the professor has reached a new level of exasperation.

20. Two examples of hyperbole are used to show the lengths to which the professor will go to have the student see cells. What is the professor

prepared to do first?

21. What does the professor swear to do if the student doesn't see cells through the microscope?

22. The professor begins a sentence which he doesn't finish. "In twenty-two years of botany, I—" What do you think he was going to say?

23. Why did the professor abruptly stop talking?

The author makes an allusion to a famous actor, Lionel Barrymore, to make the professor's behavior more vivid for the reader. An **allusion** is a reference to a famous person or event that makes a comparison and gives the reader a new perspective on the subject.

24. What effect did these scenes with the student have on the professor?

CONCLUDING PARAGRAPH (par. 5)

The last paragraph of an essay may summarize, express a reaction, offer an opinion, or reach a conclusion about what has happened. Here, the first sentence continues the exaggerated tone of the previous paragraph and acts as a transition to introduce the topic of this paragraph.

25. What phrase is an example of exaggeration?

26. What is the topic of the paragraph?

27. What did the student see with most adjustments?

28. With one particular adjustment the student sees something unusual. Describe what he sees.

29. What is the student's response to this sight?

30. Describe the instructor's face when he notices the student's activity.

31. The narrator uses three descriptive words that appeal to our sense of sound and signal a mood change in the professor. List these words.

32. The professor's mood changes from happy and hopeful to:

33. What did the student see through the microscope, and then draw?

34. How did this happen?

35. The story reaches a climax which leads the reader to draw a conclusion about the narrator. What conclusion have you reached?

36. The author's tone, his attitude toward the subject is:
    a. serious
    b. humorous
    c. dreary
    d . angry

37. The author uses transitional words and phrases to link ideas in this essay. List at least five.

38. The author's primary purpose in this selection is to:

    a. inform
    b. persuade
    c. entertain

The Active Reading exercise can be scored using the answer key and grading grid. Enter your grade in the progress chart.

GUIDED WRITING

The Guided Writing section at the end of this chapter (page 45) provides topics and plans for writing narrative paragraphs and essays. Select a topic and write a short essay by following the writing plan that begins on page 47. Continue work in this chapter until you finished all three Active Reading and Guided Writing activities.

DADDY TUCKED THE BLANKET
by Randall Williams

Randall Williams was a reporter for The Alabama Journal *when he wrote this autobiographical essay about growing up poor. In this narrative he uses examples to illustrate how the environment of poverty creates not only physical but emotional hardships. The shabby houses of his childhood are symbolic of the deteriorating relationship between his mother and father. Mr. Williams shows us how members of his family reacted to one another and to the environment created by poverty.*

Word Alert

abuse	mistreatment
affluent	wealthy
articulate	able to speak clearly
Depression, the	a period of economic hardship in the U.S. (1929–1941)
deteriorating	becoming worse
futility	the quality of being useless
grandeur	magnificence
humiliating	lowering the pride or dignity of someone
psyche	the mind; soul or self
sheer	utter, pure
shiftless	incapable; inefficient, lazy
teetering	wavering; moving unsteadily

About the time I turned 16, my folks began to wonder why I didn't   1
stay home any more. I always had an excuse for them, but what I didn't
say was that I had found my freedom and I was getting out.

I went through four years of high school in semirural Alabama and   2
became active in clubs and sports; I made a lot of friends and became a
regular guy, if you know what I mean. But one thing was irregular about
me: I managed those four years without ever having a friend visit at
my house.

I was ashamed of where I lived. I had been ashamed for as long as I   3
had been conscious of class.

4   We had a big family. There were several of us sleeping in one room, but that's not so bad if you get along, and we always did. As you get older, though, it gets worse.

5   Being poor is a humiliating experience for a young person trying hard to be accepted. Even now—several years removed—it is hard to talk about. And I resent the weakness of these words to make you feel what it was really like.

6   We lived in a lot of old houses. We moved a lot because we were always looking for something just a little better than what we had. You have to understand that my folks worked harder than most people. My mother was always at home, but for her that was a full-time job—and no fun either. But my father worked his head off from the time I can remember in construction and shops. It was hard, physical work.

7   I tell you this to show that we weren't shiftless. No matter how much money Daddy made, we never made much progress up the social ladder. I got out thanks to a college scholarship and because I was a little more articulate than the average.

8   I have seen my Daddy wrap copper wire through the soles of his boots to keep them together in the wintertime. He couldn't buy new boots because he had used the money for food and shoes for us. We lived like hell, but we went to school well-clothed and with a full stomach.

9   It really is hell to live in a house that was in bad shape 10 years before you moved in. And a big family puts a lot of wear and tear on a new house, too, so you can imagine how one goes downhill if it is teetering when you move in. But we lived in houses that were sweltering in summer and freezing in winter. I woke up every morning for a year and a half with plaster on my face where it had fallen out of the ceiling during the night.

10   This wasn't during the Depression; this was in the late 60's and early 70's.

11   When we boys got old enough to learn trades in school, we would try to fix up the old houses we lived in. But have you ever tried to paint a wall that crumbled when the roller went across it? And bright paint emphasized the holes in the wall. You end up more frustrated than when you began, especially when you know that at best you might come up with only enough money to improve one of the six rooms in the house. And we might move out soon after, anyway.

The same goes for keeping a house like that clean. If you have a house *12*
full of kids and the house is deteriorating, you'll never keep it clean.
Daddy used to yell at Mama about that, but she couldn't do anything. I
think Daddy knew it inside, but he had to have an outlet for his rage
somewhere, and at least yelling isn't as bad as hitting, which they never
did to each other.

But you have a kitchen which has no counter space and no hot water, *13*
and you will have dirty dishes stacked up. That sounds like an excuse, but
try it. You'll go mad from the sheer sense of futility. It's the same thing in
a house with no closets. You can't keep clothes clean and rooms in order
if they have to be stacked up with things.

Living in a bad house is generally worse on girls. For one thing, they *14*
traditionally help their mother with the housework. We boys could get
outside and work in the field or cut wood or even play ball and forget
about living conditions. The sky was still pretty.

But the girls got the pressure, and as they got older it became worse. *15*
Would they accept dates knowing they had to "receive" the young man
in a dirty hallway with broken windows, peeling wallpaper and a cracked
ceiling? You have to live it to understand it, but it creates a shame which
drives the soul of a young person inward.

I'm thankful none of us ever blamed our parents for this, because it *16*
would have crippled our relationships. As it worked out, only the relationship between our parents was damaged. And I think the harshness which
they expressed to each other was just an outlet to get rid of their anger at
the trap their lives were in. It ruined their marriage because they had no
one to yell at but each other. I knew other families where the kids got the
abuse, but we were too much loved for that.

Once I was about 16 and Mama and Daddy had had a particularly *17*
violent argument about the washing machine, which had broken down.
Daddy was on the back porch—that's where the only water faucet was—
trying to fix it and Mama had a washtub out there washing school clothes
for the next day and they were screaming at each other.

Later that night everyone was in bed and I heard Daddy get up from *18*
the couch where he was reading. I looked out from my bed across the hall
into their room. He was standing right over Mama and she was already
asleep. He pulled the blanket up and tucked it around her shoulders and
just stood there and tears were dropping off his cheeks and I thought I
could faintly hear them splashing against the linoleum rug.

19   Now they're divorced.

20   I had courses in college where housing was discussed, but the sociologists never put enough emphasis on the impact living in substandard housing has on a person's psyche. Especially children's.

21   Small children have a hard time understanding poverty. They want the same things children from more affluent families have. They want the same things they see advertised on television, and they don't understand why they can't have them.

22   Other children can be incredibly cruel. I was in elementary school in Georgia—and this is interesting because it is the only thing I remember about that particular school—when I was about eight or nine.

23   After Christmas vacation had ended, my teacher made each student describe all his or her Christmas presents. I became more and more uncomfortable as the privilege passed around the room toward me. Other children were reciting the names of the dolls they had been given, the kinds of bicycles and the grandeur of their games and toys. Some had lists which seemed to go on and on for hours.

24   It took me only a few seconds to tell the class that I had gotten for Christmas a belt and a pair of gloves. And then I was laughed at—because I cried—by a roomful of children and a teacher. I never forgave them, and that night I made my mother cry when I told her about it.

25   In retrospect, I am grateful for that moment, but I remember wanting to die at the time.

ACTIVE READING

The Active Reading exercise gives you an opportunity to reread the essay with a critical eye. By answering the questions that follow, you will extend and sharpen your understanding of the selection. This activity will help you become a more efficient reader and a more effective writer.

INTRODUCTORY PARAGRAPHS (par. 1–3)

In paragraphs one, two, and three we are introduced to the narrator, some elements of the setting, and given background information about a conflict that exists. The author gets our attention by letting us know that there is something unusual about the person who is telling the story.

1. **Who** is the story about?
2. **Where** does the story take place?
3. **When** does the story take place: past, present, or future?
4. In **what** two ways is the narrator a "regular guy?"
5. **What** was "irregular" about him?

The third paragraph, consisting of two sentences, is set apart to emphasize the narrator's feelings about the subject of the essay.

6. **Why** did he act in such an irregular way?
7. **How** long had he felt this way?
8. Define the word *class* as used in context.

DEVELOPMENT PARAGRAPH *(par. 4–5)*

Paragraph four provides additional background for the setting. We learn that the narrator was from a big family, that several children slept in one room, and they all got along well. In paragraph five, the narrator clearly states the thesis of the essay and offers his personal reflections.

9. What is the thesis of the essay?
10. What are his current feelings about his past experience?

DEVELOPMENT PARAGRAPHS *(par. 6–8)*

Paragraphs six, seven, and eight illustrate the ways in which the parents sacrificed for their children.

11. Give four examples of the parents' efforts to care for their children.
12. Did all of this hard work change their social class?
13. How did the narrator change his own social status?

DEVELOPMENT PARAGRAPH *(par. 9–15)*

Paragraphs nine through fifteen tell about many of the physical hardships associated with living in poverty. The author does this by offering examples and describing in detail the discomforts and frustrations experienced by the family as a result of being poor. The narrator appeals to the senses as a way of involving the reader in his experience.

Words and phrases from these paragraphs are listed below. Decide which sense is being appealed to in each: sight, sound, taste, smell, or touch.

14. an old house that is teetering when you move in

15. houses that were sweltering in summer and freezing in winter

16. woke up every morning with plaster on my face

17. where it (plaster) had fallen out of the ceiling during the night

18. paint a wall that crumbled when a roller went across it

19. bright paint emphasized the holes in the wall

20. a kitchen with no counter space, and no hot water will have dirty dishes stacked up

21. a house with no closets . . . and everything stacked up

22. a dirty hallway with broken windows, peeling wallpaper, and a cracked ceiling

DEVELOPMENT PARAGRAPH (par. 10)

This paragraph, consisting of a single sentence, emphasizes the great difference that exists between the narrator and his contemporaries. The narrator compares the poverty of his childhood with that of the Depression. During the Depression, poverty was nothing to be ashamed of because so many people were poor.

23. During what time period did the Depression occur? (see Word Alert)

24. During what years does the story take place?

DEVELOPMENT PARAGRAPHS (par. 11–15)

In paragraphs eleven through fifteen, the narrator tells us how poverty affected him and his family psychologically. We see how the emotional strain the family experiences is caused by the deteriorating environment in which they live. This cause and effect relationship is illustrated throughout the essay.

25. How did the boys feel when they tried to fix up the old houses they lived in?

26. How did yelling at the mother help the father?

27. According to the narrator, how did the lack of counter space and hot water in the kitchen, and no closets for storage of clothes, affect the family emotionally?

28. Why was there greater pressure on the girls as they got older?

29. What does the author say in paragraph fifteen that summarizes the emotional impact of poverty and restates the theme of the essay?

DEVELOPMENT PARAGRAPHS *(par. 16–19)*

In paragraphs sixteen through nineteen the narrator continues to tell us about the effects of poverty, with a focus on his parents' relationship.

30. Did the parents blame the children for their situation?

31. Who did they blame for their situation and why?

A broken washing machine led to a violent argument between the parents. Later that evening, the narrator sees his father standing over Mama who is already asleep. The author uses this incident to build tension and bring the story to a climax.

32. What does the father do?

33. The father reacts emotionally. What emotion does he express and how do we know this?

34. At this moment, how does the father feel about the mother?

35. Why do you think the parents got divorced?

CONCLUDING PARAGRAPHS *(par. 20–25)*

These last six paragraphs move the essay toward a resolution and a conclusion. In these closing paragraphs, the narrator writes about the effects of poverty on children, first in a general way, and then with a specific example of a personal experience.

36. What does the narrator find lacking in the sociologists' explanation of poverty?

37. The author says that small children have a hard time understanding poverty. Why?

As a way of restating the theme of the essay, the narrator tells a story that illustrates both the cruelty of children and the cruelty of poverty. In concluding, the narrator expresses his feelings about this incident that happened many years before.

38. How old is the narrator when this incident occurs? Where does it happen?

39. What are the students doing and how does the boy feel about it?

40. What does he say and do when it's his turn?

41. Why do you think the boy cried?

42. How did the children and the teacher react to his crying?

43. What would you say about the teacher's behavior?

44. How did his mother react when he told her about the incident?

45. How does the narrator feel about the treatment he received in class?

46. Although he remembers it as a painful experience, the narrator says he is grateful for the moment. How do you explain these contradictory feelings expressed by the narrator?

47. The author uses transitional words and phrases to link ideas in this essay. List at least five.

48. The author's primary purpose in this selection is to:
    a. inform
    b. persuade
    c. entertain

The Active Reading exercise can be scored using the answer key and grading grid. Enter your grade in the progress chart.

The Guided Writing section that begins on the next page provides topics and plans for writing narrative paragraphs and essays. Select a topic and write an extended essay by following the writing plan that begins on page 47.

GUIDED WRITING

This part of the chapter will help you apply what you have learned about writing narrative paragraphs and essays. Choose one of the topics listed below for each writing assignment that you do. If you want to write about something else, ask your instructor if the topic is appropriate for writing narration. Follow the plan that applies to write your composition. Submit your completed composition to the instructor for evaluation. When you receive a grade for this work, enter it in the progress chart.

WRITING TOPICS

- Write about a catastrophic event in nature such as a hurricane, tornado, flood, earthquake, or fire.

- Write about a catastrophic event in a social relationship such as the breakup of a friendship, the death of someone close to you, losing a job, or divorce in the family.

- Use humor to tell about a situation in which you appear inept, like the narrator did in "University Days."

- Tell about an amusing experience that involved you and a teacher.

- Write about a time when you felt so ashamed or humiliated that you wanted to "die."

- Tell about the environment you grew up in and how it affected relationships in your family.

PREWRITING: GENERATING IDEAS

Now that you have selected a topic, you will need to gather information and generate ideas before you begin to write. If you choose to tell about a personal experience, you will probably rely on your memory, other people's input, and your own creativity for details. Other types of narratives may require that you use reference works to collect information for your composition.

First, identify the time and place of the narrative and provide relevant background information (the setting). Next, name and briefly describe the major character(s) and decide the position of the narrator. Make a list of the events that occur in chronological order. You will be using this sequence of events to build the plot: what is happening, to whom, and why. Decide the point you wish to make and how the narrative will end. Use the information you gather and your list of events as you follow the plan for writing a narrative paragraph or essay.

WRITING PLAN: THE PARAGRAPH

1. Decide the point of view of the narrator, first or third person. Introduce your topic and get the reader's attention with a strong opening statement(s).

2. Set the tone for the paragraph, your attitude toward the subject. The tone might be serious or humorous, formal or informal.

3. Tell something about "who, what, where, when, and why" to create the setting and provide atmosphere for the narrative.

4. Develop the plot through the sequence of events. Provide details about the character(s), what is happening to them, and why. Details include descriptions, facts, examples, and explanations.

5. Write a conclusion to your paragraph that reminds the reader of the topic by summarizing, reaching a conclusion, or expressing an opinion.

6. To create unity in your writing, make sure that each sentence in the paragraph relates to the topic. Your writing will be coherent if ideas follow one another in a logical pattern and sentences flow smoothly from one to the other. Use transitions to link or connect ideas. The list of transitional words and phrases at the back of this book is for your use and reference when you write (see pages 259–264).

7. Use variety in your choice of words to maintain reader interest. Where appropriate, use **figurative language** to increase the impact of your words and to stimulate the reader's imagination. The most commonly used figures of speech are the simile, metaphor, personification, and hyperbole. Definitions of literary and rhetorical terms can be found in the Glossary on pages 265–270.

8. Create a title for your paragraph, a word or phrase that captures the reader's interest and tells what you are writing about.

9. Use the *Checklist for Revision* provided at the end of this section to help you review and revise your paragraph.

WRITING PLAN: SHORT AND EXTENDED ESSAYS

While short and extended essays are similar—both have introductory and concluding paragraphs—the extended essay has more development paragraphs. "University Days," a short narrative essay, is developed through the use of description, examples, and exaggeration. "Daddy Tucked the Blanket," an extended narrative, uses examples, description, cause and effect, and offers opinions to develop the topic. The longer essay makes use of more writing strategies to reinforce the theme of the narrative.

Introductory Paragraph(s)

1. Decide the point of view of the narrator: a character involved in the action (first person) or an observer outside the action (third person).

2. Begin with a statement that challenges the imagination of the reader. Your introductory paragraph(s) sets the tone for the essay, your attitude toward your subject. The tone might be serious or humorous, formal or informal.

3. Tell what the essay is about by introducing your topic and purpose. This is the thesis statement, the main idea to be supported throughout the essay.

4. Introduce the time and place of the narrative, including background information (setting). Introduce the characters as well as the situation or conflict. Telling something about "who, what, where, when, and why" will help to create the setting for your narrative.

5. State your plan for the development of this narrative. An extended essay may contain more than one introductory paragraph.

Development Paragraph(s)

1. Use your development paragraphs to build the plot through the sequence of events that occur. Each of these paragraphs may examine a different aspect of the plot. Let the reader know your topic or focus for each paragraph.

2. Provide specific details about the characters: names, physical appearance, actions, words, thoughts, and feelings. Tell what is happening, to whom, and why. Where appropriate, use dialogue to help the reader make inferences and draw conclusions about the characters.

3. Identify major conflicts and complications: why they happen and how they are resolved. This information will support your thesis statement, build the plot, and lead to the climax of your story.

4. If you are writing an extended narrative, you can use the development paragraphs to include more details and events, develop characters more fully, and build a more intricate plot.

5. All sentences in a paragraph should relate to the topic and to one another. All paragraphs in an essay should support the topic and follow some logical order. Use transitions to link ideas within paragraphs and to make connections between paragraphs. Refer to the list of transitional words and phrases on pages 259–264.

6. Use variety in your choice of words to maintain reader interest. Where appropriate, use figurative language to increase the impact of your words and to stimulate the reader's imagination. The most commonly used figures of speech are the simile, metaphor, personification, and hyperbole. Definitions of literary and rhetorical terms can be found in the Glossary on pages 265–270.

Concluding Paragraph(s)

1. In your conclusion, restate the thesis in some way for emphasis. If you are using examples, save the most powerful one for last.

2. The point of greatest tension in the narrative, the climax, is often presented in the conclusion of the essay.

3. Reinforce the point of your essay by summarizing, offering an opinion, or drawing a conclusion.

4. Let the reader know your feelings about what has happened.

5. More than one paragraph may be used to conclude an extended essay, as is the case with "Daddy Tucked the Blanket."

6. The checklist below will help you to review and revise your essay.

note: The title of your essay should be a word or phrase that captures the reader's attention and tells what you are writing about. Create a title for your first draft and review it before making it final.

CHECKLIST FOR REVISION

1. My paragraph/essay has a first- or third-person point of view. I begin with a strong statement that gets the reader's attention, introduce my topic, and set the tone. If I am writing an essay, my thesis statement appears in the opening paragraph(s).

2. I introduce the time and place of the narrative, the characters, some background information, and the situation or conflict.

3. I develop the plot through the sequence of events. I provide details about the characters, what is happening to them, and why. Where appropriate, I use dialogue to make inferences and draw conclusions about the characters.

4. The development paragraphs of my short and extended narratives include more details, more events, and build more intricate plots.

5. In concluding my narrative paragraph or essay, I present the climax and let the reader know the point of my story. I tell the outcome by summarizing, offering an opinion, or drawing a conclusion.

6. Sentences within each paragraph relate to the topic. In an essay, development paragraphs follow a logical order and support the thesis. I use transitions to link ideas within paragraphs and to make connections between paragraphs.

7. I use variety in my choice of words to maintain reader interest. Where appropriate, I use figurative language to increase the impact of my words and to stimulate the reader's imagination.

8. As I revise the form and content of my work, I correct errors in punctuation, capitalization, spelling, grammar, and usage.

9. The title of my paragraph or essay tells what I wrote about and captures the reader's interest.

Continue work in this chapter until you have finished all three Active Reading and Guided Writing activities.

Chapter 3

DESCRIPTION

Description is used to create impressions that are vivid, real, and lifelike for the reader. By appealing to the five senses the writer tells us how something **looks, sounds, tastes, smells,** and how it feels to the **touch**. These are five ways of describing a person, place, thing, idea, emotion, or event.

When you describe a person, you will want to use specific details that create an overall pattern or impression. Include information about a person's clothes, facial features and expressions, body language, attitudes, behavior, quirks, habits, and conversation. Dialogue will add dimensionality to your characters by having the reader experience them directly, through their words.

To describe a place, you will need to present accurate details and create an atmosphere that gives the reader a feeling of being there. For a complete description of inanimate objects and living things, study your subject carefully in order to gather all the details. Describing events is like narration in that you include information about people, places, and objects in a logical order. Ideas and emotions can be described as separate subjects or as an aspect of a person, place, thing, or event.

You can describe something objectively, impartially, by sticking to the facts without evaluating them, and letting your readers infer their own meaning. This is characteristic of technical and scientific descriptions which usually aim for objectivity. You can also describe something subjectively, so that your reader feels a certain way and experiences the emotional impact of the subject.

Description captures sensory impressions that can decay in seconds and translates them into written language that may last forever. Description is used both as a primary writing strategy and as a way to support other forms of writing. For example, description may be used in narration to establish the setting of a story, in exposition to develop the steps in an analysis, and in persuasion to clarify the evidence of an argument.

This chapter contains three reading selections, all examples of descriptive writing. The first is a paragraph, the second a short essay, and the third a longer piece. Each is followed by an Active Reading exercise that helps you to understand the form and content of the reading model. The Guided Writing section at the end of this chapter will help you to create three original pieces of writing using description.

Chapter Selections

Cannery Row *by John Steinbeck*

Return to Paradise *by James Michener*

This Way for the Gas, Ladies and Gentlemen *by Tadeusz Borowski*

CANNERY ROW

by John Steinbeck

John Steinbeck (1902-1968) was born and raised in California and attended Stanford University. Variously employed as a fruit-picker, painter, caretaker, surveyor, and reporter, he is regarded as one of the great American writers of the twentieth century. He has written novels, short stories, plays, and screenplays. Among the many honors bestowed on him were the Pulitzer Prize (1940) for his novel The Grapes of Wrath, *an Oscar nomination for best original story (1944) for "Lifeboat," and the Nobel Prize for literature in 1962. Throughout his long and controversial career, John Steinbeck extolled the virtues of the American dream while he warned against what he believed to be the evils of an increasingly materialistic American society. The excerpt presented here is from his novel* Cannery Row *(1945) about life in a fishing community on the California coast.*

Word Alert

barnacles	small, hard-shelled aquatic animals that attach themselves to rocks and boats
bellow	to make a loud, deep, hollow sound characteristic of a bull; to shout, to roar
buoy	an anchored float that marks a channel or a reef; a beacon
calcareous	containing calcium carbonate, chalky; growing in soil impregnated with lime
limpets	sea mollusks that cling tenaciously to rocks and timber
obscured	hidden or concealed
protean	bacteria in decaying organic matter; derived from Proteus, a Greek sea god capable of assuming different forms
sepia	a dark-brown ink or pigment made from the secretion of the cuttlefish
sperm and ova	mature male and female germ cells that can reproduce when fused; also known as male and female gametes

Then the creeping murderer, the octopus, steals out, slowly, softly, moving like a gray mist, pretending now to be a bit of weed, now a rock, now a lump of decaying meat while its evil goat eyes watch coldly. It oozes and flows toward a feeding crab, and as it comes close its yellow eyes burn and its body turns rosy with the pulsing color of anticipation and rage. Then suddenly it runs lightly on the tips of its arms, as ferociously as a charging cat. It leaps savagely on the crab, there is a puff of black fluid, and the struggling mass is obscured in the sepia cloud while the octopus murders the crab. On the exposed rocks out of water, the barnacles bubble behind their closed doors and the limpets dry out. And down to the rocks come the black flies to eat anything they can find. The sharp smell of iodine from the algae, and the lime smell of calcareous bodies and the smell of powerful protean, smell of sperm and ova fill the air. On the exposed rocks the starfish emit semen and eggs from between their rays. The smells of life and richness, of death and digestion, of decay and birth, burden the air. And salt spray blows in from the barrier where the ocean waits for its rising-tide strength to permit it back into the Great Tide Pool again. And on the reef the whistling buoy bellows like a sad and patient bull.

ACTIVE READING

The Active Reading exercise gives you an opportunity to reread the paragraph with a critical eye. By answering the questions that follow, you will extend and sharpen your understanding of the selection. This activity will help you become a more efficient reader and a more effective writer. The author's use of **imagery** to introduce his subject gives this paragraph a very dramatic beginning that grabs the reader's attention. Imagery is the use of words, phrases, and figures of speech that help a reader picture or imagine sensations and ideas. The use of images makes description interesting and exciting.

1. What subject is introduced at the beginning of this paragraph?
2. Is the subject a person, place, thing, idea, emotion, or event?
3-7. Find five phrases in the first sentence that describe the octopus as dangerous, disguised, or fearsome.
8. What feeling or mood does the author create with the first sentence?
9. Identify the phrase in the first sentence that is a simile, tell what two things are being compared, and state the characteristic they share.

References to movement and color in the first four sentences draw a clear picture of how the octopus approaches and catches its prey. This part of the paragraph takes place in the water and appeals primarily to sight and touch; our sense of hearing and smell is minimal under water.

10-18. List nine phrases that describe the movement of the octopus, in the order that they occur. These movements climax with the murder of the crab.

19. Now, list five references to color that describe the changing appearance of the octopus.

It is in the second part of this paragraph that the octopus and the crab are shown to be actors in a much larger drama which is unfolding in the tide pool. By appealing to the five senses, the author describes the activity that takes place out of the water on the exposed rocks. Indicate the activity of each animal or object in items 20-24 below, and the sense to which the author is appealing.

20. barnacles

21. limpets

22. black flies

23. starfish

24. buoy

25. The buoy bellows like a sad and patient bull. What figure of speech is this?

26-29. Life on the rocks above the tidal pool is described by repeated references to the sense of smell. List four of these and tell the source, if given.

30-32. In a summary statement, the author describes the smells associated with the life cycle in and around the tidal pool. What aspects of the life cycle does he address?

33. Which aspects of the life cycle refer indirectly to the murder of the crab by the hungry octopus?

34. Although it appears near the end of the paragraph, this summary statement serves as a topic sentence; it expresses the point the author wishes to make. What is the topic of this paragraph?

The author concludes the paragraph by painting a picture of the ocean about to rise over the barrier reef and reclaim the Great Tidal Pool, making it part of the ocean once more. The cycle of life and death in the tidal pool is determined by the ebb and flow of the ocean tides.

35. The last sentence makes a reference to sound. What makes the sound?

36. Does the narrator have a first or third person point of view in this paragraph?

37. Is description used as a primary writing strategy in this paragraph? If not, what strategy does the use of description support?

38. The author uses transitional words and phrases to link ideas in this paragraph. List at least five.

39. The author's primary purpose in this selection is to:

   a. inform
   b. persuade
   c. entertain

The Active Reading exercise can be scored using the answer key and grading grid. Enter your grade in the progress chart.

GUIDED WRITING

The Guided Writing section at the end of this chapter (page 74) provides topics and plans for writing descriptive paragraphs and essays. Select a topic and write a paragraph by following the writing plan on page 75.

Continue work in this chapter until you have finished all three Active Reading and Guided Writing activities. Upon completion, you will have written three new compositions for your portfolio (one paragraph and two essays). Record grades in your progress chart and, if available, on the Academic Credit Statement in your *Writing Portfolio Organizer*.

RETURN TO PARADISE

by James A. Michener

James Michener was born in 1907 in New York. He grew up in Pennsylvania, and was graduated from Swarthmore College in 1929. During World War II, Michener was a naval officer, stationed in the Solomon Islands. Stranded on a small island with nothing to do, he wrote. The result was a collection of stories called Tales of the South Pacific, *which won the Pulitzer Prize for fiction in 1948, and was made into the Broadway musical "South Pacific." Nearly all of his stories are built around some well-known historical event that has occurred in either Asia or the Pacific. "South Pacific," "Return to Paradise," "The Bridges at Toko-Ri," "Sayonara," and "Hawaii" are motion picture versions of his works. In this excerpt from* Return to Paradise, *Michener brings the South Pacific alive with his rich description of life in the tropics.*

Word Alert

aloft	above; at a great height
Australian Outback	isolated rural country of Australia
barren	bare; desolate
boisterous	noisy, rowdy; expressive of exuberance and high spirits
Bora Bora	an island in the South Pacific northwest of Tahiti
Canaques	French for Kanakas, meaning South Sea Islanders
chicory	an herb: the roasted root is used to flavor coffee while the plant is used in salads
convoluted	coiled, twisted; involved and intricate
coral	calcerous skeletal deposit; if it's attached and growing, it is alive
Fiji	islands in the Southwest Pacific; an independent dominion that is part of the British Commonwealth
flamboyant	showy, ornate; given to dashing display
kava	an alcoholic drink made from kava which is a pepper plant
keenly	extremely sensitive; astute, aware of

kookaburra	a bird native to Australia that is about the size of a crow and has a call resembling loud laughter
lagoon	a shallow channel or pond near a larger body of water
languid	sluggish or listless, slow moving
neighing	to make the loud, prolonged cry of a horse
New Caledonia	an island in the Southwest Pacific governed by France
New Guinea	an island northeast of Australia
Noumea	a city and port in New Caledonia
Pan	the Greek god of shepherds and hunters, and the traditional inventor of the panpipe
plaintive	melancholy or sad; suffering
plumes	feathers; material, as a tuft of hair worn as an ornament; probably a reference to the horses' manes
provincial	relating to or coming from a province, a district, or a part of a country
Rabaul	a city at the eastern end of New Britain that is part of New Guinea
rejuvenating	to make youthful again; renew, reinvigorate
Sepik natives	a tribe whose home is along the Sepik River in Papua, New Guinea
subtler	more delicate; more refined
Tahiti	an island in the South Pacific
temporal	finite time as opposed to eternity; relating to an earthly life
Tonga	a Pacific island east of Fiji that is part of the British Commonwealth
writhe	to move or proceed with twists and turns; to twist as if from pain or struggling

1 The South Pacific sharpens the perceptions of a man and brings him closer to an elemental nature. It may seem contradictory, but in the languid tropics one spends more time contemplating those great good things of sound and sight and smell.

This time I saw some things I had missed before. The mountains of New Caledonia, great glowing red hills rising from green valleys, were brilliantly beautiful. On the Australian Outback, across absolutely barren wilderness, I saw from aloft a herd of wild horses galloping with their heads stretched forward and their plumes flying. I saw the lagoon at Bora Bora, nestling beneath the volcano, sleeping within the protecting rim of coral. I can't forget that curious and half-revolting sight in Tonga, where entire trees were covered with sacred bats, squirming, furry, flying creatures whose chatter was never silenced. I remember the gay color of the provincial square in Noumea, where the flamboyant trees were aflame and where Canaques danced beneath them, shuffling for hours at a time while frenzied natives beat upon gasoline tins until the night throbbed. 2

There were strange things to feel, too. There was the brain coral that grows along the edge of the reef, a huge ball of rock covered with softly convoluted folds, living and delicate to the touch. I used to lie upon them and they would clutch my belly and keep me from slipping down the face of the reef. I remember the giant Rabaul snails, bigger than my fist, crawling over my fingers, no part of them moving, yet with everything in motion. Or the indescribable shock of those cold tropical shower baths where you would expect to relish anything cool—but not that cold! And what I liked best, the feel of the kava bowl in Fiji, a coconut shell worn grayish-brown by many hands over many years, cool to the touch yet containing a bite as the kava hit my gums. 3

Of the tropic sounds none can compare with the thunder of surf upon the distant reef, where the coral halts the vast waves in full flight so that they writhe into the air like monstrous horses along the rim of a Greek bowl, neighing and thrashing their forefeet. The most unbelievable sound, of course, was the laughter of the kookaburra birds in Australia. I heard them at least a hundred times but never without wanting to laugh along with them, for their shattering cry is totally boisterous. There was a subtler sound that came in time to represent the jungle. A crowd of Sepik natives had been flown down to our plantation in New Guinea, and in their homesick huts they played endlessly upon their reed pipes of Pan. Sometimes they played for twenty hours at a stretch, four plaintive notes weaving a haunted spell. If I were to hear that monotonous tune tonight, I would be back in New Guinea—and I would like that. 4

5   There were good things to taste, too, such as the juicy mangoes in Tahiti that drip bright yellow stains upon your chin. The classic taste was the sun-sweet pineapple of New Guinea, which was more acid and memorable than I've ever known before or since. It clung to my fingers for a day as if reluctant to let me forget how good the feast had been.

6   But in human beings it is the sense of smell—least regarded of the senses—which is most powerful in evoking memories; so that now if I smell burnt chicory, I am in Fiji. If I smell clean ocean fish, I'm in the Tahiti market. Or a whiff of burnt sulfur can pitch me back into the sugar factories of Queensland. . . . I have tried to imprison the smell of ripe vanilla oils as they drift across Raiatea on some dewy morning. . . . But the queenly fragrance of the tropics is the tender perfume of frangipani blossoms when dew is on them. The frangipani is a miraculous tree which bears a multitude of creamy white flowers whose petals shade into a golden amber where they join the stem. And there they hide as lovely a fragrance as we know.

7   But rejuvenating as it is to feel oneself close to nature, that alone is never enough. Along with the timelessness of natural things must go a concern with temporal events if a man expects to live with any decency in his world. If the South Pacific were merely an escape from reality it would be nothing but a pleasant grave; but that is not the case, for when I am in the South Pacific I am each day more keenly an American. And from that restful vantage of islands and coral I sometimes discover things I did not know before.

ACTIVE READING

The Active Reading exercise gives you an opportunity to reread the essay with a critical eye. By answering the questions that follow, you will extend and sharpen your understanding of the selection. This activity will help you become a more efficient reader and a more effective writer.

INTRODUCTORY PARAGRAPH   *(par. 1)*

The opening paragraph introduces the subject of the essay, the author's thesis (the point he wants to make), and a plan for the development of the essay.

    1. What is the subject of this essay?

    2. What thesis does the writer intend to develop and prove in this essay?

3. How does the author plan to develop the essay?

4. What words reveal this plan?

5. What seems contradictory to the author?

6. What inference can you draw about American culture based on the narrator's beliefs?

DEVELOPMENT PARAGRAPH *(par. 2)*

7. Identify the sense to which the author appeals in this paragraph?

The author's references to places, people, animals, and things come alive for the reader because he uses descriptive words or phrases to paint a picture. In the exercise below, match the place, person, animal, or thing with its appropriate description. For each numbered item, write the letter that is a match.

8. hills   a. flamboyant . . . were aflame

9. valleys   b. galloping

10. wilderness   c. at Bora Bora, nestling beneath the volcano

11. wild horses   d. sacred

12. plumes   e. barren

13. lagoon   f. throbbed

14. coral   g. frenzied . . . beat upon gasoline tins

15. bats   h. protecting rim of

16. creatures   i. gay color of the

17. provincial square j. great glowing red

18. trees   k. squirming, furry, flying

19. Canaques   l. green

20. natives   m. danced beneath them, shuffling for hours

21. night   n. flying

DEVELOPMENT PARAGRAPH *(par. 3)*

22. What sense does the author say he will appeal to in this paragraph?

23. Describe completely the brain coral that grows along the edge of the reef?

24. How does the narrator touch these coral covered rocks and how do they affect him?

25. How does the narrator describe the Rabaul snails?

26. How does the author describe his feelings about the tropical shower baths?

27. How does the narrator describe the kava bowl?

28. What produces the taste (bite) the narrator experiences?

    a. the lingering taste of coconut

    b. the time-worn taste of people's hands

    c. the taste of the kava drink

DEVELOPMENT PARAGRAPH *(par. 4)*

29. What sense does the narrator appeal to in this paragraph?

30. Of the sounds listed below, which one is <u>not</u> used to describe the surf?

    a. thunder

    b. wheels turning

    c. horses neighing

    d . horses thrashing their feet

31. How is the sound of the surf created?

32. Write the simile that the narrator uses in this paragraph.

33. What two things are being compared in this simile?

34. What is the similarity between waves and horses?

35. The sound the kookaburra birds make is similar to what human sound?

36. What did the narrator feel like doing when he heard them?

37. How does he describe the sounds the birds make?

38. The more subtler sound is made by whom?

39. What instrument do they play?

40. The narrator says of the Sepik natives, ". . . they played endlessly upon their reed pipes of Pan." This might be considered an example of what figure of speech?

41. Actually, what was the longest amount of time they could play for and what sounds did they make?

42. What place did the narrator associate with this sound?

43. The narrator says their tune is monotonous, yet if he were to hear it he'd be back in New Guinea and would like that. What inference can you draw from this?

DEVELOPMENT PARAGRAPH *(par. 5)*

This short paragraph appeals to taste.

44. The narrator mentions two characteristics of mangoes from Tahiti. What are they?

45. The narrator mentions three characteristics of pineapple from New Guinea. What are they?

DEVELOPMENT PARAGRAPH *(par. 6)*

The author uses this paragraph to appeal to the sense of smell. For each numbered item, write the letter of the place that comes to mind for the narrator when he experiences that smell.

46. burnt chicory	a. Queensland
47. frangipani blossoms	b. Raiatea
48. clean ocean fish	c. Fiji
49. burnt sulphur	d. the tropics
50. ripe vanilla oils	e. Tahiti

CONCLUDING PARAGRAPH *(par. 7)*

Everything leading up to this last paragraph is focused on how the narrator, through his five senses, got to know the South Pacific. In this conclusion, the author makes reference indirectly to his thesis statement and tells how he feels about his experience.

51. How does the author feel about being close to nature?

52. With what does the author say man must be concerned?

53. According to the author, if the South Pacific were merely an escape from reality what would it be like?

54. While the South Pacific may be an escape from the author's American reality, it has its own reality and culture. How does this awareness affect the author?

55. From his vantage point in the South Pacific, the author says he discovers things he did not know before. What discoveries might you infer he is talking about?

56. Is description used as a primary writing strategy in this essay? If not, what strategy does the use of description support?

57. The author uses transitional words and phrases to link ideas in this essay. List at least five.

58. The author's primary purpose in this selection is to:
    a. inform
    b. persuade
    c. entertain

The Active Reading exercise can be scored using the answer key and grading grid. Enter your grade in the progress chart.

GUIDED WRITING

The Guided Writing section at the end of this chapter (page 74) provides topics and plans for writing descriptive paragraphs and essays. Select a topic and write a short essay by following the writing plan that begins on page 76. Continue work in this chapter until you have finished all three Active Reading and Guided Writing activities.

THIS WAY FOR THE GAS, LADIES AND GENTLEMEN

by Tadeusz Borowski

Tadeusz Borowski (1922-1951) was born in the Soviet Ukraine to Polish parents. Borowski's literary efforts were shaped by his wartime experiences as an inmate and survivor of the Nazi concentration camps at Auschwitz and Dachau. This Way for the Gas, Ladies and Gentlemen, *a collection of Borowski's stories, presents a fierce portrayal of human brutality. In the following excerpt from the title story the narrator, a prisoner himself, is a member of the labor gang called the "Canada men." Their job is to help process new arrivals at the concentration camp. Through the use of extensive description, the reader witnesses the betrayal of one prisoner by another in the struggle for survival. The ultimate irony in Borowski's life lies in the circumstances of his death: after surviving the gas chambers of Auschwitz, he committed suicide by asphyxiation at the age of twenty- nine.*

Word Alert

also los	in German, *lets go* or *so go*
Canada men	members of the labor gang, prisoners themselves, who helped to unload the incoming transports of people destined for the gas chambers in the concentration camp
jawohl	in German, *yes*
Mamele	in Yiddish, *Mama*
meine Herrschaften	in German, *ladies and gentleman*
multicoloured	of various colors; British spelling
Reich	in German, *Empire*
S.S.	in German, an abbreviation for *Schutzstaffel*, an elite unit of Nazis created to serve as body guard to Adolf Hitler and later expanded to take charge of central security, policing action, and extermination of "undesirables"
Sosnowiec-Bedzin	two mining towns in southern Poland
stupefied	astonished; amazed
verboten	in German, *it is forbidden*
verstanden	in German, *understood*

1   "The transport is coming," somebody says. We spring to our feet, all eyes turn in one direction. Around the bend, one after another, the cattle cars begin rolling in. The train backs into the station, a conductor leans out, waves his hand, blows a whistle. The locomotive whistles back with a shrieking noise, puffs, the train rolls slowly alongside the ramp. In the tiny barred windows appear pale, wilted, exhausted human faces, terror-stricken women with tangled hair, unshaven men. They gaze at the station in silence. And then, suddenly, there is a stir inside the cars and a pounding against the wooden boards.

2   "Water! Air!"—weary, desperate cries.

3   Heads push through the windows, mouths gasp frantically for air. They draw a few breaths, then disappear; others come in their place, then also disappear. The cries and moans grow louder.

4   A man in a green uniform covered with more glitter than any of the others jerks his head impatiently, his lips twist in annoyance. He inhales deeply, then with a rapid gesture throws his cigarette away and signals to the guard. The guard removes the automatic from his shoulder, aims, sends a series of shots along the train. All is quiet now. Meanwhile, the trucks have arrived, steps are being drawn up, and the Canada men stand ready at their posts by the train doors. The S.S. officer with the briefcase raises his hand.

5   "Whoever takes gold, or anything at all besides food, will be shot for stealing Reich property. Understand? *Verstanden*?"

6   "*Jawohl*!" we answer eagerly.

7   "*Also los*! Begin!"

8   The bolts crack, the doors fall open. A wave of fresh air rushes inside the train. People . . . inhumanly crammed, buried under incredible heaps of luggage, suitcases, trunks, packages, crates, bundles of every description (everything that had been their past and was to start their future). Monstrously squeezed together, they have fainted from heat, suffocated, crushed one another. Now they push towards the opened doors, breathing like fish cast out on the sand.

9   "Attention! Out, and take your luggage with you! Take out everything. Pile all your stuff near the exits. Yes, your coats too. It is summer. March to the left. Understand?"

10   "Sir, what's going to happen to us?" They jump from the train on to the gravel, anxious, worn-out.

11   "Where are you people from?"

"Sosnowiec-Bedzin. Sir, what's going to happen to us?" They repeat 12
the question stubbornly, gazing into our tired eyes.

"I don't know, I don't understand Polish." 13

It is the camp law: people going to their death must be deceived to the 14
very end. This is the only permissible form of charity. The heat is tremendous. The sun hangs directly over our heads, the white, hot sky quivers, the air vibrates, an occasional breeze feels like a sizzling blast from a furnace. Our lips are parched, the mouth fills with the salty taste of blood, the body is weak and heavy from lying in the sun. Water!

A huge, multicoloured wave of people loaded down with luggage 15
pours from the train like a blind, mad river trying to find a new bed. But before they have a chance to recover, before they can draw a breath of fresh air and look at the sky, bundles are snatched from their hands, coats ripped off their backs, their purses and umbrellas taken away.

"But please, sir, it's for the sun, I cannot. . ." 16

"*Verboten!*" one of us barks through clenched teeth. There is an S.S. 17
man standing behind your back, calm, efficient, watchful.

"*Meine Herrschaften*, this way, ladies and gentlemen, try not to throw 18
your things around, please. Show some goodwill," he says courteously, his restless hands playing with the slender whip.

"Of course, of course," they answer as they pass, and now they walk 19
alongside the train somewhat more cheerfully. A woman reaches down quickly to pick up her handbag. The whip flies, the woman screams, stumbles, and falls under the feet of the surging crowd. Behind her, a child cries in a thin little voice "*Mamele!*"—a very small girl with tangled black curls.

The heaps grow. Suitcases, bundles, blankets, coats, handbags that 20
open as they fall, spilling coins, gold, watches; mountains of bread pile up at the exits, heaps of marmalade, jams, masses of meat, sausages; sugar spills on the gravel. Trucks, loaded with people, start up with a deafening roar and drive off amidst the wailing and screaming of the women separated from their children, and the stupefied silence of the men left behind. They are the ones who had been ordered to step to the right—the healthy and the young who will go to the camp. In the end, they too will not escape death, but first they must work.

ACTIVE READING

The Active Reading exercise gives you an opportunity to reread the essay with a critical eye. By answering the questions that follow, you will extend and sharpen your understanding of the selection. This activity will help you become a more efficient reader and a more effective writer.

INTRODUCTORY PARAGRAPHS *(par. 1–3)*

In the opening sentence someone speaks and what they say gets our attention. People spring to their feet to watch, making the reader curious about the train that is coming. In this first paragraph, the author introduces certain elements of the setting with descriptive references that appeal to sight, sound, and touch.

1. What kind of cars make up this train and, therefore, what do you expect to see?

2. What do we see the conductor doing? Hear him doing?

3. What sounds are made by the locomotive?

4. Describe the faces you see in the tiny, barred windows.

5. How does the narrator describe the women? The men?

6. The first paragraph ends with a noise. What is it?

7. This scene is punctuated by weary, desperate cries for:

8. By appealing to touch and sound, the third paragraph gives us a feeling for the life and death experience at hand. What are the people doing?

INTRODUCTORY PARAGRAPHS *(par. 4–7)*

Paragraphs four to seven introduce characters and dialogue that help us to infer the setting, the time, and place of these events.

9. What war is taking place?

10. What is the setting for this story?

11. What three words or phrases in these paragraphs help the reader to make this inference?

The author describes the appearance, actions, and words of an S.S. officer and his effect on others. For each word or phrase in items 12-20, identify the sense to which it appeals (sight, sound, taste, smell, touch).

12. a green uniform covered with more glitter

13. jerks his head impatiently

14. lips twist in annoyance

15. he inhales deeply

16. with a rapid gesture throws his cigarette away

17. signals to the guard

18. guard removes automatic from shoulder, aims

19. sends a series of shots along the train

20. all is quiet now

21. What inferences can be made about the reason why it is suddenly quiet?

When the S.S. officer is described as impatient and annoyed, the author is using **irony**. Irony is the contrast between appearance and reality. In reality, the feelings of impatience and annoyance expressed by the officer more rightfully belong to the people stuffed into cattle cars.

22. The description in paragraph 4, along with the dialogue in paragraphs 5, 6, and 7, establishes the relationships among the various people mentioned. Arrange these people according to the status hierarchy. Who takes orders from whom?

The setting and mood are established in the first seven paragraphs. **Mood** is the atmosphere or feeling that a writer creates in a work through the choice of setting, imagery, details, descriptions, and other evocative words. The mood created here is tense, filled with fear and desperation. This is no ordinary train depot and these are no ordinary passengers.

DEVELOPMENT PARAGRAPH *(par. 8)*

In paragraph eight the author uses sight, sound, and touch to get the reader to experience the feelings of the people on the train. For each word or phrase below identify the sense, or senses, to which the author appeals.

23. the bolts crack

24. the doors fall open

25. a wave of fresh air rushes inside

26. people inhumanly crammed

27. buried under incredible heaps of luggage

28. monstrously squeezed together

29. fainted from heat

30. suffocated

31. crushed one another

32. they push towards the opened doors

33. breathing like fish cast out on the sand

34. What two living things are compared in the simile in question 33 and how are they alike?

DEVELOPMENT PARAGRAPHS *(par. 9–14)*

Using a writer's technique known as **foreshadowing**, the author gives clues or hints about what is to happen in the story. On the train people are treated like cargo and when they exit are required to leave their belongings behind. This gross mistreatment, horrible in itself, pales by comparison to the fate that awaits them.

In paragraphs nine through fourteen, the author uses dialogue and description to give more information about the new arrivals, and to establish the relationship between them and the Canada men. Both groups are prisoners in a concentration camp. By giving orders, the Canada men establish themselves as superior to the people from the train.

35. What orders are the people given as they exit the train?

36. Someone asks, "Sir, what's going to happen to us?" How does the narrator avoid answering this question?

37. When they ask again, how does the narrator avoid answering the question a second time?

38. Why does the narrator avoid answering their questions?
    a. he doesn't know the answer
    b. he doesn't understand Polish
    c. he doesn't want to hurt them
    d. he is not allowed to tell them

39. The narrator refers to this camp law as "the only permissible form of charity." What does he mean?

40. While this deception may appear charitable, what was a more likely reason for such a rule?

The fact that the new arrivals do not know their fate, and the reader does, is an example of **dramatic irony**. This occurs when the reader is aware of something about which the characters involved know nothing.

At this point in paragraph fourteen, the separation between the Canada men and the new prisoners narrows. The Canada men, despite their superior status, are depicted as sharing the experience of the new arrivals. This is done primarily through references to touch and taste. The narrator uses the word *our* to emphasize his identification with the new prisoners. The Canada men, even though they are members of the labor gang, could be put to death with the other prisoners at any time.

Identify each phrase below as appealing to touch, taste, or sight.

41. the heat is tremendous

42. the sun hangs directly over our heads

43. the white, hot sky quivers

44. the air vibrates

45. an occasional breeze feels like a sizzling blast from a furnace

46. our lips are parched

47. the mouth fills with the salty taste of blood

48. the body is weak and heavy from lying in the sun

49. Water!

50. The simile in question 45 compares what two things?

51. The reference to a "sizzling blast from a furnace" hints at the eventual fate of prisoners in this camp. This writer's technique is known as:

The great majority of the new arrivals in the concentration camp were taken from the train depot to the gas chambers where they were murdered with poison gas. The bodies were taken to ovens where they were cremated. This was the eventual fate of prisoners in the camp.

DEVELOPMENT PARAGRAPH *(par. 15)*

The author describes the new arrivals as " A huge, multicoloured wave of people." This is a comparison between two unlike things where one is said to be the other.

52. What kind of figurative language is the writer using?

53. What two things are being compared?

54. People pour from the train "like a blind, mad river trying to find a new bed." What kind of figurative language is the writer using?

55. What two things are being compared?

56. How is this group of people similar to a river trying to find a bed?

57. As the new arrivals disembark the train, the Canada men swing into action under the watchful eyes of an S.S. officer. What do the Canada men do to these people?

DEVELOPMENT PARAGRAPHS *(par. 16–19)*

Paragraphs sixteen through nineteen use dialogue and appeal to sound and touch to remind the reader of the hierarchy of authority. The presence of the S.S. officers keeps the Canada men snarling at the new arrivals.

"Meine Herrschaften, this way, ladies and gentlemen, try not to throw your things around, please. Show some goodwill, he says courteously, his restless hands playing with the slender whip."

This is an example of **verbal irony**, a contrast between what is said and what is meant. The S.S. officer's sarcasm, his sneering, taunting attitude, is in sharp contrast to his "kind" words.

58. How do the people respond to his words at first?

59. What seemingly harmless move by a new arrival exposes the S.S. officer's deception and cruelty?

Identify the use of sight, sound, or touch in each of the words or phrases listed below.

60. the whip flies

61. the woman screams

62. [the woman] stumbles

63. [the woman] falls under the feet of the surging crowd

64. a child cries in a thin, little voice, "Mamele!"

65. a very small girl with tangled black curls

CONCLUDING PARAGRAPH *(par. 20)*

The concluding paragraph uses examples, vivid details, and description to summarize what happens, with a focus on the different kinds of separations that occur.

66. What is the first thing people are separated from?

67. The long list of possessions appeals to what senses?

68. What other separations occur?

69. Description of these separations is accomplished using references to sound. In what ways do we hear the people being separated?

70. What happens to the healthy and young men who are left behind?

71. What do you think happens to the women and children?

72. What is the point of view of the narrator, first or third person?

73. Did he survive the concentration camp and how do you know?

74. Is description used as a primary writing strategy in this essay? If not, what strategy does the use of description support?

75. The author uses transitional words and phrases to link ideas in this essay. List at least five.

76. The author's primary purpose in this selection is to:
    a. inform
    b. persuade
    c. entertain

The Active Reading exercise can be scored using the answer key and grading grid. Enter your grade in the progress chart.

GUIDED WRITING

The Guided Writing section that begins on the next page provides topics and plans for writing descriptive paragraphs and essays. Select a topic and write an extended essay by following the writing plan that begins on page 76.

GUIDED WRITING

This part of the chapter will help you apply what you have learned about writing descriptive paragraphs and essays. Choose one of the topics listed below for each writing assignment that you do. If you want to write about something else, ask your instructor if the topic is appropriate for writing description. Follow the plan that applies to write your composition. Submit your completed composition to the instructor for evaluation. When you receive a grade for this work, enter it in the progress chart.

WRITING TOPICS

- Describe an event you witnessed that was dramatic or spellbinding, like Steinbeck's description of the octopus stalking and killing the crab.

- Describe a place where you have spent time close to nature: a mountain, a river, a canyon, a forest, an ocean, a desert, a jungle, etc.

- Choose a culture different than your own that you have experienced personally, read about, or have been told about, and describe it in detail.

- In "Return to Paradise," James Mitchener makes a convincing case for travel to the South Pacific. Select a place and describe it so that you persuade your readers to want to go there.

- Using ample description and dialogue, create a period or event in history which illustrates man's inhumanity to man: the Holocaust, the Trail of Tears (Cherokee Indians), the Spanish Inquisition, the Salem Witch Trials, the Killing Fields of Cambodia, the Slave Auction. Remember to include real people who express real feelings.

- Was there ever a time you did something to hurt another person: out of fear, out of guilt, out of a deep sense of loyalty, or for money? Describe the setting and the people involved. Tell the story by describing how people look, their actions, thoughts, and feelings. Use dialogue where appropriate.

PREWRITING: GENERATING IDEAS

Now that you have selected a topic, you will need to gather information and generate ideas before you begin to write. If you choose to describe something based on experience, you will probably rely on your memory, other people's input, and your own creativity for details. Other types of description may require that you use reference works to collect information for your composition.

When you describe a person, place, thing, or idea, you will be creating vivid images for the reader by appealing to the five senses. List the ways in which your subject appeals to one or more of the following: sight, sound, taste, smell, and touch. You may decide to focus on one, some, or all of the five senses to describe your subject. Keep the five senses in mind as you follow the plan for writing a descriptive paragraph or essay.

WRITING PLAN: THE PARAGRAPH

1. Decide the point of view of the narrator, first or third person. Begin with a strong image that gets the reader's attention. Introduce your topic at the beginning of the paragraph.

2. Set the tone for the paragraph, your attitude toward the subject. The tone might be serious or humorous, formal or informal.

3. Create atmosphere for your paragraph by using words and phrases that help the reader experience your subject.

4. Appeal to as many of the five senses as necessary to develop your topic adequately and reinforce the point you want to make in this paragraph.

5. Write a conclusion to your paragraph that includes description and presents an overview, summarizes, or expresses an opinion.

6. To create unity in your writing, make sure that each sentence in the paragraph relates to the topic. Your writing will be coherent if ideas follow one another in a logical pattern and sentences flow smoothly from one to the other. Use transitions to link or connect ideas. The list of transitional words and phrases at the back of this book is for your use and reference when you write (see pages 259–264).

7. Use variety in your choice of words to maintain reader interest. Where appropriate, use figurative language to increase the impact of your words and to stimulate the reader's imagination. The most commonly used figures of speech are the simile, metaphor, personification, and hyperbole. Definitions of literary and rhetorical terms can be found in the Glossary on pages 265–270.

8. Create a title for your paragraph, a word or phrase that captures the reader's interest and tells what you are writing about.

9. Use the *Checklist for Revision* provided at the end of this section to help you review and revise your paragraph.

WRITING PLAN: SHORT AND EXTENDED ESSAYS

While short and extended essays are similar—both have introductory and concluding paragraphs—the extended essay has more development paragraphs. "Return to Paradise," a short essay, is developed through appeals to the five senses and the use of examples. In "This Way for the Gas, Ladies and Gentlemen," the author uses extensive description to augment his narrative.

Introductory Paragraph(s)

1. Decide your point of view. Is the narrator of the essay involved in the action (first person), or an observer outside the action (third person)?

2. Use a strong image or images to get the reader's attention. Tell what the essay is about by introducing your topic and purpose. This is the thesis statement, the main idea to be supported throughout the essay.

3. Use vivid details to introduce the setting and create a mood. The introductory paragraph(s) will set the tone for the essay, your attitude toward the subject.

4. State your plan for the development of this essay. An extended essay may contain more than one introductory paragraph.

Development Paragraph(s)

1. Each development paragraph can be used to examine a different aspect of your subject. For example, in "Return to Paradise," each development paragraph appeals to one of the five senses. Let the reader know your topic or focus for each new paragraph.

2. Create atmosphere in your development paragraphs by using imagery: words and phrases that help the reader experience your subject.

3. Appeal to as many of the five senses as necessary to develop the topic adequately and reinforce the point you want to make in your essay.

4. If you are writing an extended descriptive essay, use the development paragraphs to include more details and paint a more complete picture for the reader.

5. All sentences in a paragraph should relate to the topic and to one another. All paragraphs in an essay should support the topic and follow some logical order. Use transitions to link ideas within paragraphs and to make connections between paragraphs. Refer to the list of transitional words and phrases on pages 259–264.

6. Use variety in your choice of words to maintain reader interest. Where appropriate, use figurative language to increase the impact of your words and to stimulate the reader's imagination. The most commonly used figures of speech are the simile, metaphor, personification, and hyperbole. Definitions of literary and rhetorical terms can be found in the Glossary on pages 265–270.

Concluding Paragraph(s)

1. In your conclusion, restate the thesis in some way for emphasis. If you are using examples, save the most powerful one for last.

2. Use vivid details and descriptions to summarize, offer an opinion, or reach a conclusion that reinforces the point of your essay.

3. Let the reader know how you feel about the subject you are describing. Provide details that account for these feelings.

4. More than one paragraph may be used to conclude an extended essay.

5. The checklist below will help you to review and revise your essay.

note: The title of your essay should be a word or phrase that captures the reader's attention and tells what you are writing about. Create a title for your first draft and review it before making it final.

CHECKLIST FOR REVISION

1. My paragraph/essay has a first- or third-person point of view. I begin with a strong statement that gets the reader's attention, introduce my topic, and set the tone. If I am writing an essay, I state my thesis in the opening paragraph(s).

2. I use vivid details to introduce the setting and create a mood. I appeal to the five senses and use imagery to paint a picture for the reader. Each development paragraph examines a different aspect of my subject.

3. In an extended essay, I use the development paragraphs to include ample details and examples.

4. In concluding my paragraph or essay, I use description to present an overview, summarize, offer an opinion, or reach a conclusion that reinforces my point.

5. I let the reader know how I feel by providing details about the subject that account for my feelings.

6. Sentences within each paragraph relate to the topic. Development paragraphs follow a logical order and support the point of the essay. I use transitions to link ideas within paragraphs and to make connections between paragraphs.

7. I use variety in my choice of words to maintain reader interest. Where appropriate, I use figurative language to increase the impact of my words and to stimulate the reader's imagination.

8. As I revise the form and content of my work, I correct errors in punctuation, capitalization, spelling, grammar, and usage.

9. The title of my paragraph or essay tells what I wrote about and captures the reader's interest.

Continue work in this chapter until you have finished all three Active Reading and Guided Writing activities.

Chapter 4

ILLUSTRATION

Effective writing in any form depends upon illustration, examples that provide details and facts. When you give an example, you offer specific information about a general category. France is an example of the category, *country*, while the Pacific is an example of the category, *ocean*. Examples make writing vivid and illustrate the points you wish to make.

Examples are used mainly to support other writing strategies. Rarely will you find a piece of writing based solely on illustration. Randall Williams uses examples to support his narrative about growing up poor in "Daddy Tucked the Blanket." James Michener includes examples in "Return to Paradise," his descriptive essay about the South Pacific.

In later chapters, strategies that focus on explanation will use examples in support of their main points. These strategies include process analysis, comparison and contrast, classification, definition, and cause and effect. When you write persuasively you may also use examples to illustrate your position.

If you are writing about a personal experience you will need to provide the examples from memory. If you are unfamiliar with the subject, you will need to gather examples from the experience of others or from books. In either case, if the examples you use are well chosen and relevant, the reader is likely to accept your assertions.

Whether your purpose is to narrate, describe, explain, or persuade, use examples that are appropriate and accurate. Be sure these examples support your thesis and illustrate the points you are trying to make. While quality is more important than quantity, you will need to present enough examples to illustrate your point. Your writing will be more convincing if you offer specific examples rather than broad generalizations.

This chapter contains three reading selections, all examples of illustrative writing. The first is a paragraph, the second a short essay, and the third a longer piece. Each is followed by an Active Reading exercise that helps you to understand the form and content of the reading model. The Guided Writing section at the end of this chapter will help you to create three original pieces of writing using illustration.

Chapter Selections

Sweet Potato Pie *by Eugenia Collier*

Tricks! Treats! Gangway! *by Ray Bradbury*

Secrets of the Centenarians *by N. Larina*

SWEET POTATO PIE

by Eugenia Collier

Born in Baltimore in 1928, Collier attended Howard University, Columbia University, and the University of Maryland. Much of her professional career has been spent as an English professor, most recently at Howard University. Her poems and stories appeared regularly in Negro Digest, Black World, TV Guide, *and* The New York Times. *Her short story "Marigolds" won the 1969 Gwendolyn Brooks Award for Fiction. Collier has also written scholarly articles on African American literature. She wrote "Sweet Potato Pie" as a gift of love to an old friend. His family, she says, "exemplified the strength of the black family . . . so often assailed, put-upon, oppressed, but still prevailing because of their own toughness of spirit and love for each other." In the excerpt presented here, Collier uses examples to describe the culture of Harlem.*

Word Alert

ancestral	related to or from ancestors
boisterous	rowdy, noisy, exuberant, high-spirited
epic	extending beyond the usual in size or scope
flitting	to move about rapidly and nimbly
Garvey Day	in honor of Marcus Garvey (1887–1940) who preached black nationalism and pride in the 1920s
Harlem	One of the largest African American communities in the United States, Harlem is a residential and business section of Manhattan in New York City. In recent years, it has diversified with the influx of Latinos and continental Africans.
hawkers	those that hawk wares; peddlers
livid	discolored by bruising
mythic	imaginary or fictitious
ominously	having a menacing or threatening aspect
panorama	an unlimited view of all visible objects over a wide area
saucily	flippant and bold in manner or attitude
saunter	stroll; to walk in an idle or leisurely manner
savor	to delight in, to enjoy, to relish

siren songs an alluring utterance or appeal, especially one that is seductive or deceptive

throngs crowds

Whenever I come to Harlem I feel somehow as if I were coming home—to some mythic ancestral home. The problems are real, the people are real—yet there is some mysterious epic quality about Harlem, as if all black people began and ended there, as if each had left something of himself. As if in Harlem the very heart of blackness pulsed its beautiful tortured rhythms. Joining the throngs of people that saunter Lenox Avenue late afternoons, I headed for Charley's apartment. Along the way I savored the panorama of Harlem—women with shopping bags trudging wearily home; little kids flitting saucily through the crowd; groups of adolescent boys striding boldly along—some boisterous, some ominously silent; tables of merchandise spread on the sidewalks with hawkers singing their siren songs of irresistible bargains; a blaring microphone sending forth waves of words to draw passersby into a restless bunch around a slender young man whose eyes have seen Truth; defeated men standing around on street corners or sitting on steps, heads down, hands idle; posters announcing Garvey Day; "Buy Black" stamped on pavements; store windows bright with things African; stores still boarded up, a livid scar from last year's rioting. There was a terrible tension in the air; I thought of how quickly dry timber becomes a roaring fire from a single spark.

ACTIVE READING

The Active Reading exercise gives you an opportunity to reread the paragraph with a critical eye. By answering the questions that follow, you will extend and sharpen your understanding of the selection. This activity will help you become a more efficient reader and a more effective writer.

1. The narrator begins by telling us the setting for this paragraph and how she feels about it. What place is the author writing about?

2. The narrator says she feels as if she is coming home. What kind of a home?

The narrator says that even though the problems and people are real, there is "some mysterious epic quality" about the place. This gets the reader's attention which is maintained by the author's use of examples to illustrate her point.

3–5. What three examples of this mysterious quality does the author present?

6. "Joining the throngs of people that saunter Lenox Avenue late afternoons, I headed for Charley's apartment." This sentence serves which of the following purposes?

   a. shows the narrator as part of the group
   b. acts as a transition from a general description to specific examples
   c. takes the reader from the abstract to the concrete
   d. all of the above

7. The narrator says, "Along the way, I savored the panorama of Harlem—" Does she experience this as pleasant or unpleasant? What word in this statement tells you so?

The author describes the sights and sounds of Harlem. This panorama is made vivid for the reader with examples that illustrate the "beautiful tortured rhythms" of Harlem. Identify the people or things described by the phrases below.

8. _____ with shopping bags trudging wearily home

9. _____ flitting saucily through the crowd

10. _____ striding boldly along—some boisterous, some ominously silent

11. _____ spread on the sidewalks

12. _____ singing their siren songs of irresistible bargains

13. _____ sending forth waves of words

14. _____ into a restless bunch

15. _____ whose eyes have seen Truth

16. _____ standing around on street corners or sitting on steps, heads down, hands idle

17. _____ announcing Garvey Day

18. _____ stamped on pavements

19. _____ bright with things African

20. _____ still boarded up

21. _____ from last year's rioting

Throughout the paragraph we see the rhythms of Harlem as both beautiful and tortured. At the end, the author summarizes by describing the atmosphere on the street and by offering her opinion.

22. What word best describes the feeling in the air?

   a. tense
   b. joyful
   c. relaxed
   d. sad

23. In closing the narrator says, "I thought of how quickly dry timber becomes a roaring fire from a single spark." What opinion is the author expressing here?

   a. large amounts of dry timber in the street are dangerous
   b. people should be careful when handling matches
   c. people in Harlem are like dry timber ready to ignite and riot again
   d. all of the above

24. To what does the author compare "a terrible tension in the air?"

   a. dry timber
   b. a roaring fire
   c. a single spark
   d. all of the above

25. The author uses transitional words and phrases to link ideas in this paragraph. List at least five.

26. The author's primary purpose in this selection is to:

   a. inform
   b. persuade
   c. entertain

The Active Reading exercise can be scored using the answer key and grading grid. Enter your grade in the progress chart.

GUIDED WRITING

The Guided Writing section at the end of this chapter (page 98) provides topics and plans for writing paragraphs and essays that use examples. Select a topic and write an illustrative paragraph by following the writing plan on page 99. Continue work in this chapter until you have finished all three Active Reading and Guided Writing activities.

TRICKS! TREATS! GANGWAY!

by Ray Bradbury

Born in Waukegan, Illinois in 1920, Bradbury graduated from high school in Los Angeles, and worked as a newsboy to support himself while he was writing. He started writing fantasy and science fiction full-time in 1943. The Martian Chronicles (1950), an account of man's colonization of Mars, is widely regarded as his most outstanding work. It blends many of his major themes including freedom versus conformity, and the idea of space as a frontier wilderness, a place where man sets out on a quest for self-discovery and spiritual renewal. Among his most well-known short story collections are The Illustrated Man (1951), Fahrenheit 451 (1953), The Golden Apples of the Sun (1953), and Dandelion Wine (1957). His work has appeared in more than seven hundred anthologies, and he has written for magazines, film, and television. His work has been recognized with numerous awards and prizes. In the excerpt presented here, Bradbury recalls Halloween in the old-fashioned Midwestern town of his childhood.

Word Alert

banshee	a female spirit in Gaelic folklore whose appearance or wailing warns of approaching death
bereavements	mourning the loss of loved ones
caldron	a large kettle or boiler
corn shocks	a pile of Indian corn stalks set up in a field to dry
disemboweled	with the entrails or insides removed
gizzards	the part of a bird's digestive system located in the throat area that grinds the food
lurks	sneaks; those that lie in wait in a place of concealment for an evil purpose
papier-mâché	paper or newsprint that, when combined with glue or other liquids, can be molded into objects
sappy	silly; foolishly or immaturely sentimental
scrabble	to scramble or clamber; to claw about clumsily or frantically
serpentines	like a serpent in form or movement; coils
tripe	stomach tissue of hoofed mammals that chew their cud, such as sheep, giraffes, deer, and camels
viscera	internal organs of the body such as the heart, liver, or intestines

1   **H**alloweens I have always considered wilder and richer and more important than even Christmas morn. The dark and lovely memories leap back at me as I see once again my ghostly relatives, and the lurks and things that creaked stairs or sang softly in the hinges when you opened a door. . . .

2   My grandparents' home, then, was a caldron to which we might bring hickory sticks that looked like witches' broken arms and leaves from the family graveyard out where the banshee trains ran by at night souling the air with bereavements. To their house, upstairs and down, must be fetched corn shocks from fields just beyond the burying tombs, and pumpkins. And from Woolworth's, orange-black crepe serpentines, and bags of black confetti which you tossed on the wind, yelling, "A witch just sneezed!" and papier-mâché masks that smelled like a sour dog's fur after you had snuffed in and out while running. All of it had to be fetched, carried, touched, held, sniffed, crunched along the way. . . .

3   The whole house had to be done over in a few short, wildly laughing hours. All staircases must be eliminated by grabbing leaves out of dining-room tables and covering the steps so you could only scrabble and slip up and then slide, shrieking, down, down, down, into night. The cellar must be mystified with sheets hung on lines in a ghostly maze through which giggling and screaming banshees must blunder and flee, children suddenly searching for mothers, and finding spiders. The icebox must be stashed with chicken viscera, beef hearts, ox tongues, tripe, chicken legs, and gizzards, so that at the height of the party the participants, trapped in the coal cellar, might pass around the "parts" of the dead witch: "Here's her heart! . . . Here's her finger! . . . Here's her eyeball!"

4   Then, everything set and placed and ready, you run out late from house to house to make certain-sure that each boy-ghost remembers, that each girl-become-witch will be there tomorrow night. Your gorilla fangs in your mouth, your winged cape flapping, you come home and stand in front of your grandparents' house and look at how great and spooky it has become, because your sappy aunt and your loony brother and you yourself have magicked it over, doused the lights, lit all the disemboweled pumpkins and got it ready like a dark beast to devour the children as they arrive through its open-mouth door tomorrow night. . . .

5   But the party was almost unimportant, wasn't it? Preparation was 70 percent of the lovely, mad game. As with most holidays, the getting set, the gathering sulfur for the explosion, was sweeter, sadder, lovelier than the stampede itself.

ACTIVE READING

The Active Reading exercise gives you an opportunity to reread the essay with a critical eye. By answering the questions that follow, you will extend and sharpen your understanding of the selection. This activity will help you become a more efficient reader and a more effective writer.

INTRODUCTORY PARAGRAPH   *(par. 1)*

The author introduces the subject in a thesis statement that gets the reader's attention by making a comparison. The details he offers and the evocative words he uses in this paragraph help to create a mood and an overview for the essay. Throughout, the author combines narrative and descriptive strategies with examples to illustrate the wildness and richness of his Halloween experience.

1. What is the subject of the essay?

2. What two holidays are compared?

3. What is the author's thesis statement?

While the author does not offer a specific plan, the mood he creates lets the reader know the essay will be about his Halloween experience.

4–6. List three phrases that help to create the mood for this essay.

DEVELOPMENT PARAGRAPH *(par. 2)*

The author tells us about the wildness and richness of Halloween using vivid examples to illustrate his point.

7. What was the setting for Halloween?

8. The metaphor in the first sentence of this paragraph compares what two fundamentally different things?

The nature of a metaphor is to show how two fundamentally different things are alike. A caldron is a kettle used for boiling and brewing. The caldron is a real thing, with **literal** meaning. Symbolically, the grandparents' home is a caldron in that it holds the Halloween "brew" of decorations the narrator and his cohorts collected. This is an example of **figurative** language.

9–14. The remainder of the paragraph provides examples of things the narrator and his friends brought to the grandparents' house to decorate for Halloween. Name them.

The examples above appeal to our senses in order to get us in the mood, to scare us. For items 15–24 below, identify the sense to which each description appeals.

15. looked like witches' broken arms

16. from the family graveyard

17. where the banshee trains ran by at night souling the air with bereavements

18. from fields just beyond the burying tombs, and pumpkins

19. orange-black

20. black confetti

21. you tossed on the wind

22. yelling, "A witch just sneezed!"

23. smelled like a sour dog's fur after you had snuffed in and out while running

24. All of it had to be fetched, carried, touched, held, sniffed, crunched along the way.

DEVELOPMENT PARAGRAPH *(par. 3)*

The narrator uses examples to illustrate the topic of this paragraph and to reinforce the thesis of the essay, that Halloween was great fun.

25. What is the topic sentence for this paragraph?

26–28. What three parts of the house or objects in it were transformed for the occasion?

29–31. What is done to each part or object?

32–34. What is the anticipated effect of each redecoration?

DEVELOPMENT PARAGRAPH *(par. 4)*

Once everything was set and placed and ready, there were still other things to be done. This paragraph provides examples of things the narrator did after the house was prepared for the party.

35. How were boys and girls invited to the party?

36. What did the narrator wear to deliver invitations?

37. How does the narrator view his handiwork?

38. Who is responsible for this change?

39. How does he summarize what they did?

40. What simile does the narrator use to describe the way the house looks?

41. What two things are being compared in this simile?

42. How is a dark beast similar to a house decorated for Halloween?

CONCLUDING PARAGRAPH *(par. 5)*

43. The author offers his opinion that the [Halloween] party was almost unimportant. What does he think is more important than the party?

He reinforces this point with an **analogy**, a form of comparison showing a similarity between things that are otherwise unalike. The analogy below (item #44) takes the form *a:b : : c:d.* A definition for this analogy can be stated as: *a is to b as c is to d.* Find the word in the reading model that best completes the comparison.

44. Preparation for the party : gathering sulphur : : the party : _____

45. What does the narrator say about "getting set" for Halloween?

46. The author uses transitional words and phrases to link ideas in this essay. List at least five.

47. The author's primary purpose in this selection is to:
    a. inform
    b. persuade
    c. entertain

The Active Reading exercise can be scored using the answer key and grading grid. Enter your grade in the progress chart.

GUIDED WRITING

The Guided Writing section at the end of this chapter (page 98) provides topics and plans for writing illustrative paragraphs and essays. Select a topic and write a short essay by following the writing plan that begins on page 100.

Continue work in this chapter until you have finished all three Active Reading and Guided Writing activities. Upon completion, you will have written three new compositions for your portfolio (one paragraph and two essays). Record grades in your progress chart and, if available, on the Academic Credit Statement in your *Writing Portfolio Organizer*.

Note:

The selection you will read on the following page, titled "Secrets of the Centenarians: How Soviet Georgians Stay Young," was written prior to the 1991 dissolution of the Soviet Union, also known as the Union of Soviet Socialist Republics. The U.S.S.R., which stretched from Eastern Europe across Asia, was originally formed in the 1920s by fifteen republics, including Russia. As a result, certain terms in the selection are no longer current or applicable. For example, Leningrad, a large Russian city, was renamed St. Petersburg. Soviet Georgia, one of the fifteen republics, is now known as Georgia. This is just one example of how rapidly our world is changing, even in the time it takes for you to read this selection.

SECRETS OF THE CENTENARIANS:
How Soviet Georgians Stay Young
by N. Larina

N. Larina was a staff writer for Literaturnaya Gazeta, *Russia's most respected journal of intellectual commentary. Still in existence today, this publication has been an important voice of politics, literature, science, and history written by Russians, for Russians. Over the years,* The Literary Gazette *gave us a portrait of Soviet society that was not always attractive, but one that accurately reflected the Soviet Union's position and role in the world. The article excerpted and presented here discusses a topic of interest to everyone regardless of their politics, how to live a long life.*

Word Alert

academician	a member of an academy for promoting science, art, or literature; a member of an institution of learning
centenarian	a person that is at least 100 years old
commentary	an explanation or an expression of opinion
diverse	differing from one another; unlike
edible	fit to be eaten
Edison, Thomas A.	(1847–1931) American inventor. Among his inventions were the telegraph, the phonograph, the lightbulb, the system for distributing electricity, and motion pictures.
gerontology	study of aging and the problems of the aged
Leningrad	After the dissolution of the U.S.S.R. in 1991, Leningrad was renamed St. Petersburg, its original name earlier in Russian history. St. Petersburg is a major seaport, rail junction, and industrial, cutural, and scientific center.
manifestation	demonstration of the existence or presence of a person, object, or quality
matsoni	in Russian, a homemade yogurt that is eaten by Soviet Georgians on a daily basis
Buonarroti, Michelangelo	(1475–1564) Italian sculptor, painter, architect, and poet known as *Michelangelo*. The painting on the ceiling of the Sistine Chapel in Rome and two sculptures, *David* and the *Pieta*, are among his best known works.

Newton, Sir Isaac	(1642–1727) English mathematician and physicist considered by many to be the greatest scientist that ever lived. In a two-year period, 1664–1666, he discovered the law of universal gravitation and that white light is composed of all the colors of the spectrum.
obsolete	no longer in use; outmoded
physiology	the biological science of essential life processes, functions, and activities
resolutely	marked by firm determination; resolved
Soviet Georgia	After the dissolution of the U.S.S.R. in 1991, Soviet Georgia was renamed Georgia. This mountainous republic is known for its teas, citrus fruit, tobacco, wine grapes, and silk produced from its mulberry trees. The region has a rich literary and cultural history that goes back to the fifth century.
Tolstoy, Leo	(1828–1910) Russian novelist and philosopher considered to be one of the world's greatest writers. His two greatest novels are *War and Peace*, about Napoleon's invasion of Russia, and *Anna Karenina*, about the tragedy of a woman's faith in romantic love.
unanimous	having the agreement and consent of all; being of one mind
Voltaire, François	(1694–1778) French philosopher and author who was one of the towering geniuses in literary and intellectual history. Voltaire's practical philosophy was one of common sense and his writings, characterized by brevity and wit, often attacked the established institutions of his time.

1   **W**hat is the key to a hearty long life? *Literaturnaya Gazeta* asked this and other questions of some of our country's oldest residents. On the basis of answers received, we have sketched a portrait of the longliver, and we also offer commentary by Academician D. Chebotarev, Director of the Institute of Gerontology. Fifty-two per cent of our respondents were 96 to 115 years old and 8 per cent were between 116 and 132.

2   The poll showed that longlivers are unanimous on at least one principle: if you want a long life, engage in physical labor. "Whoever keeps com-

pany with his pillow will not live long," says 108-year-old Sona Aligyzy Kerimova. "I have always gotten up at 5 a.m. sharp." Ninety-year-old Sergei Ivanovich Khokhlov from Kuibyshev Province reports that he shovels snow, carries firewood and water, and from time to time works as a porter at the railroad station. And 109-year-old Sarkis Airapetovich Ogadzhanyan always sleeps in the open air. For three-quarters of the year he uses no head covering.

In the mountains of Abkhazia, in Soviet Georgia, it is not unusual to   3
meet an old man hiking mile after mile to visit a neighbor. But wait. One is not supposed to call the honored elders here old people. "Longlivers" is the preferred term because an "old person" is someone who has grown old, while a longliver lives long without growing old.

As for diet, it turned out that only 22 per cent restrict their foods, and   4
these restrictions usually involve meat. The remaining 78 per cent consume the most diverse edible substances: onions, garlic, tomatoes, cucumbers, eggplant, beans, walnuts, buttermilk, *matsoni*, honey, meat, and of course spring water—although all agree that overeating is dangerous.

Half of the longlivers we heard from consider themselves fairly strong.   5
A. Ivanova from Leningrad has never had medical treatment. Natalya Ivanovna Pankratova, 100 years old, from Kuibyshev, still reads without glasses. Onik Osadzhanovna Oganyan can thread a needle herself. Sergei Ivanovich Khokhlov, ninety years old, reports that he has no gray hairs and "all my teeth are intact except one." When the medical commission came to Mardakert District to hold examinations, it turned out that the 132-year-old Arakelyan did not even have a medical card. Asked what illnesses she had had, she replied: "There was no time to be ill. I spent my whole life raising children, grandchildren, and great grandchildren, and I have more than seventy of them."

As Dmitry Chebotarev points out, the longlivers denied themselves   6
pleasures the rest of us often abuse. Most of them never smoked or drank alcoholic beverages. "Many longlivers are resolutely—I would even say, aggressively—set against chemical medications," he said.

For a long time old age itself was viewed as an illness. Now this   7
viewpoint has become obsolete. It has changed because of studies focusing on the physiology of the aging organism and the aging process of healthy people. Studying them affords an opportunity to determine what changes in the functions of the organism are a manifestation of illness, and what changes are a result of age.

8   It is not one's calendar age but his biological age that determines how long a person should work. Some people in active creative work are involved until the last days of their lives. History knows a multitude of examples. "I think about nothing but work day and night," wrote Michelangelo, who lived to be eighty-nine. Add Newton, Edison, Voltaire, and Tolstoy, and there is every reason to conclude that the more intensive the involvement with mental labor, the longer mental capacities are retained. While there is no cure for old age, those who uncover the secrets of long life stay healthy and "young."

ACTIVE READING

The Active Reading exercise gives you an opportunity to reread the essay with a critical eye. By answering the questions that follow, you will extend and sharpen your understanding of the selection. This activity will help you become a more efficient reader and a more effective writer.

INTRODUCTORY PARAGRAPH *(par. 1)*

The author begins the paragraph by asking a question that gets our interest.

1. What question is asked?
2. Who answered this and other questions?
3. Where do these people live?
4. Who conducted this survey?
5. What is the purpose of this survey and the essay?
6. What percent of the respondents were 96 years of age, or older?

DEVELOPMENT PARAGRAPH *(par. 2)*

The first sentence introduces the topic of this paragraph and prepares the reader for the examples that follow.

7. The poll shows that longlivers are unanimous on at least one principle. What is it?

The author introduces us to three people who are longlivers and follow this principle. The first makes a statement from which the reader must make an inference.

8. What does 108-year-old Sona say about long life?

9. What do you think her statements mean?

10. How does 90-year-old Sergei from Kuibyshev Province prolong his life?

11. The third longliver is 109-year-old Sarkis. What does he do to stay healthy?

DEVELOPMENT PARAGRAPH *(par. 3)*

This paragraph further develops the premise that physical activity is essential to long life and defines the term "longlivers."

12. What other physical activity promotes long life?

13. The difference between a "longliver" and an "old person" is that:
    a. an "old person" grows old without living a long time.
    b. an "old person" is someone who has grown old, while a "longliver" lives long without growing old.
    c. a "longliver" is someone who is old before their time.
    d. a "longliver" is immortal and will never die.

DEVELOPMENT PARAGRAPH *(par. 4)*

14. What is the subject of this paragraph?

15. In what way, if any, do some longlivers restrict their diet?

16. List five examples of the foods longlivers eat.

17. What do all longlivers believe about food?

DEVELOPMENT PARAGRAPH *(par. 5)*

This paragraph provides several examples of longlivers who are remarkably strong and healthy.

18. In what way is A. Ivanova from Leningrad strong?

19. What is remarkable about 100-year-old N.I. Pankratova?

20. What ability does O.O. Oganyan possess?

21. In what way is 90-year-old S.I. Khokhlov healthy?

22. How does 132-year-old Arakelyan explain her good health?

DEVELOPMENT PARAGRAPH *(par. 6)*

This paragraph gives examples of the things longlivers avoid in order to be healthy.

    23. Name three things longlivers don't do.

DEVELOPMENT PARAGRAPH *(par. 7)*

This paragraph looks at changing viewpoints about old age.

    24. How was old age viewed for many years?

    25. What has caused this viewpoint to become obsolete?

    26. Scientists study what causes change in the functions of the organism (person). These changes are attributed to one of two things. What are they?

    27. What can you infer is the reason for scientists wanting to distinguish between changes that are due to illness and those that are due to aging?

CONCLUDING PARAGRAPH *(par. 8)*

The subject of the concluding paragraph is work and old age. How long a person works, the author believes, should be determined by the biological age of the body rather than calendar age.

    28. Based on the essay, which of the following do you think best defines biological age?

        a. the amount of wear and tear the body shows
        b. the actual number of years lived
        c. the number of years worked
        d. the number of years retired

    29. The author says that history provides many examples of people who worked until the last days of their lives. Name five such people.

    30. The author draws a conclusion about mental activity in the form of a cause and effect statement. What is it?

The last sentence, rewritten below, also contains a cause and effect statement. One part is marked (a) and the other is marked (b). Identify each phrase as either the cause or effect part of the statement. Remember, the *cause* is the reason why and the *effect* is the result or outcome. Ask yourself, "What leads to what?"

    31. (a) Those who uncover the secrets of long life (b) stay healthy and young.

32. The author uses transitional words and phrases to link ideas in this essay. List at least five.

33. The author's primary purpose in this selection is to:
   a. inform
   b. persuade
   c. entertain

The Active Reading exercise can be scored using the answer key and grading grid. Enter your grade in the progress chart.

GUIDED WRITING

The Guided Writing section that begins on the next page provides topics and plans for writing illustrative paragraphs and essays. Select a topic and write an extended essay by following the writing plan that begins on page 100.

GUIDED WRITING

This part of the chapter will help you apply what you have learned about writing paragraphs and essays that use examples. Choose one of the topics listed below for each writing assignment that you do. If you want to write about something else, ask your instructor if the topic is appropriate for writing that uses examples. Follow the plan that applies to write your composition. Submit your completed composition to the instructor for evaluation. When you receive a grade for this work, enter it in the progress chart.

WRITING TOPICS

- Describe or tell about a place filled with people and action. Use examples to illustrate the panorama of life that makes this place memorable.

- Describe a visit to a fair or marketplace. Use examples that stimulate the senses: sight, sound, taste, smell, and touch.

- Choose a holiday experience to tell about and use examples to show how and why it was special for you.

- Tell about pretending to be somebody other than who you are: dressing up for Halloween or acting in a play. Was there a time when you needed to present yourself as somebody else or were mistaken for another person? Use examples to illustrate one of these situations.

- Write about a person whose lifestyle you admire and tell why. Offer examples that illustrate the most important aspects of the way this person lives.

- Write about an elderly person that you know who might be characterized as a longliver. Give examples of his/her prescription for a long life.

PREWRITING: GENERATING IDEAS

Now that you have selected a topic, you will need to gather information and generate ideas before you begin to write. If you are writing about a personal experience you will probably rely on your memory, other people's input, and your own creativity for generating examples. Other topics may require that you use reference works to collect information for your composition.

First, decide the major point(s) of your paragraph or essay. Then create a list of examples for each point that you wish to make. Use this list as you follow the plan for writing an illustrative paragraph or essay. Every writing strategy can use examples to illustrate points the writer wishes to make. "Sweet Potato Pie" is a descriptive paragraph that uses many examples to give the reader a panoramic view of Harlem. "Tricks! Treats! Gangway!" uses examples to tell a story about Halloween. "The Secrets of the Centenarians" uses many examples to explain how it is possible for people to live long lives.

WRITING PLAN: THE PARAGRAPH

1. Decide the point of view of the narrator, first or third person. Write an introduction that gets the reader's attention and present your topic at the beginning of the paragraph.

2. Whatever primary writing strategy you choose, use as many examples as necessary to develop your topic adequately and reinforce the point you want to make.

3. In a narrative, provide specific details about what is happening, to whom, and why. In a descriptive paragraph, appeal to as many of the five senses as you can. If you are explaining a process, present facts and explanations.

4. Write a conclusion to your paragraph that restates the topic and presents an overview, summarizes, or expresses an opinion.

5. To create unity in your writing, make sure that each sentence in the paragraph relates to the topic. Your writing will be coherent if ideas follow one another in a logical pattern and sentences flow smoothly from one to the other. Use transitions to link or connect ideas. The list of transitional words and phrases at the back of this book is for your use and reference when you write (see pages 259–264).

6. Use variety in your choice of words to maintain reader interest. Where appropriate, use figurative language to increase the impact of your words and to stimulate the reader's imagination. The most commonly used figures of speech are the simile, metaphor, personification, and hyperbole. Definitions of literary and rhetorical terms can be found in the Glossary on pages 265–270.

7. Create a title for your paragraph, a word or phrase that captures the reader's interest and tells what you are writing about.

8. Use the *Checklist for Revision* at the end of this section to help you review and revise your paragraph.

WRITING PLAN: SHORT AND EXTENDED ESSAYS

While short and extended essays are similar—both have introductory and concluding paragraphs—the extended essay has more development paragraphs. "Tricks! Treats! Gangway!" is a short essay that uses description and examples. "Secrets of the Centenarians" is an extended essay that explains and supports its thesis about longlivers with many examples.

Introductory Paragraph(s)

1. Decide the narrator's point of view. Is the narrator of the essay involved in the action (first person), or an observer outside the action (third person)?

2. Write an attention-getting opener for your essay. Tell what the essay is about by introducing your topic and purpose. This is the thesis statement, the main idea to be supported throughout the essay.

3. Use your introductory paragraph(s) to set the tone for the essay, your attitude toward the subject. The tone of an essay might be serious or humorous, formal or informal.

4. State your plan for the development of this essay. An extended essay may contain more than one introductory paragraph.

Development Paragraph(s)

1. Each development paragraph can be used to examine a different aspect of your subject. Let the reader know your topic or focus for each new paragraph.

2. Set the tone for the paragraph, your attitude toward the subject. The tone might be serious or humorous, formal or informal.

3. Whatever primary writing strategy you choose, use as many examples as necessary to develop your topic adequately and reinforce the points you want to make.

4. In a narrative, provide specific details about what is happening, to whom, and why. In a descriptive essay, appeal to as many of the five senses as you can. If you are explaining a process, present facts and explanations.

5. If you are writing an extended essay, use the development paragraphs to include more details and examples that support and illustrate your thesis.

6. All sentences in a paragraph should relate to the topic and to one another. All paragraphs in an essay should support the topic and follow some logical order. Use transitions to link ideas within paragraphs and to make connections between paragraphs. Refer to the list of transitional words and phrases on pages 259–264.

7. Use variety in your choice of words to maintain reader interest. Where appropriate, use figurative language to increase the impact of your words and to stimulate the reader's imagination. The most commonly used figures of speech are the simile, metaphor, personification, and hyperbole. Definitions of literary and rhetorical terms can be found in the Glossary on pages 265–270.

Concluding Paragraph(s)

1. Restate the thesis in some way for emphasis. Use your most powerful example(s) in your conclusion for greatest impact.

2. Present an overview, summarize the major points, offer an opinion, or reach a conclusion that reinforces the point of your essay.

3. More than one paragraph may be used to conclude an extended essay.

4. The checklist below will help you to review and revise your essay.

note: The title of your essay should be a word or phrase that captures the reader's attention and tells what you are writing about. Create a title for your first draft and review it before making it final.

CHECKLIST FOR REVISION

1. My paragraph/essay has a first- or third-person point of view. I begin with a strong statement that gets the reader's attention, introduce my topic, and set the tone. If I am writing an essay, my thesis statement appears in the opening paragraph(s).

2. My pararaph or essay includes enough examples to develop the topic adequately and reinforce major points. Each development paragraph examines a different aspect of my subject.

3. In a narrative I provide specific details about what is happening, to whom, and why. When writing description, I appeal to the five senses. In explaining a process, I present facts and explanations.

4. In an extended essay, I use the development paragraphs to include more details and examples that support and illustrate the thesis.

5. In concluding my paragraph or essay I present an overview, summarize, offer an opinion, or reach a conclusion that reinforces my point. I use my most powerful example(s) here for greatest impact.

6. Sentences within each paragraph relate to the topic. Development paragraphs follow a logical order and support the point of the essay. I use transitions to link ideas within paragraphs and to make connections between paragraphs.

7. I use variety in my choice of words to maintain reader interest. Where appropriate, I use figurative language to increase the impact of my words and to stimulate the reader's imagination.

8. As I revise the form and content of my work, I correct errors in punctuation, capitalization, spelling, grammar, and usage.

9. The title of my paragraph or essay tells what I wrote about and captures the reader's interest.

Continue work in this chapter until you have finished all three Active Reading and Guided Writing activities.

Chapter 5

PROCESS ANALYSIS

Exposition is writing that informs the reader by explaining facts and ideas so that they are easily understood. The subject of your explanation might be a person, place, thing, event, or idea. The key patterns of exposition are **process analysis**, **comparison and contrast**, **classification**, **definition**, and **cause and effect**. This chapter focuses on process analysis, while later chapters concentrate on the other expository strategies.

Process analysis explains how something is done, how something works, or how something occurs. A process is a series of steps leading to a result. Something as simple as preparing a meal or as complex as forming a company to sell food both involve steps in a process. Analysis divides something into parts in order to understand the whole. A process analysis essay presents steps in chronological order, shows how each step is related to the others, and explains how you get from the beginning to the end of the process.

Because process writing always involves a series of steps or events that must occur in proper order, the basic structure of the paper will be chronological. To write effective process analysis paragraphs and essays, organize your paper as follows. First, present an overview of the topic and define any technical terms. Next, indicate the sequence of steps in the process with appropriate examples. Conclude with a discussion or explanation of the outcome or results.

It is important that you know as much as you can about a process, through research or firsthand knowledge, before you begin writing. Make yourself an expert on the topic you choose, so that you can clearly and thoroughly explain the process to your audience. To keep the interest of your readers, provide as much information as they need to know to understand the process. At the same time, try not to overwhelm them with excessive detail.

Process papers use transitions as markers to each step or stage in the process. Transitions like *first, second,* and *third* can be added to the beginnings of sentences or paragraphs to identify the order of each stage in the process. Transitions like *before, after,* or *sometimes* can be used to show time relationships when explaining a process. In order to write process analysis, you will need to use transitional words and phrases that express time relationships. A list of these transitions can be found on pages 259–260.

This chapter contains three reading selections, all of which use process analysis to explain facts and ideas. The first is a paragraph, the second a short essay, and the third a longer piece. Each is followed by an Active Reading exercise that helps you to understand the form and content of the reading model. The Guided Writing section at the end of this chapter will help you to create three original pieces of writing using process analysis.

Chapter Selections

How to Kill a Wasp *by H. Allen Smith*

The Birth and Death of Islands *by Rachel Carson*

Exercise: A New Dietary Requirement *by Jane Brody*

HOW TO KILL A WASP
by H. Allen Smith

H. Allen Smith (1907–1976) was born in McLeansboro, Illinois, and began working as a newspaper reporter at the age of fifteen. He joined the United Press in New York City as a feature writer in 1929, and worked for the New York World-Telegram *until 1941 before devoting himself to his own writing. For the next three decades Smith wrote about a series of odd, wacky characters who appeared in collections of humorous anecdotes, observations, and essays. His books include* Low Man on a Totem Pole *(1941),* We Went Thataway *(1949),* The Compleat Practical Joker *(1953),* How to Write Without Knowing Nothing *(1961), and* Poor H. Allen Smith's Almanac *(1965). Presented here is an excerpt from "How to Kill A Wasp," a good example of Smith's light and humorous style. Taken from* The Best of H. Allen Smith *(1972), Smith calls on the expertise of a favorite character, Mr. Buttolph, to explain the dangerous process of killing a wasp.*

Word Alert

ball peen   the round head of a hammer that is opposite the face and is used for bending, shaping, or cutting the material struck

sidle   to move sideways, especially in a furtive or indirect way

playing possum   to pretend to be asleep or dead

"Don't ever think," Mr. Buttolph explained, "that you can handle a wasp the way you handle a fly. You've got to plan a campaign—figure out just exactly how you're going to proceed against him, and hope he doesn't get you while you're mapping your plans. Keep your eye on him, *but don't let him know you're looking at him.* Quietly assemble your equipment. A rubber fly swatter. Thick gloves. Put a hat on. Turn your shirt collar up and button it. Keep a ball peen hammer handy. Then go after him—but don't go directly at him. Sidle up to him. Pretend you're just walking in his direction by accident. Say something to throw him off guard, like, 'Now, I wonder what I did with those glasses.' Watch him out of the corner of your eye, and if he starts to wiggle or flap his legs ease away from him, back off, and wait a while. Give him a chance to settle down.

Go outdoors and practice with the rubber swatter. Drive a tack in the wall and stand off and swat at it—develop your aim, because that's important. God help you if you ever swing at a wasp and miss him. Now, go back in and locate him again and see what sort of a mood he's in. If he's at ease, sidle up to him and when you're sure of your position, when you're certain that you've got the proper range, bust him one as hard as you can. If he falls to the floor, jump on him, stomp him—even then he may get up off the floor and stab you. Hit him with the hammer. Don't take your eye off him. No matter that he's lying there like a corpse. He may be playing possum. Get a newspaper and wrap him up in it and then set fire to it. After that it *may* be that he won't bother you again."

ACTIVE READING

The Active Reading exercise gives you an opportunity to reread the paragraph with a critical eye. By answering the questions that follow, you will extend and sharpen your understanding of the selection. This activity will help you become a more efficient reader and a more effective writer.

The groups of sentences numbered 1 through 8 below are from the model paragraph. These groups have been rearranged so that they are not in the right sequence. In the correct order, they form the expository paragraph you have just read.

Without looking back at the model, reorganize the groups of sentences that follow to form a paragraph that clearly explains how one goes about killing a wasp. First, look for the topic sentence. Next, look for transitional words which serve as clues to the order of the sentences.

Write a letter for each sentence group below, indicating its correct order in the paragraph. For example, write the letter *A* for the group that should come first in the paragraph. Use the letters *B* through *H* to order the remaining groups of sentences.

1. _____ Now, go back in and locate him again and see what sort of a mood he's in. If he's at ease, sidle up to him and when you're sure of your position, when you're certain that you've got the proper range, bust him one as hard as you can.

2. _____ Keep your eye on him, *but don't let him know you're looking at him.*

3. _____ Then go after him—but don't go directly at him. Sidle up to him. Pretend you're just walking in his direction by accident. Say something to throw him off guard, like, 'Now, I wonder what I did with those glasses.'

4. _____ "Don't ever think," Mr. Buttolph explained, "that you can handle a wasp the way you handle a fly. You've got to plan a campaign— figure out just exactly how you're going to proceed against him, and hope he doesn't get you while you're mapping your plans.

5. _____ If he falls to the floor, jump on him, stomp him—even then he may get up off the floor and stab you. Hit him with the hammer.

6. _____ Quietly assemble your equipment. A rubber fly swatter. Thick gloves. Put a hat on. Turn your shirt collar up and button it. Keep a ball peen hammer handy.

7. _____ Don't take your eye off him. No matter that he's lying there like a corpse. He may be playing possum. Get a newspaper and wrap him up in it and then set fire to it. After that it *may* be that he won't bother you again."

8. _____ Watch him out of the corner of your eye, and if he starts to wiggle or flap his legs ease away from him, back off, and wait a while. Give him a chance to settle down. Go outdoors and practice with the rubber swatter. Drive a tack in the wall and stand off and swat at it—develop your aim, because that's important. God help you if you ever swing at a wasp and miss him.

The author gets the reader's attention in the first sentence of the paragraph by making a comparison between the handling (killing) of wasps and flies. The second sentence offers a plan for explaining the process of killing a wasp.

9. In preparing to kill a wasp, what must you do first?

10. What equipment will you need?

11. When you go after the wasp, is it best to go at him directly or indirectly? Why?

12. What do you do if the wasp starts to wiggle and flap his legs?

13. How would you go about developing your aim to kill a wasp?

14. What two conditions are necessary before you attack a wasp?

15. What should you do after you hit the wasp and he falls to the floor?

16. According to the author, how do you make sure he's dead?

17. Why does the author recommend this last step?

18. What is the author's tone, his attitude toward his subject in this paragraph?

19. What is the mood (atmosphere and feeling) created in this paragraph?

20. What literary device does the author use to create the tone and mood of this selection?

21. The author uses transitional words and phrases to link ideas in this paragraph. List at least five.

22. The author's primary purpose in this selection is to:

    a. inform
    b. persuade
    c. entertain

The Active Reading exercise can be scored using the answer key and grading grid. Enter your grade in the progress chart.

GUIDED WRITING

The Guided Writing section at the end of this chapter (page 123) provides topics and plans for writing paragraphs and essays using process analysis. Select a topic and write a paragraph by following the writing plan on page 124.

Continue work in this chapter until you have finished all three Active Reading and Guided Writing activities. Upon completion, you will have written three new compositions for your portfolio (one paragraph and two essays). Record grades in your progress chart and, if available, on the Academic Credit Statement in your *Writing Portfolio Organizer*.

THE BIRTH AND DEATH OF ISLANDS

by Rachel Carson

Rachel Carson (1907–1964) was born in Springfield, Pennsylvania. She received degrees from Pennsylvania College for Women and Johns Hopkins University, completing further graduate study at the Marine Biological Laboratory, Woods Hole, Massachusetts. She taught at several universities and worked as an aquatic biologist for the U.S. Fish and Wildlife Service. A world-renowned writer and conservationist, she received many awards and honors including the George Westinghouse Science Writing Award, the National Book Award, and the Conservationist of the Year Award from the National Wildlife Federation, for her book The Silent Spring *(1962). "The Birth and Death of Islands" is excerpted from* The Sea Around Us *(1951), a number one nonfiction best seller, which was made into a film that won an Academy Award for best documentary in 1952. In the selection presented here, Ms. Carson explains the process of island formation with drama in every sentence.*

Word Alert

catastrophic	a violent and sudden change in a feature of the earth; a disaster
continent	one of the seven great divisions of land on the globe; mainland
ejecta	material expelled from a volcano
ephemeral	lasting a short time; transient
expanse	something spread out typically over a wide area; an extensive stretch of land or sea
fissure	a narrow opening or crack of considerable length and depth
fundamentally	basically; essentially
intrusion	to enter by force; a geological intrusion
molten	fused or liquefied by heat; melted
paradox	a seemingly contradictory statement that may nonetheless be true
rampart	a wall-like ridge of rock fragments, earth, or debris; a protective barrier
shoal	a sand bank or sand bar that is just below the water

terrestrial	relating to land, as distinct from air or water; earthly
travail	hard work, effort; agony, torment; strenuous physical exertion
tuff	volcanic rock fused together by heat; rock fragments
vessel	ship; large boat

1   Millions of years ago, a volcano built a mountain on the floor of the Atlantic. In eruption after eruption, it pushed up a great pile of volcanic rock, until it had accumulated a mass a hundred miles across at its base, reaching upward toward the surface of the sea. Finally its cone emerged as an island with an area of about two hundred square miles. Thousands of years passed, and thousands of thousands. Eventually the waves of the Atlantic cut down the cone and reduced it to a shoal—all of it, that is, but a small fragment which remained above water. This fragment we know as Bermuda.

2   With variations, the life story of Bermuda has been repeated by almost every one of the islands that interrupts the watery expanses of the oceans far from land. For these isolated islands in the sea are fundamentally different from the continents. The major land masses and the ocean basins are today much as they have been throughout the greater part of geologic time. But islands are ephemeral, created today, destroyed tomorrow. With few exceptions, they are the result of the violent, explosive, earth-shaking eruptions of submarine volcanoes, working perhaps for millions of years to achieve their end. It is one of the paradoxes in the ways of earth and sea that a process seemingly so destructive, so catastrophic in nature, can result in an act of creation.

3   Islands have always fascinated the human mind. Perhaps it is the instinctive response of man, the land animal, welcoming a brief intrusion of earth in the vast, overwhelming expanse of sea. Here in a great oceanic basin, a thousand miles from the nearest continent, with miles of water under our vessel, we come upon an island. Our imaginations can follow its slopes down through darkening waters to where it rests on the sea floor. We wonder why and how it arose here in the midst of the ocean.

4   The birth of a volcanic island is an event marked by prolonged and violent travail: the forces of the earth striving to create, and all the forces of the sea opposing. The sea floor, where an island begins, is probably

nowhere more than about fifty miles thick—a thin covering over the vast bulk of the earth. In it are deep cracks and fissures, the result of unequal cooling and shrinkage in past ages. Along such lines of weakness the molten lava from the earth's interior presses up and finally bursts forth into the sea. But a submarine volcano is different from a terrestrial eruption, where the lava, molten rocks, gases, and other ejecta are hurled into the air through an open crater. Here on the bottom of the ocean the volcano has resisting it all the weight of the ocean water above it. Despite the immense pressure of, it may be, two or three miles of sea water, the new volcanic cone builds upward toward the surface, in flow after flow of lava. Once within reach of the waves, its soft ash and tuff are violently attacked, and for a long period the potential island may remain a shoal, unable to emerge. But, eventually, in new eruptions, the cone is pushed up into the air and a rampart against the attacks of the waves is built of hardened lava.

Navigator's charts are marked with numerous recently discovered submarine mountains. Many of these are the submerged remnants of the islands of a geologic yesterday. The same charts show islands that emerged from the sea at least fifty million years ago, and others that arose within our own memory. Among the undersea mountains marked on the charts may be the islands of tomorrow, which at this moment are forming, unseen, on the floor of the ocean and are growing upward toward its surface.

5

ACTIVE READING

The Active Reading exercise gives you an opportunity to reread the essay with a critical eye. By answering the questions that follow, you will extend and sharpen your understanding of the selection. This activity will help you become a more efficient reader and a more effective writer.

INTRODUCTORY PARAGRAPH (par. 1)

The introduction tells in chronological order the story of how islands are formed. In this overview, the author uses a specific island as an example of how every island is created. The author's words establish a dramatic tone that continues throughout the selection.

1. What island is the subject of this paragraph?

2. When did the process of island formation begin?

3. Where did the process of this island's formation begin?

4. How did the island develop?

5. In what form did the island emerge?

6. How large was the surface area?

7. How did the waves of the Atlantic shape the island?

8. How long did this take?

9. What remains of this process today?

The tone of the first paragraph gives the reader a sense of the enormity of events, and the seemingly endless period of time over which these events have occurred.

DEVELOPMENT PARAGRAPH *(par. 2)*

The author introduces this paragraph with the thesis statement of the essay, "With variations, the life story of Bermuda has been repeated by almost every one of the islands that interrupt the watery expanses of the oceans far from land." The rest of the paragraph uses comparison and contrast, as well as cause and effect, to explain the process of island formation.

10. Islands are compared to what other land mass?

11. How are islands and continents similar?

12. How do islands and continents differ?

In the sentences below, one part is marked (*a*) and the other is marked (*b*). Identify each phrase as either the cause or effect part of the statement. Remember, the *cause* is the reason why and the *effect* is the result or outcome. Ask yourself, "What leads to what?"

13. (a) Islands are the result of (b) the violent, explosive, earth-shaking eruptions of submarine volcanoes, working perhaps for millions of years to achieve their end.

14. (a) It is one of the paradoxes in the ways of earth and sea that a process seemingly so destructive, so catastrophic in nature, (b) can result in an act of creation.

15. A **paradox** is a seemingly contradictory statement that on closer examination proves to be true. In the last sentence of the paragraph the author presents a paradox. What is it?

DEVELOPMENT PARAGRAPH *(par. 3)*

The author sets a tone of wonderment and awe for this paragraph with the proposition that "Islands have always fascinated the human mind."

16. What is the reason the author gives for people feeling relieved when they sight an island?

17. Human beings have feelings of awe and wonderment about the origins of islands. Find five phrases the author uses that evoke these feelings.

18. The author switches to first person point of view in this paragraph. How do we know that this switch has occurred?

19. What is the author's purpose in switching to first person?

DEVELOPMENT PARAGRAPH *(par. 4)*

This paragraph expands on the theme of the essay, dealing mainly with the birth of an island. The author presents the steps in this process in chronological order. The specific details and explanations she provides help us to understand this monumental event.

The six groups of sentences numbered *20* through *25* below are from paragraph four of the essay. These groups have been rearranged so that they are not in their right sequence. In the correct order, they form a paragraph that explains the birth of a volcanic island.

Without looking back at the model, reorganize the groups of sentences that follow so that they form paragraph four of the essay. First, look for the topic sentence. Next, look for transitional words that serve as clues to the order of the sentences.

Write a letter for each sentence group to indicate its correct order in the paragraph. For example, write the letter *A* for the group that should come first in the paragraph. Use the letters *B* through *F* to order the remaining groups of sentences.

20. _____ Despite the immense pressure of, it may be, two or three miles of seawater, the new volcanic cone builds upward toward the surface, in flow after flow of lava.

21. _____ In it are deep cracks and fissures, the result of unequal cooling and shrinkage in past ages. Along such lines of weakness the molten lava from the earth's interior presses up and finally bursts forth into the sea.

22. _____ The birth of a volcanic island is an event marked by prolonged and violent travail: the forces of the earth striving to create, and all the forces of the sea opposing. The sea floor, where an island begins, is probably nowhere more than about fifty miles thick—a thin covering over the vast bulk of the earth.

23. _____ But, eventually, in new eruptions, the cone is pushed up into the air and a rampart against the attacks of the waves is built of hardened lava.

24. _____ But a submarine volcano is different from a terrestrial eruption, where the lava, molten rocks, gases, and other ejecta are hurled into the air through an open crater. Here on the bottom of the ocean the volcano has resisting it all the weight of the ocean water above it.

25. _____ Once within reach of the waves, its soft ash and tuff are violently attacked, and for a long period the potential island may remain a shoal, unable to emerge.

CONCLUDING PARAGRAPH *(par. 5)*

The essay ends with a brief discussion of navigational charts and what they tell us about islands. The author concludes with a reference to the future that lets the reader know this process will continue indefinitely.

26. The charts are marked with numerous recently discovered submarine mountains. Which of the following best defines them?

   a. the islands of tomorrow forming, unseen, on the floor of the ocean
   b. the submerged remnants of the islands of a geologic yesterday
   c. both of the above
   d. small continents formed from terrestrial eruptions

27. What do these same charts show about islands that have emerged from the sea?

28. The author uses transitional words and phrases to link ideas in this paragraph. List at least five.

29. The author's primary purpose in this selection is to:

   a. inform
   b. persuade
   c. entertain

The Active Reading exercise can be scored using the answer key and grading grid. Enter your grade in the progress chart.

GUIDED WRITING

The Guided Writing section at the end of this chapter (page 123) provides topics and plans for writing paragraphs and essays using process analysis. Select a topic and write a short essay by following the writing plan that begins on page 125. Continue work in this chapter until you have finished all three Active Reading and Guided Writing activities.

EXERCISE:
A NEW DIETARY REQUIREMENT
by Jane Brody

Jane Brody was born in Brooklyn, New York in 1941. She received degrees from Cornell University and the University of Wisconsin. In 1965 she began writing stories on medicine and biology for The New York Times. *Her columns on popular medicine were designed to help people understand how their bodies worked and how to stay well. In her widely syndicated column, "Personal Health," she wrote about a variety of topics including nutrition, disease, medication, exercise, and health-related news. Among her honors for writing is the 1978 Science Writer's Award. Brody's books include* Jane Brody's Nutrition Book *(1981),* Jane Brody's The New York Times Guide to Personal Health *(1982), and* Jane Brody's Good Food Book *(1985). All of her books focus on how ordinary people can attain good health through their own common sense. Presented here is an excerpt from her essay on the necessity of regular exercise as essential to weight loss and good health.*

Word Alert

adverse	harmful or bad
ailment	a bodily disorder or chronic disease
arthritis	painful inflammation of the body's joints
besiege	to cause worry or distress; beset
biochemical	characterized by, produced by, or involving chemical reactions in living organisms
chronic	marked by long duration or frequent occurrence; habitual
diabetes	a disease characterized by inadequate secretion or utilization of insulin by the pancreas
euphoric	a feeling of elation or well-being
lame	weak or ineffective
metabolism	the rate at which the body burns calories or energy; for the individual, metabolism is influenced by exercise, food, and the temperature of the environment
osteoporosis	thinning of the bone due to insufficient production of calcium
pike	as in "turnpike"; 20 years down the pike means "down the road" or 20 years later

prevalent	widely accepted or practiced
sedentary	doing or requiring much sitting; settled
stabilize	to hold steady; make stable, steadfast, or firm
tempered	moderated, adjusted; controlled by

Our species evolved on the move. Recent research on the effects of exercise and the consequences of sedentary living has shown that physical activity is crucial to the proper processing of foods that we eat. In fact, most of the chronic and often life-threatening ailments that besiege Americans in epidemic proportions could be tempered by regular exercise. Among them are heart disease, diabetes, high blood pressure, arthritis, and osteoporosis. But let's face it: most people are not motivated to exercise by what it may do for them 20 years down the pike. What gets people like me out moving every day is what exercise does for me right now, especially how it allows me to enjoy eating without gaining. I, along with millions of Americans, have discovered that exercise is the key to permanent and painless weight control. . . .

According to one prevalent theory of weight control, your normal (that is, usual) body weight is like water—it constantly seeks its own level. The weight at which you stabilize when you make no special effort to gain or lose is called your body's *set point*. When your weight drops below that set point, chemical signals of starvation seem to trigger a corrective system into action to bring you back to "normal," even though normal by your definition means fat. This may be a major reason behind the failure of diets to produce long-lasting weight loss for most people. Only a few highly controlled individuals seem able to fight their set point indefinitely. But before you conclude that keeping weight off is hopeless if it means a constant battle against an unseen biochemical enemy, the set-point theory offers you an out. Through exercise, you can safely and permanently lower your set point (as long as you keep exercising) so that you will now stabilize at a lower weight.

Everybody knows that exercise uses calories, and that the harder and longer you exercise, the more calories your body will burn. But when people look at how hard they would have to work to get rid of the calories in just one piece of pie a la mode (running fast for an hour or sawing wood for 2), not to mention what it takes to lose a pound (walking for 16 hours or swimming hard for 7), many sit down in self-defeat. The effort

1

2

3

required hardly seems to pay. But what most people don't realize is that exercise does far more than just burn calories while you're exercising. Vigorous exercise also revs up the body engine—raises its idling speed, as it were—so that *your body continues to use extra calories for up to 15 hours after you stop exercising.* If you exercise twice a day—once in the morning and once in the evening—you get the calorie-burning bonus all day long, even while you sleep. Even if your metabolism is normally on the slow side, exercise can boost it permanently by 20 percent to 30 percent. . . .

4   The weight-control benefits of exercise go far beyond its direct effect on how many calories your body uses. Vigorous exercise also suppresses your appetite. After a hard run or an hour of tennis, for example, you may find you don't get hungry for an hour or more. And although you may eat more when you exercise, chances are the extra calories will be significantly less than what you used up through exercise. A study by Dr. Peter Wood at Stanford University Medical School showed that very active people consume about 600 calories more than their sedentary counterparts but weigh on the average 20 percent less.

5   Furthermore, exercise is a natural relaxant and produces a lasting euphoric effect. This, in turn, reduces the chances that you'll eat to relieve such emotions as tension, anxiety, anger, frustration, boredom, and depression. The good feelings induced by vigorous exercise most likely result from a natural tranquilizing chemical, beta-endorphin, that is released in the brain in response to exercise. This chemical is the body's equivalent of morphine or Valium minus the expense and adverse side effects associated with drugs. The release of beta-endorphin may account for the addictive quality of exercise and the fact that many exercise enthusiasts report that they don't feel as good when they are not able to exercise. . . .

6   The real problem with exercise for most people is not a failure to realize that it's good for them but an unwillingness to work it into their daily lives, the most common excuse being "I don't have time." People have always managed to find time for the things they really want to do. Finding time for exercise, then, starts with a realization of its importance and a decision—a commitment—to make it a regular part of your life. Just as you brush your teeth every day, eat every day, and sleep every day, you can exercise every day. After a while, you may find, as I did, with regular moderate exercise you get more rest from less sleep and you work so

much more efficiently that you actually have *more* time now that you've given up some time to exercise.

ACTIVE READING

The Active Reading exercise gives you an opportunity to reread the essay with a critical eye. By answering the questions that follow, you will extend and sharpen your understanding of the selection. This activity will help you become a more efficient reader and a more effective writer.

INTRODUCTORY PARAGRAPH *(par. 1)*

The author begins with the sentence, "Our species evolved on the move." This stimulates thinking about the way we live today compared to the way we lived early in our evolution. In the distant past, humans were of necessity active and on the move as hunters and gatherers. With the advent of agriculture we tended to stay in one place, still physically active. Today, the comforts of our advanced civilization give us the option of being sedentary. For many people exercise is the only way to be physically active.

The second sentence of the paragraph is a cause and effect statement. The first part of the sentence tells us about research in which people who exercise were compared with people who are sedentary. The second part of the sentence tells us the outcome of the research.

1. What is the function of this sentence in the essay?
2. If foods are not processed properly, what can happen?
3. The author believes that exercise can reduce the chances of our developing certain kinds of diseases in the future. What are they?
4. What motivates millions of Americans, including the author, to exercise regularly?

DEVELOPMENT PARAGRAPH *(par. 2)*

The author uses this paragraph to discuss one prevalent theory of weight control. She uses a simile to illustrate the theory.

5. What two things are compared in the simile?
6. In what way are these two similar?

7. Define the term *set point* as it refers to body weight.

Below are two parts of a cause and effect statement from the paragraph. One is marked (*a*) and the other is marked (*b*). Identify each phrase as either the cause or effect part of the statement. Remember, the *cause* is the reason why and the *effect* is the result or outcome. Ask yourself, "What leads to what?"

8. (a) When your weight drops below your set point (b) chemical signals of starvation seem to trigger a corrective system into action to bring you back to "normal," even though normal by your definition means fat.

9. Suppose your normal weight, your set point, is 150 pounds and you have recently lost 20 pounds through dieting. Regardless of the kind of diet you used, how will your body respond?

10. What do you need to do to stabilize at the lower weight of 130 pounds?

DEVELOPMENT PARAGRAPH *(par. 3)*

The second paragraph of the essay introduces the set point theory while the third paragraph explains how you lower your set point through exercise.

11. The author begins this paragraph by telling us two things everyone knows about exercise. What are they?

Below are two parts of a cause and effect statement from the paragraph. One is marked (*a*) and the other is marked (*b*). Identify each phrase as either the cause or effect part of the statement. Remember, the *cause* is the reason why and the *effect* is the result or outcome. Ask yourself, "What leads to what?"

12. (a) When people look at how hard they would have to work to get rid of the calories in just one piece of pie a la mode (b) many sit down in self-defeat.

13. The author also offers examples of what one has to do to work off calories. What do you have to do to lose the calories gained by eating one piece of pie a la mode?

14. What do you have to do to lose one pound?

In restating her point of view, the author expresses a common attitude that people have towards losing weight through exercise.

15. What does she say in this restatement?

16. What is it that most people don't realize about exercise?

17. What does vigorous exercise do?

18. What do you have to do to get a calorie-burning bonus all day long, even while you sleep?

19. What conclusion does the author reach?

Here is a summary of what the author is saying:

If exercise boosts your metabolism permanently so that you are burning 20 to 30 percent more calories, you will lose weight. You will also establish a lower set point for your body which will enable you to maintain a lower weight without feeling starved.

20. Now reread paragraph three. Does the topic sentence appear at the beginning, middle, or end of this paragraph?

DEVELOPMENT PARAGRAPH *(par. 4)*

In paragraph three we learned that exercise burns calories and lowers your body's set point. In this paragraph, the author talks about the indirect effects of exercise on weight control.

21. How else does vigorous exercise affect the body?

22. What example of this does the author offer?

23. What other way does vigorous exercise affect the body?

24. What does research about very active people show?

DEVELOPMENT PARAGRAPH *(par. 5)*

Paragraph five continues the main idea introduced in paragraph four, that exercise produces several indirect effects that help control weight.

25. What feeling does exercise produce?

26. How do our emotions affect our eating habits?

27. Do we eat less or more when we experience the euphoric effect of exercise?

28. What natural tranquilizing chemical causes the euphoric effect of exercise?

29. Where and how is this chemical produced in the body?

30. What other chemicals synthesized and sold as prescription drugs have an effect similar to beta-endorphins?

31. What drawbacks do prescription drugs have that beta-endorphins do not have?

32. The author infers that the release of beta-endorphins during exercise produces a positive addiction. What fact does the author offer to illustrate this point?

CONCLUDING PARAGRAPH *(par. 6)*

In this last paragraph the author examines the nature of commitment to exercise.

33. Do people realize that exercise is good for them?

34. What is the most common excuse for not exercising?

35. According to the author, is this excuse justifiable?

36. What must you do in order to find time for exercise?

37. Exercise should become a routine like what other activities?

38-39. The author reinforces the point of this paragraph with a reference to her own experience. She found two additional benefits of exercise to share with the reader. What are they?

40. The author concludes by showing a relationship between exercise and time. How does she express this relationship?

41. The author uses transitional words and phrases to link ideas in this paragraph. List at least fifteen.

42. The author's primary purpose in this selection is to:

   a. inform

   b. persuade

   c. entertain

The Active Reading exercise can be scored using the answer key and grading grid. Enter your grade in the progress chart.

The Guided Writing section that begins on the next page provides topics and plans for writing paragraphs and essays using process analysis. Select a topic and write an extended essay by following the writing plan that begins on page 125.

GUIDED WRITING

This part of the chapter will help you apply what you have learned about writing paragraphs and essays using process analysis. Choose one of the topics listed below for each writing assignment that you do. If you want to write about something else, ask your instructor if the topic is appropriate for writing process analysis. Follow the plan that applies to write your composition. Submit your completed composition to the instructor for evaluation. When you receive a grade for this work, enter it in the progress chart.

WRITING TOPICS

- In "How to Kill a Wasp" the author provides a serious analysis of the method he uses, even though the subject is intended to be amusing. Using a similar approach, explain how you would get rid of a pest.

- Explain how to do something at which you are particularly skilled, or choose one of the following and explain the process involved: scuba diving, skate boarding, jogging, hang gliding, ice skating, riding a horse, administering first aid for choking, administering CPR, roping a calf, driving a tractor.

- Explain how the earth is constantly being reshaped by one of the following natural processes: earthquakes, erosion (tides and winds), temperature changes, flooding, or glacial movement.

- Explain the major changes that took place in the formation of our planet, Earth, in each of the four geologic eras: Cenozoic, Mesozoic, Paleozoic, and Precambrian.

- Explain how you went about improving yourself in some way: losing weight, exercising, a change in your eating habits, quitting smoking, reducing stress. Detail the process you followed to achieve your goals.

- Explain how exercise may help to prevent one or more of the following physical disorders: heart disease, diabetes, high blood pressure, arthritis, osteoporosis.

PREWRITING: GENERATING IDEAS

Now that you have selected a topic, you will need to gather information and generate ideas before you begin to write. If you are writing about a personal experience you will probably rely on your memory, other people's input, and your own creativity for generating facts, explanations and examples. Other topics may require that you use reference works to collect this information for your composition.

Determine the major steps involved in the process you plan to explain and list them in chronological order. It is important to show how one step leads to the next. Use this list as you follow the plan for writing a paragraph or essay using process analysis. Any technical terms should be defined as they are presented in your composition.

WRITING PLAN: THE PARAGRAPH

1. Decide the point of view of the narrator, first or third person. Write an introduction that gets the reader's attention, and present your topic at the beginning of the paragraph.

2. Set the tone for the paragraph, your attitude toward the subject. The tone might be serious or humorous, formal, or informal.

3. Present the steps of the process in chronological order, and explain each clearly and thoroughly. It is important that you show how one step leads to the next. Define any technical terms for the reader. Use facts, explanations, and examples where appropriate.

4. While process analysis is your primary writing strategy, you can also use description, illustration, cause and effect, comparison and contrast, and definition to reinforce the points you want to make.

5. Write a conclusion to your paragraph that restates the topic and presents an overview, summarizes, or expresses an opinion.

6. To create unity in your writing, make sure that each sentence in the paragraph relates to the topic. Your writing will be coherent if ideas follow one another in a logical pattern and sentences flow smoothly from one to the other. Use transitions to link or connect ideas. The list of transitional words and phrases at the back of this book is for your use and reference when you write (see pages 259–264).

7. Use variety in your choice of words to maintain reader interest. Where appropriate, use figurative language to increase the impact of your words and to stimulate the reader's imagination. The most commonly used figures of speech are the simile, metaphor, personification, and hyperbole. Definitions of literary and rhetorical terms can be found in the Glossary on pages 265–270.

8. Create a title for your paragraph, a word or phrase that captures the reader's interest and tells what you are writing about.

9. Use the *Checklist for Revision* at the end of this section to help you review and revise your paragraph.

WRITING PLAN: SHORT AND EXTENDED ESSAYS

While short and extended essays are similar—both have introductory and concluding paragraphs—the extended essay has more development paragraphs. "The Birth and Death of Islands" uses examples, comparison and contrast, cause and effect, and description to explain the process of island formation. In "Exercise: A New Dietary Requirement," the author explains and supports her thesis about exercise with cause and effect, definition, examples, and comparison and contrast.

Introductory Paragraph(s)

1. Decide the narrator's point of view. Is the narrator of the essay involved in the action (first person), or an observer outside the action (third person)?

2. Write an introduction that is thought provoking for the reader. Tell what the essay is about by introducing your topic and purpose. This is the thesis statement, the main idea to be supported throughout the essay.

3. Use your introductory paragraph(s) to set the tone for the essay, your attitude toward the subject. The tone might be serious or humorous, formal or informal.

4. State your plan for the development of this essay. An extended essay may contain more than one introductory paragraph.

Development Paragraph(s)

1. Each development paragraph can be used to examine a different aspect of your subject. Let the reader know your topic or focus for each new paragraph.

2. Present the steps of the process in chronological order, and explain each clearly and thoroughly. It is important to show how one step leads to the next.

3. Provide enough facts, explanations, and examples to develop your topic adequately. Define any technical terms for the reader.

4. While process analysis is your primary writing strategy, you can also use description, illustration, cause and effect, comparison and contrast, and definition to reinforce the points you want to make.

5. If you are writing an extended essay, use the development paragraphs to include more details that support your thesis.

6. All sentences in a paragraph should relate to the topic and to one another. All paragraphs in an essay should support the topic and follow some logical order. Use transitions to link ideas within paragraphs and to make connections between paragraphs. Refer to the list of transitional words and phrases on pages 259–264.

7. Use variety in your choice of words to maintain reader interest. Where appropriate, use figurative language to increase the impact of your words and to stimulate the reader's imagination. The most commonly used figures of speech are the simile, metaphor, personification, and hyperbole. Definitions of literary and rhetorical terms can be found in the Glossary on pages 265–270.

Concluding Paragraph(s)

1. Restate the thesis in some way for emphasis. Present an overview, summarize the major points, offer an opinion, or reach a conclusion that reinforces the point of your essay.

2. More than one paragraph may be used to conclude an extended essay.

3. Use the checklist below to help you review and revise your essay.

note: The title of your essay should be a word or phrase that captures the reader's attention and tells what you are writing about. Create a title for your first draft and review it before making it final.

CHECKLIST FOR REVISION

1. My paragraph/essay has a first- or third-person point of view. I begin with a strong statement that gets the reader's attention, introduce my topic, and set the tone. If I am writing an essay, I state my thesis in the opening paragraph(s).

2. I present the steps of the process in chronological order, then explain each clearly and thoroughly. I show how one step leads to the next.

3. Technical terms are defined for the reader. My pararaph or essay includes enough facts, explanations, and examples to develop the topic adequately and reinforce major points. Each development paragraph explains different aspects of the process.

4. In an extended essay, I use the development paragraphs to include more details that support the thesis.

5. In concluding my paragraph or essay I present an overview, summarize, offer an opinion, or reach a conclusion that reinforces my point.

6. Sentences within each paragraph relate to the topic. Development paragraphs follow a logical order and support the point of the essay. I use transitions to link ideas within paragraphs and to make connections between paragraphs.

7. I use variety in my choice of words to maintain reader interest. Where appropriate, I use figurative language to increase the impact of my words and to stimulate the reader's imagination.

8. As I revise the form and content of my work, I correct errors in punctuation, capitalization, spelling, grammar, and usage.

9. The title of my paragraph or essay tells what I wrote about and captures the reader's interest.

Continue work in this chapter until you have finished all three Active Reading and Guided Writing activities.

128

Chapter 6

COMPARISON
AND
CONTRAST

In comparison and contrast, characteristics of two subjects are examined for the purpose of identifying their similarities and differences. In making comparisons we look for similarities between two or more things, people, places, or ideas; contrast involves finding differences. When you write a paper using this strategy, you can focus on just the similarities, just the differences, or discuss both.

Comparison and contrast makes sense only if the subjects belong to the same general category and share some obvious characteristics or aspects. For example, you might compare cities such as San Francisco and Boston, or sports such as basketball and football, or household pets like cats and dogs. Make sure that there is sufficient reason for making the comparison or contrast, that it reveals something new or interesting or important about the subjects.

Comparison and contrast is often an excellent way of explaining something to your reader. For example, you can compare a gecko, a small insect-eating lizard, with a crocodile, a large carnivorous reptile. Your explanation can reinforce the reader's understanding of both creatures. Once you have chosen subjects to be compared and contrasted, make a list of the characteristics they share. This will help you to generate the information for your paper.

The two basic strategies for organizing a comparison and contrast essay are the **alternating** and **block** patterns. The alternating pattern explains the two subjects by discussing shared characteristics side by side, pointing out similarities and differences. This pattern is particularly effective in longer essays where the writer wants to demonstrate many points of comparison. The block pattern, also known as the **divided** pattern, presents all of the information about one subject first, and then all the information about the other subject second. The advantage of the block pattern is that it presents each subject as a unified whole.

Writers often combine the two patterns for writing comparison and contrast. You might begin an essay with the divided pattern in order to provide an overview of the two subjects. Then you would shift to the alternating pattern for a more detailed comparison between subjects. Whichever pattern you use, be sure your two subjects belong to the same category and that your essay examines their shared characteristics.

This chapter contains three reading selections, all of which use comparison and contrast as a writing strategy. The first is a paragraph, the second a short essay, and the third a longer piece. Each is followed by an Active Reading exercise that helps you to understand the form and content of the reading model. The Guided Writing section at the end of this chapter will help you to create three original pieces of writing using comparison and contrast.

Chapter Selections

Free to Fly Inside the Cage *by Michael Kramer*

About Discipline *by Bruno Bettelheim*

The Transaction *by William Zinsser*

FREE TO FLY INSIDE THE CAGE:
A visitor discovers a country still scarred by Tiananmen but looking beyond the bars
by Michael Kramer

Michael Kramer was born in 1945 and is a graduate of Amherst College and Columbia Law School. He has worked as an editor and political writer for New York *magazine, as editor and publisher of* More, *a journalism review, and as chief political correspondent for* U.S. News & World Report. *The author of several books, he is regarded by his colleagues as one of the most energetic and intelligent reporters around. Presented here is an excerpt from his article that appeared in* Time *magazine. He wrote about China in the aftermath of the world-shaking events that occurred in Beijing, the capital of the People's Republic of China. In June, 1989, millions of students and workers demonstrated peacefully for democratic change in Beijing's traditional center for power, Tiananmen Square. Several thousand people were killed or injured by the People's Army on orders of Deng Xiaoping and the Communist Party leadership. The paradox here is that the people were killed by the People's Army, an act that contradicts basic communist ideology. In the excerpt below, Kramer compares and contrasts other contradictory aspects of Chinese life.*

Word Alert

bourgeois	relating to the middle class; marked by a concern for material interest, respectability, and a tendency toward mediocrity; dominated by commercial and industrial interests
break-dancing	a type of acrobatic dancing that uses the entire body to do a series of fast and complex moves
capitalism	an economic system characterized by private or corporate ownership of capital goods, by investments that are determined by private decision rather than by state control, and by prices, production, and the distribution of goods that are determined mainly by competition in a free market
civic	relating to a citizen, a city, citizenship, or civil affairs
civility	courtesy, politeness
Deng Xiaoping	Chinese Communist leader

ghost marriage	This is an ancient Chinese ritual in which two sets of parents arrange the marriage of their deceased children. The bodies of the children are unearthed and a formal wedding takes place, including gifts for the parents of the "bride." The Chinese, who believe in life after death, arrange the "marriage" in the hope that their children will be happy in the afterlife.
incongruities	made up of incompatible, inconsistent, or discordant parts or qualities
intractable	difficult to govern or manage
liberalism	liberal views and policies, especially in regard to political or social questions; open-minded, tolerant
modernity	contemporary, up to date, recent, modern
paradox	a statement that is seemingly contradictory or opposed to common sense and yet may be true
reserve	restraint or caution in one's words or actions
Shanghai	city and port in east China at the mouth of the Yangtze River
Sichuan	province in south central China
socialism	a system or condition of society in which the means of production are owned and controlled by the state
socialist	one who advocates or practices socialism
tai chi	a Chinese system of exercise, characterized by slow, stylized movement

It is impossible, after just five weeks "inside," to say what China is like. It is possible only to meet some people, sketch some scenes, let some voices tell their stories. And if, up close, childhood impressions fade, enough incongruities and paradoxes survive to concentrate the mind. Like the newspapers that urge "bitter struggle" against "bourgeois liberalism" while trumpeting the pleasures of disco dancing on the same page. Like the never ending loop of music in the lobby of a hotel in Sichuan province that alternates between a Rod Stewart oldie (*Sailing*) and a socialist goody (*Without the Communist Party There would Be No New China*). Like the young man break-dancing to a blaring Madonna album amid a few hundred elderly tai chi practitioners at a Shanghai park. Like the reserve and civility evident in personal relations that rarely translate to civic responsibility. Like the more intractable tensions of incorporating the best of capitalism while preserving socialism—tensions that have arisen because of, rather than in spite of, Deng's economic reforms. Like everything about the ghost marriage and those who celebrate it. All this and more reflect the clash of modernity and tradition and the exquisite balancing acts required when a nation persists in pursuing contradictory notions of culture, economics, and politics at the same time.

ACTIVE READING

The Active Reading exercise gives you an opportunity to reread the paragraph with a critical eye. By answering the questions that follow, you will extend and sharpen your understanding of the selection. This activity will help you become a more efficient reader and a more effective writer.

Throughout this selection the author looks at the contrasting or contradictory aspects of China. First, he examines what is possible and impossible to know about China.

1. How long had the author been in China when he wrote this article?
2. In what way is the title "Free to Fly Inside the Cage" an example of verbal irony?
3. What word in the subtitle evokes an image of being in prison?
4. What is impossible to know about China after just five weeks?
5. What does the author believe is possible after five weeks in China?

In his first two sentences the author introduces the topic, China. In the next sentence, he tells us that he will focus on the incongruities and paradoxes that exist there. The remainder of the paragraph presents examples that highlight the contrasts between modern and traditional China.

Listed below are aspects of Chinese life that the author uses in comparing and contrasting modern and traditional ways. Refer to the reading selection to complete the chart.

Aspects of Chinese Life	Modern	Traditional
6. newspapers		
7. hotel lobby music		
8. exercise		
9. tensions of the economic system		
10. ghost marriage		

11. In his concluding sentence, what does the author say is required when a nation persists in pursuing contradictory notions of culture, economics, and politics at the same time?

12. The author uses transitional words and phrases to link ideas in this paragraph. List at least five.

13. What general category is being examined in this selection?

14. Which writing pattern, alternating or block, does the author use for this paragraph of comparison and contrast?

15. The author's primary purpose in this selection is to:

    a. inform

    b. persuade

    c. entertain

The Active Reading exercise can be scored using the answer key and grading grid. Enter your grade in the progress chart.

GUIDED WRITING

The Guided Writing section at the end of this chapter (page 146) provides topics and plans for writing paragraphs and essays using comparison and contrast. Select a topic and write a paragraph by following the writing plan that begins on page 147. Continue work in this chapter until you have finished all three Active Reading and Guided Writing activities.

ABOUT DISCIPLINE
by Bruno Bettelheim

Bruno Bettelheim (1903–1990) was born in Vienna, Austria and received a Ph.D. in psychology in 1938. He came to the United States in 1939 after having endured a harrowing year in German concentration camps. He summarized his observations of life in the camps in a landmark article, "Individual and Mass Behavior in Extreme Situations." As the death camps were liberated, his article gained worldwide renown and became required reading for all officers in the United States military. Bettelheim is a world authority on the treatment of childhood emotional disorders, especially autism and juvenile psychosis. He received the National Book Award for The Uses of Enchantment: The Meaning and Importance of Fairy Tales *(1976). Among his other books are* Love Is Not Enough: The Treatment of Emotionally Disturbed Children *(1950),* The Informed Heart: Autonomy in a Mass Age *(1960), and* A Good Enough Parent: A Book on Child Rearing *(1987). The selection presented here, excerpted from his last book, compares and contrasts the maternal behavior of Japanese and Americans.*

Word Alert

deliberations	to think, to ponder issues and decisions carefully, to consider thoroughly
disciplined	an orderly pattern of behavior marked by or possessing discipline; self-control
enhance	to heighten, to make greater as in value, desirability, or attractiveness
inculcate	to teach or impress by frequent repetitions or admonitions
refrain	to keep oneself from doing or indulging in something; restrain, abstain
superfluous	extra, extravagant; exceeding what is sufficient or necessary

To be disciplined requires self-control. To be controlled by others and to accept living by their rules or orders makes it superfluous to control oneself. When the more important aspects of a child's actions and behavior are controlled by, say, his parents or teachers, he will see no need to learn to control himself; others do it for him.

2   How parents in other cultures try to inculcate self-control in their children can be instructive. Consider, for example, a study designed to find out why young Japanese do much better academically than Americans. When the researchers studied maternal behavior they saw clear differences between the Japanese and the Americans. Typically, when young American children ran around in supermarkets, their mothers—often annoyed—told them, "Stop that!" or "I told you not to act this way!" Japanese mothers typically refrain entirely from telling their children what to do. Instead they ask them questions, such as "How do you think it makes the storekeeper feel when you run around like this in his store?" or "How do you think it makes me feel when my child runs around as you do?"

3   Similarly, the American mother, wanting her child to eat what he was supposed to eat, would order the child to do so or tell him that he ought to eat it because it was good for him. The Japanese mother would ask her child a question, such as "How do you think it makes the man who grew these vegetables for you to eat feel when you reject them?" or "How do you think it makes these carrots that grew so that you could eat them feel when you do not eat them?" Thus from a very early age the American child is told what to do, while the Japanese child is encouraged not only to consider other persons' feelings but to control himself on the basis of his own deliberations.

4   The reason for the higher academic achievement of Japanese youngsters may well be that the Japanese child in situations important to his mother is invited to think things out on his own, a habit that stands him in good stead when he has to master academic material. The American child, in contrast, is expected to conform his decisions and actions to what he is told to do. This expectation certainly does not encourage him to do his own thinking.

5   The Japanese mother does not just expect her child to be able to arrive at good decisions. She also makes an appeal to her child not to embarrass her. In the traditional Japanese culture losing face is among the worst things that can happen to a person. When a mother asks, "How do you think it makes me—or the storekeeper—feel when you act this way?" she implies that by mending his ways the child does her, or the storekeeper, a very great favor. To be asked to do one's own thinking and to act accordingly, as well as to be told that one is able to do someone a favor, enhances

one's self-respect, while to be ordered to do the opposite of what one wants is destructive of it.

ACTIVE READING

The Active Reading exercise gives you an opportunity to reread the essay with a critical eye. By answering the questions that follow, you will extend and sharpen your understanding of the selection. This activity will help you become a more efficient reader and a more effective writer.

INTRODUCTORY PARAGRAPH *(par. 1)*

In this first paragraph the author asks us to consider the question of self-control as compared to control by others. The author suggests two causal relationships that illustrate his thesis.

In the each of the sentences below, one part is marked (*a*) and the other is marked (*b*). Identify each phrase as either the cause or effect part of the statement. Remember, the *cause* is the reason why and the *effect* is the result or outcome. Ask yourself, "What leads to what?"

1. (a) To be disciplined (b) requires self-control
2. (a) When a child's actions and behavior are controlled by others, (b) he will see no need to learn to control himself.
3. If self-control leads to disciplined behavior, what inference can you make about control by others and what that leads to?

DEVELOPMENT PARAGRAPHS *(par. 2–4)*

4. What is the topic that the author develops in these paragraphs?
5. What question does the author want us to consider?
6. Research that compared Japanese and Americans found clear differences in behavior. What kind of behavior was compared?

Listed below are aspects or characteristics of children's behavior. The author compares and contrasts responses to these behaviors by Japanese and American mothers. Refer to the reading selection to complete the chart below.

Children's Behavior	Japanese Mother's Response to Child	American Mother's Response to Child
7. running around in supermarket		
8. not eating certain foods at mealtime		
9. in early childhood		
10. academic achievement		

11. What inference would you make about the tone of voice the Japanese mother uses when she asks questions?

   a. scolding
   b. nurturing

12. What is the basis for your answer to the above question?

13. What inference would you make about the tone of voice the American mother uses when she issues orders?

   a. scolding
   b. nurturing

14. What is the basis for your answer to the above question?

CONCLUDING PARAGRAPH (par. 5)

15. In addition to expecting her child to make good decisions, what else does the Japanese mother expect?

16. What is one of the worst things that can happen to a person in traditional Japanese culture?

17. What is implied in the questions that the mother asks of the child?

In summarizing, the author draws certain conclusions about self-respect. He says that self-respect is enhanced when you think on your own, act accordingly, and can do someone a favor. Self-respect is damaged when you are ordered to do the opposite of what you want to do.

18. On the whole, what does the author say the Japanese child learns from his mother?

19. On the whole, what does the author say the American child learns from his mother?

20. The author uses transitional words and phrases to link ideas in this essay. List at least five.

21. What general category is being examined in this selection?

22. Which writing pattern, alternating or block, does the author use for this essay of comparison and contrast?

23. The author's primary purpose in this selection is to:
    a. inform
    b. persuade
    c. entertain

The Active Reading exercise can be scored using the answer key and grading grid. Enter your grade in the progress chart.

GUIDED WRITING

The Guided Writing section at the end of this chapter (page 146) provides topics and plans for writing paragraphs and essays using comparison and contrast. Select a topic and write a short essay by following the writing plan that begins on page 148.

Continue work in this chapter until you have finished all three Active Reading and Guided Writing activities. Upon completion, you will have written three new compositions for your portfolio (one paragraph and two essays). Record grades in your progress chart and, if available, on the Academic Credit Statement in your *Writing Portfolio Organizer*.

THE TRANSACTION

by William Zinsser

William Zinsser was born in 1922 in New York City and educated at Princeton University. He worked for The New York Herald Tribune *from 1946 to 1959 as a feature writer, drama editor, film critic, and editorial writer. Zinsser was a free-lance writer until he joined the English faculty of Yale University in 1970. Among his many books,* On Writing Well: An Informal Guide to Writing Nonfiction *(1976) is best known. In this widely used textbook, he advised college students that "Words are the only tools that you will be given. Learn to use them with originality and care. Value them for their strength and their infinite diversity. Good nonfiction writing follows certain rules: Simplify. Be clear. Get rid of pomposity in your writing. Above all, be yourself." In the selection presented here, Zinsser compares a professional writer's view with that of a person who writes for enjoyment.*

Word Alert

arduous	difficult, strenuous; demanding great physical or mental effort, labor, or endurance
avocation	hobby; an activity pursued in addition to one's regular work or profession, usually for enjoyment
bewildered	puzzled, confused, perplexed
Bohemian	a person, writer, or artist living an unconventional life
drone	one who performs dull and monotonous tasks
glamorous	romantic and exciting
gusto	an overabundance of vigor and enthusiasm
luxurious	exceedingly rich or magnificent; sumptuous, opulent
mime	to act a part with mimic, gesture, and action, usually without words
remote	small in degree; slight, distant
revelation	something that is revealed, especially an enlightening or astonishing disclosure
solitary	alone; being at once single and isolated
symbolism	in writing, the use of concrete objects or things to represent other things or ideas
vocation	regular occupation or profession, especially one for which an individual is particularly suited or qualified

Several years ago a school in Connecticut held "a day devoted to the arts," and I was asked if I would come and talk about writing as a vocation. When I arrived I found that a second speaker had been invited— Dr. Brock (as I'll call him), a surgeon who had recently begun to write and had sold some stories to national magazines. He was going to talk about writing as an avocation. That made us a panel, and we sat down to face a crowd of student newspaper editors and reporters, English teachers and parents, all eager to learn the secrets of our glamorous work.

Dr. Brock was dressed in a bright red jacket, looking vaguely Bohemian, as authors are supposed to look, and the first question went to him. What was it like to be a writer?

He said it was tremendous fun. Coming home from an arduous day at the hospital, he would go straight to his yellow pad and write his tensions away. The words just flowed. It was easy.

I then said that writing wasn't easy and it wasn't fun. It was hard and lonely, and the words seldom just flowed.

Next Dr. Brock was asked if it was important to rewrite. Absolutely not, he said. "Let it all hang out," and whatever form the sentences take will reflect the writer at his most natural.

I then said that rewriting is the essence of writing. I pointed out that professional writers rewrite their sentences repeatedly and then rewrite what they have rewritten. I mentioned that E.B. White and James Thurber were known to rewrite their pieces eight or nine times.

"What do you do on days when it isn't going well?" Dr. Brock was asked. He said he just stopped writing and put the work aside for a day when it would go better.

I then said that the professional writer must establish a daily schedule and stick to it. I said that writing is a craft, not an art, and that the man who runs away from his craft because he lacks inspiration is fooling himself. He is also going broke.

"What if you're feeling depressed or unhappy?" a student asked. "Won't that affect your writing?"

10   Probably it will, Dr. Brock replied. Go fishing. Take a walk.

11   Probably it won't, I said. If your job is to write every day, you learn to do it like any other job.

12   A student asked if we found it useful to circulate in the literary world. Dr. Brock said that he was greatly enjoying his new life as a man of letters, and he told several luxurious stories of being taken to lunch by his publisher and his agent at Manhattan restaurants where writers and editors gather. I said that professional writers are solitary drones who seldom see other writers.

13   "Do you put symbolism in your writing?" a student asked me.

14   "Not if I can help it," I replied. I have an unbroken record of missing the deeper meaning in any story, play or movie, and as for dance and mime I have never had even a remote notion of what is being conveyed.

15   "I *love* symbols!" Dr. Brock exclaimed, and he described with gusto the joys of weaving them through his work.

16   So the morning went, and it was a revelation to all of us. At the end Dr. Brock told me he was enormously interested in my answers—it had never occurred to him that writing could be hard. I told him I was just as interested in *his* answers—it had never occurred to me that writing could be easy. (Maybe I should take up surgery on the side.)

17   As for the students, anyone might think that we left them bewildered. But in fact we probably gave them a broader glimpse of the writing process than if only one of us had talked. For of course there isn't any "right" way to do such intensely personal work. There are all kinds of writers and all kinds of methods, and any method that helps somebody to say what he wants to say is the right method for him.

ACTIVE READING

The Active Reading exercise gives you an opportunity to reread the essay with a critical eye. By answering the questions that follow, you will extend and sharpen your understanding of the selection. This activity will help you become a more efficient reader and a more effective writer.

INTRODUCTORY PARAGRAPH *(par. 1)*

The first paragraph sets the scene for a panel discussion on writing in which the author took part with another writer. In a conversational tone, Zinsser begins by telling us where and when the discussion takes place and who is involved.

1. Where and when does this discussion take place?

2. What had the school planned?

3. What topic was the author asked to discuss?

4. Who else was invited to speak?

5. What was this speaker's topic?

6. Who was the audience for this presentation?

DEVELOPMENT PARAGRAPH *(par. 2)*

This paragraph serves as a transition to the direct comparisons that are made throughout the development of the essay.

7. The first question from the audience was addressed to Dr. Brock. Why, according to the author?

8. What was the first question?

DEVELOPMENT PARAGRAPHS *(par. 3–16)*

Listed below are aspects or characteristics of the writer's life. The narrator compares and contrasts his own viewpoint with that of his fellow presenter, Dr. Brock. Refer to the reading selection to complete the chart on the next page.

Aspects of a Writer's Life	Dr. Brock	Mr. Zinsser
9. reason for writing		
10. What is it like to be a writer?		
11. opinion about importance of rewriting		
12. what to do when writing isn't going well		
13. Does feeling depressed or unhappy affect writing?		
14. contacts in the literary world		
15. use of symbolism in writing		
16. what these writers learned from each other		

17. With these development paragraphs in mind, do you think the narrator's reference to writing as "glamorous work" is serious or sarcastic?

The author uses examples to illustrate different points of view about writing. The reader's understanding of abstract ideas is enhanced through examples that use concrete details.

18. Dr. Brock said writing was tremendous fun. What example does he offer to illustrate this point of view?

19. Mr. Zinsser presents the view that rewriting is the essence of writing. What examples does he use?

20. Dr. Brock told the audience he greatly enjoyed his new life as a man of letters. How does he illustrate this?

21. How does Mr. Zinsser express his view of symbolism?

22. What tone does the author use in his remarks about symbolism?

23. As a result of the panel discussion, the author had two revelations. First, it had never occurred to him that writing could be easy. What was the second "revelation?"

24. What is the tone of his second revelation?

CONCLUDING PARAGRAPH (par. 17)

25. What effect does the author think the panel discussion had on the audience?

26. According to the author is there a right way to write?

27. What method does the author advocate a writer use?

28. Is the tone of this concluding paragraph sarcastic or serious?

29. Overall, is the tone of this essay serious or humorous?

30. What general category is being examined in this selection?

31. Which writing pattern, alternating or block, does the author use for this essay of comparison and contrast?

32. The author uses transitional words and phrases to link ideas in this essay. List at least five.

33. The author's primary purpose in this selection is to
    a. inform
    b. persuade
    c. entertain

The Active Reading exercise can be scored using the answer key and grading grid. Enter your grade in the progress chart.

The Guided Writing section that begins on the next page provides topics and plans for writing paragraphs and essays using comparison and contrast. Select a topic and write an extended essay by following the writing plan that begins on page 148.

GUIDED WRITING

This part of the chapter will help you apply what you have learned about writing paragraphs and essays using comparison and contrast. Choose one of the topics listed below for each writing assignment that you do. If you want to write about something else, ask your instructor if the topic is appropriate for writing comparison and contrast. Follow the plan that applies to write your composition. Submit your completed composition to the instructor for evaluation. When you receive a grade for this work, enter it in the progress chart.

WRITING TOPICS

- Identify a culture, other than China, in which the traditional and modern exist side by side. Compare and contrast the old with the new.

- Compare and contrast the major aspects of capitalism with socialism as economic systems.

- Choose two cultures and compare and contrast their mechanisms for social control: how people are socialized to follow the prevailing beliefs, mores, and norms of each society. Or, you may choose two subcultures within a society to compare and contrast.

- Think about the way you were raised as a child. Compare and contrast this with the way you plan to raise, or are raising your children.

- In "The Transaction" the man who wrote for a living found the process to be a difficult one, while the man whose hobby was writing found the experience enjoyable. Compare and contrast two activities that you regularly engage in, one that you consider work and the other that you consider fun.

- We often find ourselves comparing the real with the ideal. Compare and contrast the real with the ideal in one of the following: jobs, friendships, parents, relatives, school, housing, dating, marriage, leisure time, physical appearance, or personality.

PREWRITING: GENERATING IDEAS

Now that you have selected a topic, you will need to gather information and generate ideas before you begin to write. If you are writing about a personal experience you will probably rely on your memory, other people's input, and your own creativity. Other topics may require that you use reference works to collect this information for your composition.

In order to compare and contrast two subjects, you will need to develop a list of the characteristics, or aspects, they have in common. Use this list to make a chart that compares and contrasts your two subjects in terms of their shared characteristics. Decide which pattern you will use in your composition, alternating or block. The alternating pattern compares your subjects side by side, one aspect at a time. The block pattern discusses all aspects of one subject first, and then makes comparisons by discussing all aspects of the other subject. Refer to the chart as you follow the plan for writing a paragraph or essay using comparison and contrast.

WRITING PLAN: THE PARAGRAPH

1. Decide the point of view of the narrator, first or third person. Write an introduction that gets the reader's attention and present your topic at the beginning of the paragraph.

2. Set the tone for the paragraph, your attitude toward the subject. The tone might be serious or humorous, formal or informal.

3. Use the chart you have created to help you compare and contrast each aspect of your two subjects. Use facts, description, definition, explanation, and examples where appropriate.

4. If you use the alternating pattern, discuss one aspect at a time for both subjects. If you use the block pattern, discuss all the aspects of one subject first and then make comparisons to the other subject.

5. Write a conclusion to your paragraph that restates the topic and presents an overview, summarizes, or expresses an opinion.

6. To create unity in your writing, make sure that each sentence in the paragraph relates to the topic. Your writing will be coherent if ideas follow one another in a logical pattern and sentences flow smoothly from one to the other. Use transitions to link or connect ideas. The list of transitional words and phrases at the back of this book is for your use and reference when you write (see pages 259–264).

7. Use variety in your choice of words to maintain reader interest. Where appropriate, use figurative language to increase the impact of your words and to stimulate the reader's imagination. The most commonly used figures of speech are the simile, metaphor, personification, and hyperbole. Definitions of literary and rhetorical terms can be found in the Glossary on pages 265–270.

8. Create a title for your paragraph, a word or phrase that captures the reader's interest and tells what you are writing about.

9. Use the *Checklist for Revision* at the end of this section to help you review and revise your paragraph.

WRITING PLAN: SHORT AND EXTENDED ESSAYS

While short and extended essays are similar—both have introductory and concluding paragraphs—the extended essay has more development paragraphs. "About Discipline" compares and contrasts Japanese and American maternal behavior using cause and effect, examples, and explanations. In "The Transaction" the author compares and contrasts two writers and their views about writing. His essay uses narration, examples, cause and effect, and description.

Introductory Paragraph(s)

1. Decide the narrator's point of view. Is the narrator of the essay involved in the action (first person), or an observer outside the action (third person)?

2. Begin with a strong statement or question that appeals to the reader's interest. Tell what the essay is about by introducing your topic and purpose. This is the thesis statement, the main idea to be supported throughout the essay.

3. Use your introductory paragraph(s) to set the tone for the essay, your attitude toward the subject. The tone might be serious or humorous, formal or informal.

4. State your plan for the development of this essay. An extended essay may contain more than one introductory paragraph.

Development Paragraph(s)

1. Each development paragraph can be used to examine a different aspect of your two subjects. Let the reader know your topic or focus for each new paragraph.

2. Use the chart you have created to help you compare and contrast each aspect of your two subjects. Use facts, description, definition, explanation, and illustration where appropriate.

3. If you use the alternating pattern, compare and contrast your subjects side by side, one aspect at a time. If you use the block pattern, discuss all aspects of one subject first, and then and then make comparisons to the other subject.

4. If you are writing an extended essay, include more comparisons and make use of other strategies to reinforce your thesis.

5. All sentences in a paragraph should relate to the topic and to one another. All paragraphs in an essay should support the topic and follow some logical order. Use transitions to link ideas within paragraphs and to make connections between paragraphs. Refer to the list of transitional words and phrases on pages 259–264.

6. Use variety in your choice of words to maintain reader interest. Where appropriate, use figurative language to increase the impact of your words and to stimulate the reader's imagination. The most commonly used figures of speech are the simile, metaphor, personification, and hyperbole. Definitions of literary and rhetorical terms can be found in the Glossary on pages 265–270.

Concluding Paragraph(s)

1. Restate the thesis in some way for emphasis. Present an overview, summarize the major points, offer an opinion, or reach a conclusion that reinforces the point of your essay.

2. More than one paragraph may be used to conclude an extended essay.

3. Use the checklist below to help you review and revise your essay.

note: The title of your essay should be a word or phrase that captures the reader's attention and tells what you are writing about. Create a title for your first draft and review it before making it final.

CHECKLIST FOR REVISION

1. My paragraph/essay has a first- or third-person point of view. My opening sentences appeal to the reader's interest, introduce my topic, and set the tone. If I am writing an essay, my thesis statement appears in the opening paragraph(s).

2. I use the chart I have created to compare and contrast each aspect of my two subjects. I use either an alternating or block pattern in my composition.

3. My pararaph or essay uses facts, description, definition, explanation, and illustration where appropriate. Each development paragraph explains different aspects of my two subjects.

4. In an extended essay, I use the development paragraphs to include more comparisons that support the thesis.

5. In concluding my paragraph or essay I present an overview, summarize, offer an opinion, or reach a conclusion that reinforces my point.

6. Sentences within each paragraph relate to the topic. Development paragraphs follow a logical order and support the point of the essay. I use transitions to link ideas within paragraphs and to make connections between paragraphs.

7. I use variety in my choice of words to maintain reader interest. Where appropriate, I use figurative language to increase the impact of my words and to stimulate the reader's imagination.

8. As I revise the form and content of my work, I correct errors in punctuation, capitalization, spelling, grammar, and usage.

9. The title of my paragraph or essay tells what I wrote about and captures the reader's interest.

Continue work in this chapter until you have finished all three Active Reading and Guided Writing activities.

Chapter 7

CLASSIFICATION

Classification sorts information into groups or categories on the basis of shared characteristics. Nearly everything is subject to classification of some kind. The Yellow Pages classifies businesses according to the products they sell or services they offer. Biology uses a highly organized system known as scientific classification to identify plants and animals. The system of classification used by the movie industry in Hollywood to rate films—*G, PG, PG-13, R,* and *NC-17*—is familiar to most people

The chief purpose of a classification essay is to explain. At a simple level, the purpose of such explanations may be to outline the various parts of the system. At a more significant level, the purpose is to define, analyze, and justify the system's organizing principle. The goal of classification is to make things easier to find, as well as easier to understand, evaluate, and use.

The easiest way to classify is to divide your subject into two major categories. The two groups are distinguished from one another by their special characteristics. If smoking is your topic, your two categories might be smokers and nonsmokers. If lifestyle is your topic, you might distinguish between city dwellers and suburbanites.

If your paragraph or essay has more than two major categories, these need to be arranged in an order or sequence. For example, you may decide to arrange your categories in order of importance or in order of complexity. Once you have ordered your categories, differentiate them from one another and present vivid examples for each major division. While the classification system may provide the basis for overall organization, one or more of the following writing techniques will also be used: illustration, definition, comparison and contrast, narration, description, and process analysis.

This chapter contains three reading selections, all of which use classification as a writing strategy. The first is a paragraph, the second a short essay, and the third a longer piece. Each is followed by an Active Reading exercise that helps you to understand the form and content of the reading model. The Guided Writing section at the end of this chapter will help you to create three original pieces of writing using classification.

Chapter Selections

The Three New Yorks *by E. B. White*
The Structure of Memory *by April Lavallee*
Stand Up for Yourself *by Bruce Baldwin*

THE THREE NEW YORKS

by E. B. White

E(Elwyn) B(Brooks) White was born in 1899 in Mount Vernon, New York and was graduated from Cornell University. He worked as a reporter for United Press, The American Legion News Service, *and the* Seattle Times. *In 1927 White began his career in journalism, working on the staff of the* New Yorker, *contributing a column to* Harper's, *and developing the prose style that earned him the reputation as America's finest essayist. His books include* The Second Tree From the Corner *(1954),* The Points of My Compass *(1962), and three classic children's stories:* Stuart Little *(1945),* Charlotte's Web *(1952), and* The Trumpet of the Swan *(1970). He has received many awards and honors including the National Institute of Arts and Letters gold medal (1960), the Presidential Medal of Freedom (1963), and the Pulitzer Prize (1978). This excerpt from "The Three New Yorks" gets us to think about the people that give New York City, or any town, its character.*

Word Alert

Consolidated Edison Company	the utility company that provides electric power for New York City
deportment	behavior or bearing; the manner in which one conducts oneself
indignity	an insult, humiliating treatment
locusts	migratory grasshoppers, often traveling in vast swarms that strip areas of all vegetation as they pass through
quest	pursuit, search
turbulence	wild commotion

There are roughly three New Yorks. There is, first, the New York of the man or woman who was born here, who takes the city for granted and accepts its size and its turbulence as natural and inevitable. Second, there is the New York of the commuter—the city that is devoured by locusts each day and spat out each night. Third, there is the New York of the person who was born somewhere else and came to New York in quest of something. Of these three trembling cities the greatest is the last—the city of final destination, the city that is a goal. It is this third city that accounts for New York's high-strung disposition, its poetical deportment, its dedication to the arts, and its incomparable achievements. Commuters give the city its tidal restlessness; natives give it solidity and continuity; but the settlers give it passion. And whether it is a farmer arriving from Italy to set up a small grocery store in a slum, or a young girl arriving from a small town in Mississippi to escape the indignity of being observed by her neighbors, or a boy arriving from the Corn Belt with a manuscript in his suitcase and a pain in his heart, it makes no difference; each embraces New York with the intense excitement of first love, each absorbs New York with the fresh eyes of an adventurer, each generates heat and light to dwarf the Consolidated Edison Company.

ACTIVE READING

The Active Reading exercise gives you an opportunity to reread the paragraph with a critical eye. By answering the questions that follow, you will extend and sharpen your understanding of the selection. This activity will help you become a more efficient reader and a more effective writer.

The author begins by identifying his classification system, three New Yorks. Each is defined in terms of the people who live and work there—New Yorkers—and their attitudes toward the city.

1. What group does he define first?

2. What characteristics does the author ascribe to this group?

3. What group is presented second?

4. What characteristics does the author ascribe to this group?

5. Which figure of speech is used in describing commuters?
   a. metaphor
   b. simile
   c. personification
   d. hyperbole

6. What is the last of the author's three groups?

7. How does the author feel about this last group and why?

8. According to the author, what does this last group contribute to New York's character?

9. The author reinforces his point of view by restating the contributions of each group to the city. What do commuters contribute?

10. What do natives contribute?

11. What do settlers contribute?

12. Why do you think the author uses the words *tidal restlessness* to describe commuters?

13. Of the three, which group's contribution does the author believe to be most important and what makes you think so?

He continues to emphasize the importance of this group's contributions by offering examples of who they are, where they come from, and why they came to New York.

14. For each of the following people, identify where they came from and why they came to New York.

    a. a farmer

    b. a young girl

    c. a boy

Each of these people touches or is touched by New York in much the same way. The author's examples make use of hyperbole (exaggeration) to illustrate the extent of the settlers' passion.

15. How does each settler embrace New York?

16. How does each settler absorb New York?

17. What does each settler generate?

18. What conclusion might you draw about the passion of the settlers?

19. The author uses transitional words and phrases to link ideas in this paragraph. List at least five.

20. The author's primary purpose in this selection is to:

    a. inform

    b. persuade

    c. entertain

The Active Reading exercise can be scored using the answer key and grading grid. Enter your grade in the progress chart.

GUIDED WRITING

The Guided Writing section at the end of this chapter (page 167) provides topics and plans for writing paragraphs and essays using classification. Select a topic and write a paragraph by following the writing plan on page 169. Continue work in this chapter until you have finished all three Active Reading and Guided Writing activities.

THE STRUCTURE OF MEMORY

by April Lavallee

April Lavallee was a college student when she wrote this paper for a psychology class. She uses classification to broadly outline the three-part division of memory to show why we remember some things but not others. Given the amount of material presented in college courses, what student would not want to learn more about the workings of our memory system?

Word Alert

msec	abbreviation for *millisecond*: one thousandth of a second (250 msec is 1/4 of a second)
phenomena	observable or significant facts or events; exceptional or unusual people, things, or occurrences
stimulus	something that arouses or provokes activity

1   George Washington was our first President; the North defeated the South in the Civil War; the Japanese bombed Pearl Harbor during World War II; and the whale is the largest living mammal. These statements have nothing in common except that practically every American knows them. Although they are unimportant to our everyday lives, we can remember facts such as these, but we cannot remember where our keys are when we are late for work. We can recite the Pledge of Allegiance, but we cannot remember the seven digits the telephone operator just gave us. Why is this?

2   The information-processing model used to describe how our memories work helps explain phenomena such as these. This model defines three principal storage structures, each of which corresponds to a stage in the processing of a stimulus. Information is first entered or registered by means of one or more of the five senses in the Sensory Register. It is held here briefly—for approximately 250 msec to 2 seconds—in raw sensory form, and eventually decays and vanishes completely.

Once the information is recognized or learned it can pass to the next storage structure—the Short-Term Memory (STM). Information is stored here as familiar, recognizable patterns. Through rehearsal (forced recall and repetition), information can be retained here for much longer than in the Sensory Register. Without rehearsal, though, the information decays just as it does in the Sensory Register. Another limitation, in addition to time, on STM is the amount of material that can be stored here at one time, even with the help of rehearsal. The generally accepted number of items that can be held in STM is seven, plus or minus two depending on the individual.

With increased repetition, information is transferred from STM to Long-Term Memory (LTM), the third of the storage structures. This structure is relatively permanent and contains all of our knowledge about the world. Apparently LTM is unlimited in the amount of information it can hold. The secret to remembering is to get the information into LTM, so next time pay attention and rehearse that telephone number or the location of your keys and sunglasses. Then you won't forget.

ACTIVE READING

The Active Reading exercise gives you an opportunity to reread the essay with a critical eye. By answering the questions that follow, you will extend and sharpen your understanding of the selection. This activity will help you become a more efficient reader and a more effective writer.

INTRODUCTORY PARAGRAPH *(par. 1)*

In this first paragraph the author asks us to consider why it is that some things are easy and others more difficult for us to remember. She begins with four facts that practically every American knows. The author uses this information in making comparison and contrast statements.

1. What general category is being examined?
2. The author compares our memory of well-known facts with our memory of daily events in our personal life. Name two things she says we have trouble remembering.

The author concludes the paragraph by asking why it is that we remember some things and not others. This question serves as a transition to the next paragraph and motivates us to read further.

DEVELOPMENT PARAGRAPH *(par. 2)*

The author answers the question posed in the first paragraph. She says that these phenomena can be explained through the use of the information-processing model which describes how our memories work.

3. The information-processing model classifies memory into how many categories?

4. What do these categories represent?

5. What is the first structure or stage in the process?

6. By what means does information enter the Sensory Register?

7. For how long is information held at this stage?

8. What happens to information at this stage?

DEVELOPMENT PARAGRAPH *(par. 3)*

9. This paragraph discusses the second structure or stage in information processing. What is this stage called?

10. When does information move from the Sensory Register to Short-Term Memory?

11. How is information stored in this structure or stage?

12. What does one have to do to retain information in Short-Term Memory?

13. A comparison of the Sensory Register and Short-Term Memory points to one difference and one similarity. What are they?

14. In what other way is Short-Term Memory limited?

15. Approximately how many items can an individual hold in Short-Term Memory?

CONCLUDING PARAGRAPH *(par. 4)*

This paragraph discusses the third structure or stage in this classification system, and answers the question that was posed in the beginning of the essay.

16. How is information transferred from Short-Term Memory to Long-Term Memory?

17. What are two characteristics of this structure?

18. In what two ways is Long-Term Memory different than Short-Term Memory?

19. What does the author say is the secret of remembering?

20. What does the author recommend you do to enhance your memory?

21. The author uses transitional words and phrases to link ideas in this essay. List at least five.

22. The author's primary purpose in this selection is to:

    a. inform

    b. persuade

    c. entertain

The Active Reading exercise can be scored using the answer key and grading grid. Enter your grade in the progress chart.

GUIDED WRITING

The Guided Writing section at the end of this chapter (page 167) provides topics and plans for writing paragraphs and essays using classification. Select a topic and write a short essay by following the writing plan that begins on page 170.

Continue work in this chapter until you have finished all three Active Reading and Guided Writing activities. Upon completion, you will have written three new compositions for your portfolio (one paragraph and two essays). Record grades in your progress chart and, if available, on the Academic Credit Statement in your *Writing Portfolio Organizer*.

STAND UP FOR YOURSELF

by Bruce A. Baldwin

Bruce A. Baldwin was born in Milton, Pennsylvania in 1943 and was educated at Pennsylvania State University and at the University of Florida. He earned a doctorate in psychology from Arizona State University and taught for many years at the University of North Carolina School of Medicine. He is currently a practicing psychologist and head of Direction Dynamics. A nationally recognized authority on Lifestyle Management, Dr. Baldwin is the author of more than 100 published articles. In his book It's All In Your Head, *Dr. Baldwin teaches effective ways to become more successful, both personally and professionally. The essay presented here is excerpted from* Beyond The Cornucopia Kids. *The author tells us about how people manipulate others and how we can avoid being manipulated.*

Word Alert

abhor	to reject vehemently; to shun
appease	to calm or pacify by giving what is demanded; to placate
armor	protective covering for defense
chinks	narrow cracks or fissures; gaps
manipulate	to control by shrewdness or deviousness to one's own advantage
martyr	one who makes a show of suffering in order to arouse sympathy
ploy	a tactic intended to gain an advantage over an opponent; something devised or contrived
prerogatives	exclusive rights or privileges; powers
profess	to declare in words and appearances only; pretend
reinforce	rewarding or strengthening behavior which makes it likely to occur again
ritual	any formal and customarily repeated act or series of acts; a detailed method of procedure faithfully or consistently followed
savvy	practical and perceptive; to have common sense
susceptible	open to influence, impressionable; inability to resist another's influence attempts

At a store, five-year-old Sam spots a toy truck. His mother knows the   *1*
ritual:

"Can I have this truck?"   *2*

"Not now."   *3*

Sam bursts into tears. "You *never* let me have anything!" he cries.   *4*
"Mrs. Brown bought Tommy a truck."

"Oh, all right," his mother says. "Just this once."   *5*

Sam is used to getting things this way. He has learned to use emo-   *6*
tional pressure to manipulate his mother. Because Sam's maneuvers work
so well, his manipulative behavior is reinforced—and will be used again.

If a child of five can manipulate others by discovering their vulnerabil-   *7*
ities, think what a savvy adult can do! This is the way it works:

Locating an emotional vulnerability, often by trial and error, the ma-   *8*
nipulator exploits that knowledge to arouse our emotions and create internal
pressure. We lose objectivity and make decisions to appease the one who
has created the pressure—rather than do what is right. Then we feel used.

But if we can recognize and reduce our weaknesses, we will feel more   *9*
in control, and our relationships will improve.

To help you close up the chinks in *your* emotional armor, consider the   *10*
following list of vulnerabilities.

1. You feel guilty. Inducing guilt is the most common form of manipu-   *11*
lation. Martyrs are masters of this kind of emotional blackmail.

2. You fear conflict or anger. Many nonassertive men and women agree   *12*
to almost anything to avoid a fight. Sometimes a person's early family life
was so filled with parental conflict that he or she learned to abhor differences of any kind. Other parents so carefully hide conflict that their
children grow up with an unrealistic idea of a "good relationship."

3. You consistently fall for a "hard luck" story. Some people become ex-   *13*
pert at the game of "woe is me." They "hook" others into taking care of
them. When confronted by this kind of manipulator, ask yourself: "Is this
person playing on my emotions? How should I respond to help him help
himself?"

Tears are also a favorite ploy. Children can turn tears off and on like a   *14*
faucet and use them selectively on the parent who is most vulnerable.
(Don't forget that some adults can cry on demand too.)

15 *4. You fall for flattery.* When little Johnny is about to be punished, he professes undying love for his parents with bear hugs and sloppy kisses. His parents melt, and Johnny gets off scot-free. Similar cons are used in adult relationships. Flattery distorts your perception and makes you want to please.

16 *5. You fear disapproval.* It's surprising how many otherwise bright and insightful people can't stand the thought of not being liked by someone. So they give in. These unrealistic adults have never learned that the price of their need for approval is self-respect—and the respect of others.

17 *6. You feel insecure in your role.* In a defined role (as parent, manager, or supervisor) you have been given responsibilities, prerogatives, and boundaries. Another person, usually one who makes an unfair or unwarranted demand, makes accusations ("You don't like me!") or threats ("I'm going to report you to your supervisor!"). The recipient of the threats becomes insecure in the assigned, defined role and gives in.

18 *7. You can't stand silence.* Here a manipulator's responses are formal, monosyllabic. As time passes, feelings of rejection grow within you. To deal with this power play, avoid participating: pressure the pouter to end the game by going about your business as usual.

19 *8. You're afraid to be different.* At work here is a feeling that if you're different, you're somehow wrong. Two facts should be considered, however. First, what everyone else is doing isn't necessarily right. Second, when your major frame of reference is other people, you lose the capacity to define and live by your own values.

20 How do you reduce your vulnerabilities? Begin by thinking about occasions when you gave in to others or felt used. What feelings were dominant? What did others say or do to arouse those emotions? Who in particular arouses such feelings?

21 Once you pinpoint situations, people, and feelings that influence your decisions, you can use two strategies to avoid being manipulated. The best is to resolve the underlying issue that makes you vulnerable. For example, you can define your role in a given situation so that no one can make you insecure. Or you can decide what you owe yourself so that others can't make you feel "selfish."

22 Even if you can't completely stifle your vulnerability, you can still resist manipulation. Define the feelings that lead to your exploitation, and then use them as cues to be cautious. For instance, if you are susceptible

to guilt, *any* feelings of guilt should make you wary. Do what is right to avoid being manipulated in spite of your feelings.

By outmaneuvering your manipulators, you regain control, and your decisions reflect what's right for you. This feels good, and others learn to respect you. It's interesting that those who are easily manipulated are well-liked but not respected. By working through your emotional weak spots, you create a basis for respect *and* approval. 23

ACTIVE READING

The Active Reading exercise gives you an opportunity to reread the essay with a critical eye. By answering the questions that follow, you will extend and sharpen your understanding of the selection. This activity will help you become a more efficient reader and a more effective writer.

INTRODUCTORY PARAGRAPHS *(par. 1–8)*

The author captures our attention by presenting a specific example in which a mother is manipulated by her five-year-old boy. The author doesn't tell us about it; he shows us how it happens through dialogue between mother and son.

1. By using the term *ritual*, what is the author telling the reader about the transaction between the mother and her son?

2. How has Sam learned to get his way?

3. What is the effect on Sam when his manipulative behavior is reinforced with a successful outcome?

4. The author draws a comparison between a child of five and a savvy adult. In what way are they similar?

5. Once having located an emotional vulnerability, how does the manipulator exploit that knowledge?

6. What does this internal pressure lead to?

7. How do people generally feel after being manipulated?

DEVELOPMENT PARAGRAPH *(par. 9)*

In this paragraph the author presents a thesis statement "... if we can recognize and reduce our weaknesses, we will feel more in control, and our relationships will improve." The remainder of the development paragraphs are grouped into one of two categories: recognizing our weaknesses and reducing our vulnerability to them.

DEVELOPMENT PARAGRAPHS *(par. 10–19)*

These development paragraphs are designed to help you recognize ways in which you may be vulnerable to manipulation by others. The author lists eight categories that he uses to classify emotional vulnerabilities and tells how to recognize them.

8. To what does the phrase "the chinks in your emotional armor" refer?

9. What is the most common form of manipulation?

10. What do we call people who are masters of this kind of emotional blackmail?

11. Another form of manipulation that works with nonassertive men and women is:

12. Why is it that some people will do almost anything to avoid a fight? Give two reasons.

13. A third form of manipulation hooks people with a "woe is me" game. What does a person playing on this vulnerability ask others to do?

14. When confronted with this type of manipulator, what two questions should you ask yourself?

15. What is a favorite ploy of children and some adults?

16. What does little Johnny do when he is about to be punished by his parents?

17. What are the effects of Johnny's behavior?

18. The author uses this example to illustrate the fourth form of manipulation, which is:

19. How does this form of manipulation work?

20. The fifth form of manipulation the author mentions is based on fear of disapproval. How does a person who needs to gain approval respond to this influence attempt?

21. What is the price one pays for this approval?

22. A sixth way of manipulating others is to make someone who occupies a defined role feel insecure. What is the first step in this manipulation?

23. If you don't give in at this point, what happens next?

24. A seventh way of manipulating others uses what technique?

25. In order to work, this technique must produce what sort of internal pressure?

26. What technique does the author suggest for dealing with this power play?

27. The eighth way of manipulating others is based on fears of being different. With what do we equate being different?

28. What two points would the author have us consider, so that we don't equate being different with being wrong?

29. Fear of disapproval and a fear of being different have which element in common:
    a. fear of conflict
    b. fear of rejection
    c. fear of flattery
    d. all of the above

30. Now that you are familiar with different ways that people manipulate others, how did Sam get his mother to buy him a truck?

DEVELOPMENT PARAGRAPHS *(par. 20–22)*

These paragraphs suggest ways to reduce your vulnerability to emotional manipulation by others. First, you have to pinpoint situations, feelings, and people that influence your decisions. Then you can use two strategies to avoid being manipulated.

31. How might you pinpoint situations?

32. How might you pinpoint feelings?

33. How might you pinpoint people?

34. According to the author, the best strategy to use to avoid being manipulated is to:

35. The author suggests two ways or techniques to help you implement this strategy. What are they?

36. These techniques will help you counter what kinds of emotional manipulations?

37. The author says that even if you can't completely stifle your vulnerability, you can still resist manipulation. How do you do this?

38. What example does the author offer to illustrate his point?

These strategies for resisting manipulation are easier stated than accomplished. We all know that breaking old habits takes practice. The first step is to be aware of your bad feelings; ask yourself why you feel this way. The second step is to identify what you want for yourself in the situation so that you won't feel guilty, be afraid of conflict or anger, feel responsible for others, be taken in by flattery, fear disapproval, feel insecure in your role, feel rejected by others' silence, or fear being different.

CONCLUDING PARAGRAPH *(par. 23)*

In his conclusion the author restates the thesis of the essay, and summarizes the positive outcomes we can achieve by outmaneuvering manipulators.

39. What sentence in this paragraph is a restatement of the author's thesis?

40. What results can you look forward to if you outmaneuver your manipulators?

41. People who are easily manipulated are:
    a. well-liked and respected
    b. not well-liked and not respected
    c. well-liked but not respected
    d. not well-liked but respected

42. "By working through your emotional weak spots, you create a basis for respect *and* approval." Why do you think the word *and* is italicized?

43. The author uses transitional words and phrases to link ideas in this essay. List at least five.

44. The author's primary purpose in this selection is to:
    a. inform
    b. persuade
    c. entertain

The Active Reading exercise can be scored using the answer key and grading grid. Enter your grade in the progress chart.

The Guided Writing section that begins on the next page provides topics and plans for writing paragraphs and essays using classification. Select a topic and write an extended essay by following the writing plan that begins on page 170.

GUIDED WRITING

This part of the chapter will help you apply what you have learned about writing paragraphs and essays using classification. Choose one of the topics listed below for each writing assignment that you do. If you want to write about something else, ask your instructor if the topic is appropriate for writing that uses classification. Follow the plan that applies to write your composition. Submit your completed composition to the instructor for evaluation. When you receive a grade for this work, enter it in the progress chart.

WRITING TOPICS

- E. B. White classifies New Yorkers as belonging to one of three groups: natives, commuters, or settlers. The thing that these people have in common is that they are all New Yorkers. The author discusses where New Yorkers come from and how they relate to the city.

  Create a classification system for people in your community or school based on one of the following topics: age, cliques, origin, ethnicity, cultural interests, level of education, or some other category.

- Choose one of the following topics with its accompanying classification system to write about.

  Lifestyles: a large city, the suburbs, a small town, and the rural countryside

  Sources of power for transportation: people power, animals, machines, and wind

  Levels of involvement in sports: watching television, attending a live sporting event, actively participating

- "The Structure of Memory" presents a classification system based on observations of the way people learn and retain information. In the same way, each of the topics below uses a classification system to explain some aspect of human behavior. Choose one of these topics to write about.

  Sigmund Freud's stages of psychosexual development

  Abraham Maslow's hierarchy of needs

  Jean Piaget's stages of cognitive development

  Elisabeth Kubler-Ross's stages of dying or loss

  Erik Erikson's stages of psychosocial development

- Scientific study relies heavily on classification. Select one of the topics below to write about.

  major systems of the human body

  the primary food groups

  the development of man

  types of clouds

  kinds of mountains

- "Stand Up for Yourself" makes use of eight categories in its system of classification. In the same way, each of the topics below can be divided into categories. Select one topic and write about it using classification.

  major world religions

  the Greek Zodiac

  the Chinese Zodiac

  kinds of government

  kinds of popular music

  types of poetry

  the writing strategies presented in this book

PREWRITING: GENERATING IDEAS

Now that you have selected a topic, you will need to gather information and generate ideas before you begin to write. If you are writing about a personal experience you will probably rely on your memory, other people's input, and your own creativity. Other topics may require that you use reference works to collect this information for your composition.

Classification sorts information into groups or categories on the basis of shared characteristics. List the major categories in your classification system, then decide on an order or sequence for these categories. Next, gather information and sort by category. You can use the information in one of two ways: (1) to outline the various parts of the system or (2) to define and explain, in depth, the system's organizing principle. Refer to your list as you follow the plan for writing a paragraph or essay using classification.

WRITING PLAN: THE PARAGRAPH

1. Decide the point of view of the narrator, first or third person. Write an introduction that gets the reader's attention and presents your point of view.

2. Set the tone for the paragraph, your attitude toward the subject. The tone might be serious or humorous, formal or informal.

3. Use the list you have created to briefly define and explain the various parts of your classification system. The system should be presented in a logical order and information properly sorted. Use explanation, definition, comparison and contrast, cause and effect, and illustration where appropriate.

4. Write a conclusion to your paragraph that restates the topic and presents an overview, summarizes, or expresses an opinion.

5. To create unity in your writing, make sure that each sentence in the paragraph relates to the topic. Your writing will be coherent if ideas follow one another in a logical pattern and sentences flow smoothly from one to the other. Use transitions to link or connect ideas. The list of transitional words and phrases at the back of this book is for your use and reference when you write (see pages 259–264).

6. Use variety in your choice of words to maintain reader interest. Where appropriate, use figurative language to increase the impact of your words and to stimulate the reader's imagination. The most commonly used figures of speech are the simile, metaphor, personification, and hyperbole. Definitions of literary and rhetorical terms can be found in the Glossary on pages 265–270.

7. Create a title for your paragraph, a word or phrase that captures the reader's interest and tells what you are writing about.

8. Use the *Checklist for Revision* at the end of this section to help you review and revise your paragraph.

WRITING PLAN: SHORT AND EXTENDED ESSAYS

While short and extended essays are similar—both have introductory and concluding paragraphs—the extended essay has more development paragraphs. "The Structure of Memory" uses classification to explain an information-processing model of memory. In this short essay, the author uses examples, comparison and contrast, definition, and explanation. "Stand Up for Yourself," an extended essay, uses classification to point out our emotional vulnerabilities, how to recognize them, and how to resist manipulation. The author supports his thesis with illustration, comparison and contrast, definition, cause and effect, and explanation.

Introductory Paragraph(s)

1. Decide the narrator's point of view. Is the narrator of the essay involved in the action (first person), or an observer outside the action (third person)?

2. Begin with a strong statement, a question, or an example that focuses the reader's interest on the subject. Tell what the essay is about by introducing your topic and purpose. This is the thesis statement, the main idea to be supported throughout the essay.

3. Use your introductory paragraph(s) to set the tone for the essay, your attitude toward the subject. The tone might be serious or humorous, formal or informal.

4. An extended essay may contain more than one introductory paragraph.

Development Paragraph(s)

1. Development paragraphs can be used to discuss the various categories of your classification system. Let the reader know the focus of each paragraph.

2. Use the list you have created to define and explain in depth your classification system. The system should be presented in a logical order and information properly sorted. Use explanation, definition, comparison and contrast, cause and effect, and illustration where appropriate.

3. If you are writing an extended essay, include more categories in your classification system and make use of other strategies to reinforce your thesis.

4. All sentences in a paragraph should relate to the topic and to one another. All paragraphs in an essay should support the topic and follow some logical order. Use transitions to link ideas within paragraphs and to make connections between paragraphs. Refer to the list of transitional words and phrases on pages 259–264.

5. Use variety in your choice of words to maintain reader interest. Where appropriate, use figurative language to increase the impact of your words and to stimulate the reader's imagination. The most commonly used figures of speech are the simile, metaphor, personification, and hyperbole. Definitions of literary and rhetorical terms can be found in the Glossary on pages 265–270.

Concluding Paragraph(s)

1. Restate the thesis in some way for emphasis. Present an overview, summarize the major points, offer an opinion, or reach a conclusion that reinforces the point of your essay.

2. More than one paragraph may be used to conclude an extended essay.

3. Use the checklist below to help you review and revise your essay.

note: The title of your essay should be a word or phrase that captures the reader's attention and tells what you are writing about. Create a title for your first draft and review it before making it final.

CHECKLIST FOR REVISION

1. My paragraph/essay has a first- or third-person point of view. My opening sentences appeal to the reader's interest, introduce my topic, and set the tone. If I am writing an essay, my thesis statement appears in the opening paragraph(s).

2. I use my list of categories to define and explain my classification system. I created a logical sequence and grouped information on the basis of shared characteristics.

3. I use explanation, definition, comparison and contrast, cause and effect, and illustration where appropriate. Each development paragraph of my essay explains a different category of my classification system.

4. In an extended essay, I use the development paragraphs to include more categories and make use of other strategies to reinforce the thesis.

5. In concluding my paragraph or essay, I restate the thesis and present an overview, summarize, offer an opinion, or reach a conclusion that reinforces my point.

6. Sentences within each paragraph relate to the topic. Development paragraphs follow a logical order and support the point of the essay. I use transitions to link ideas within paragraphs and to make connections between paragraphs.

7. I use variety in my choice of words to maintain reader interest. Where appropriate, I use figurative language to increase the impact of my words and to stimulate the reader's imagination.

8. As I revise the form and content of my work, I correct errors in punctuation, capitalization, spelling, grammar, and usage.

9. The title of my paragraph or essay tells what I wrote about and captures the reader's interest.

Continue work in this chapter until you have finished all three Active Reading and Guided Writing activities.

Chapter 8

DEFINITION

You can use definition to make clear the meaning of a word, an abstract concept, or to help identify the special qualities of a person, place, animal, object, or process. Writers often use definition when they want to explain something in detail. Definition may also be used to entertain, to persuade, to instruct, or to establish a standard. When you write an autobiographical essay for admission to college or professional school, you are defining yourself by providing the reader with information that distinguishes you from other applicants.

There are two principal kinds of definitions: short and extended. The short definition, often found in the dictionary, identifies the class to which a subject belongs and gives the subject's distinguishing characteristics. This brief definition is usually presented as a synonym, a phrase, or a sentence. For example, the definition of a *tornado* is "a violently destructive whirlwind." This identifies the tornado as a kind of "wind" that whirls and is violently destructive. The short definition reduces the subject to its most important characteristics. The advantage of the short definition is that it provides a precise meaning for a word, one that is readily understood by both readers and writers.

When writers wish to define an abstract, controversial, or complex concept, a short definition is often too limiting. Abstract concepts like *school spirit, personality,* and *conformity* cannot be adequately defined in a word, phrase, or sentence of explanation. Controversial terms like freedom, pornography, and communism also reflect the need for extended definition. The extended definition may vary in length from a paragraph or two, to an entire essay or even a whole book. Alone or in combination with other kinds of writing, extended definition is a favorite strategy of expository writers.

Writers can define by drawing analogies, likening the subject to something else. This is especially useful when explaining a concept. For example, if you are explaining the concept of a "blind date" you might say: a blind date is like a surprise package in that we hope for the best when confronted with the unknown. Writers may define by explaining the function of a person or object; function may be central to the definition. Writers can also define by using expository techniques such as comparison and contrast or classification.

This chapter contains three reading selections, all of which use definition as a writing strategy. The first is a paragraph, the second a short essay, and the third a longer piece. Each is followed by an Active Reading exercise that helps you to understand the form and content of the reading model. The Guided Writing section at the end of this chapter will help you to create three original pieces of writing using definition.

Chapter Selections

Junk *by George Stewart*
Spirituality *by John Updike*
On Being Female, Black, and Free *by Margaret Walker*

JUNK

by George Stewart

George Stewart (1895-1980) was born in Sewickley, Pennsylvania, and educated at Princeton, the University of California, and Columbia University. He taught English for almost forty years at the University of California at Berkeley. His writing includes seven novels, most notably East of the Giants *(1938),* Storm *(1941),* Earth Abides *(1949), and literature for children. He is best remembered for his many nonfiction books, each of which employs dramatic and memorable detail to document aspects of America's regional and local history. In* U.S. 40 *(1953) he shows how America's first national highway evolved from Indian trails and pioneer roads. In "Junk," excerpted from* Not So Rich as You Think *(1968), Stewart defines the word* junk *by tracing its history, and tells how its meaning changed over time.*

Word Alert

conception   idea or concept

derogatory   expressing a low opinion; degrading or disparaging

oakum   loose rope fibers impregnated with tar and used in caulking the seams of wooden ships

salt-beef   beef cured in salt or brine

salvable   capable of being saved or salvaged

Junk, both as a conception and as a term, has little history behind it. The word itself, traditionally existing only in the English language, may be traced from the fifteenth century, when it meant an old and worn rope. A seaman's term, it was probably derived from the Portuguese, in their century of notable achievement in seafaring. *Junca* means a reed in Portuguese, and of reeds a kind of cheap and inferior rope was made. Such ropes did not wear long, and so the derogatory suggestion of the word easily developed. Once worn out, these ropes were cut up to serve for oakum or boat-fenders, and *junk* thus began to assume its modern suggestion of "secondary material." By the eighteenth century, British and American seamen were applying the word in a general derogatory sense, as when salt-beef was called junk. It was also used for miscellaneous collections of worn, secondhand, and cheap goods. Shops which stocked such materials for the outfitting of seamen came to be called junk shops. Only toward the end of the nineteenth century, however, first in the United States and later in Great Britain, did the word begin to assume its modern meaning—used material, of a certain bulk and durability, chiefly conceived by the consumer as something to be got rid of, but salvable under favorable circumstances.

ACTIVE READING

The Active Reading exercise gives you an opportunity to reread the paragraph with a critical eye. By answering the questions that follow, you will extend and sharpen your understanding of the selection. This activity will help you become a more efficient reader and a more effective writer.

The author begins by letting us know he is defining a term rather than a person, place, object, or process. In this paragraph he traces the history of the word *junk*.

1. The word *junk* in English has been traced to what century?

2. What did the word mean at that time?

3. What kind of workers originally used this term?

4. The author tells us that the word was probably derived from which Portuguese word?

5. What does this word mean?

6. The author says that *junca* probably came into use during Portugal's century of notable achievement in seafaring. To what century is the author referring? Make an inference based on the passage or use an encyclopedia.

7. At that time, what did the Portuguese make from reeds?

8. What led to the derogatory meaning of the word?

9. How did the word *junk* come to suggest "secondary material?"

10. How did British and American seamen use the word *junk* in the eighteenth century?

11. Give two examples of things referred to as junk at that time.

12. What were junk shops?

13. When and where did the word begin to assume its modern meaning?

14. The author concludes by stating the modern meaning of the word *junk*. What is it?

15. The author uses transitional words and phrases to link ideas in this paragraph. List at least five.

16. The author's primary purpose in this selection is to:
    a. inform
    b. persuade
    c. entertain

The Active Reading exercise can be scored using the answer key and grading grid. Enter your grade in the progress chart.

GUIDED WRITING

The Guided Writing section at the end of this chapter (page 195) provides topics and plans for writing paragraphs and essays using definition. Select a topic and write a short essay by following the writing plan that begins on page 196.

Continue work in this chapter until you have finished all three Active Reading and Guided Writing activities. Upon completion, you will have written three new compositions for your portfolio (one paragraph and two essays). Record grades in your progress chart and, if available, on the academic Credit Statement in your *Writing Portfolio Organizer*.

SPIRITUALITY

by John Updike

John Updike was born in 1932 in Shillington, Pennsylvania. He was educated at Harvard University and attended the Euskin School of Drawing and Fine Art at Oxford. Updike is a prolific writer of novels, poetry, and short stories. Among his best known novels are The Poorhouse Fair *(1959),* Rabbit Run *(1960),* The Centaur *(1963),* Of the Farm *(1965),* Couples *(1968),* Rabbit Redux *(1971),* Marry Me: A Romance *(1976), and* The Coup *(1978). He has not only written numerous poetry and short story collections, but also been a regular contributor to anthologies, collections, magazines, and periodicals. Among his honors were a Guggenheim Fellowship in Poetry (1959), the National Book Award in fiction (1963), Fulbright Fellow (1972), and American Book Award nomination (1980). In this short essay, Updike offers a definition of spirituality, an especially elusive abstract concept.*

Word Alert

brainless	mindless, not relating to the mind; lacking intelligence, stupid
Buddha	Buddha (563–483 B.C.) taught that suffering is inherent in life and that one can be liberated from it by mental and moral self-purification. His name means "the enlightened one."
connotation	something suggested by a word or thing; implication
deduction	reaching a conclusion by reasoning; inference in which the conclusion follows necessarily from the premises
dispensable	capable of being dispensed with; unessential
Einstein	Albert Einstein (1879–1955) was an American theoretical physicist known for the formulation of the theory of relativity. He received the Nobel Prize for Physics in 1921. He is recognized as one of the greatest physicists of all times.
essence	being, entity, element; basic traits that define the character of something
gender	classification of sex; masculine and feminine
immaterial	without material body or form
impalpable	intangible; not perceptible to the touch; not easily perceived or understood by the mind

induction	the act or process of deriving general principles from particular facts or instances
intuition	knowing without the use of rational processes; immediate cognition; acute insight
metaphysical	based on abstract or speculative reasoning; excessively subtle, abstruse; supernatural
preponderance	superiority in number, power, strength, importance, or weight
quixotic	idealistic, chivalrous; having lofty romantic ideas
spirituality	the state, quality, or fact of being spiritual; concerned with the soul; belonging to a church or religion, sacred; having supernatural qualities
St. Teresa	St. Theresa of Avila was a sixteenth-century Carmelite nun and author of religious classics. She followed a program of discipline and prayer that led to frequent mystical experiences.
semicomic	somewhat comical; partially funny
spirit lamps	a lamp using alcohol or other liquid fuel
syllogisms	logic; reasoning from the general to the specific; deduction
vapors	archaic definition: hysteria or emotional depression
volatile	fleeting; ephemeral, transitory; explosive
Victorian	relating to or belonging to the period of Queen Victoria of England; 19th century England

The word *spirituality* comes, by way of *spirit*, from the Latin verb for the act of breathing, *spirare*. Spirit, then, is the principal of life within us, our invisible essence. A parallel derivation took a rather different turn in French, becoming the noun *esprit*, which came to signify the mind, the precious human gift of understanding. [1]

In English the word remains brainless, and it has diminished over the increasingly metaphysical decades to a semicomic ghost, as when we say "evil spirits," which are not to be confused with spirits of alcohol or turpentine. The concept of spirituality retains connotations of the volatile, the impalpable, the immaterial, the dispensable. It suggests the vapors, the heavenward hysteria of St. Teresa or a Victorian spiritualist, a tricky dependence upon the unseen that any man or sensible woman can do without. [2]

3   Myself, I associate spirituality with intuition, which is often labeled "feminine." The ability to make one's way among the unseen currents, to arrive at the truth while bypassing induction and deduction, to pluck things out of the air—a gender tilt in this area would help account for the female preponderance of fortune-tellers and churchgoers. A spiritual person of either sex embodies an alternative to the obvious, to bank accounts and syllogisms, to death and taxes. But there is little obvious, obviously, about being human.

4   Pressed, I would define spirituality as the shadow of light humanity casts as it moves through the darkness of everything that can be explained. I think of Buddha's smile, and Einstein's halo of hair. I think of birthday parties. I think of common politeness, and the quixotic impulse to imagine what someone else is feeling. I think of spirit lamps.

ACTIVE READING

The Active Reading exercise gives you an opportunity to reread the essay with a critical eye. By answering the questions that follow, you will extend and sharpen your understanding of the selection. This activity will help you become a more efficient reader and a more effective writer.

INTRODUCTORY PARAGRAPH *(par. 1)*

1. The author begins with a formal definition of spirituality. From what Latin word is *spirituality* derived and what does it mean?

2. How does the author define the word *spirit*?

3. What is the French word for spirit and how is it defined?

DEVELOPMENT PARAGRAPH *(par. 2)*

In this paragraph the author looks at the English meaning of the word *spirit* and the concept of spirituality. When the author refers to the meaning of the word *spirit* in English, the language he uses lends itself to more than one interpretation. This is known as **double entendre**.

4. In the first sentence of this paragraph, what two meanings are suggested by the word *brainless*?

5. The author defines the word *spiritual* in contemporary terms to mean brainless, a semicomic ghost (evil spirits), and (spirits of) alcohol or turpentine. What do these varied uses of the word illustrate?

Contemporary films illustrate the paradoxical relationship between the diminished meaning of the word *spiritual* and an increased interest in the supernatural. Ironically, the abundance of commercially successful comedy and horror films about the supernatural only serve to erode the true meaning of the word *spirituality*.

6. Name a contemporary film about the supernatural that uses a semicomic ghost as its logo, and illustrates this paradox.

7. What is the shared meaning of the words: *volatile, impalpable, immaterial?*

8. The author says these words suggest the vapors, the heavenward hysteria of St. Teresa, or a Victorian spiritualist. How does he view this behavior?

9. What judgment does the author make about this concept of spirituality?

10. The words "any man or sensible woman can do without" reflect the author's belief or opinion. The author is saying that with regard to spirituality:
    a. all men and all women are sensible
    b. some men and some women are sensible
    c. some men and all women are sensible
    d. all men and some women are sensible

11. What assumption does the author seem to be making about women in relation to men with regard to spirituality?

DEVELOPMENT PARAGRAPH *(par. 3)*

12. With what does the author associate spirituality?

The author uses three phrases to illustrate intuition: "The ability to make one's way among the unseen currents, to arrive at the truth while bypassing induction and deduction, to pluck things out of the air . . . "

13. What shared meaning in these phrases defines intuition?
    a. always attaining your goals regardless of obstacles
    b. obtaining all the facts before making decisions
    c. making the right decision based on feelings rather than on thoughts
    d. making the right decision based on thoughts rather than on feelings

14. What does the author say accounts for the preponderance of female fortune-tellers and churchgoers?

15. The author says that a spiritual person of either sex embodies an alternative to the obvious, the mundane. What four examples of "the obvious" does he offer?

16. The author says "But there is little obvious, obviously, about being human." What do you think he means?

CONCLUDING PARAGRAPH *(par. 4)*

Using imagery, the author defines spirituality as, "the shadow of light humanity casts as it moves through the darkness of everything that can be explained." There are two paradoxes in this definition. A **paradox** is a statement that seems to contradict itself but proves to be true.

17-18. Identify the two phrases from the definition of spirituality that are paradoxes.

19-20. Explain why each phrase is a paradox and what the author means.

The author offers examples that illustrate his concept of spirituality. What is there about each of the following examples in questions 21-26 that leads the author to associate them with light, spirituality, and humanity? You may need to make inferences or use an encyclopedia to answer these questions.

21. Buddha's smile

22. Einstein's halo of hair

23. birthday parties

24. common politeness

25. the quixotic impulse to imagine what someone else is feeling

26. spirit lamps

27. The author uses transitional words and phrases to link ideas in this paragraph. List at least five.

28. The author's primary purpose in this selection is to:
    a. inform
    b. persuade
    c. entertain

The Active Reading exercise can be scored using the answer key and grading grid. Enter your grade in the progress chart.

GUIDED WRITING

The Guided Writing section at the end of this chapter (page 195) provides topics and plans for writing paragraphs and essays using definition. Select a topic and write a short essay by following the writing plan that begins on page 196. Continue work in this chapter until you have finished all three Active Reading and Guided Writing Activities.

ON BEING FEMALE, BLACK, AND FREE

by Margaret Walker

Margaret Walker was born in Birmingham, Alabama in 1915. She was educated at Northwestern University and earned a doctorate at the University of Iowa. After college she worked in Chicago as a social worker, newspaper reporter, magazine editor, and member of the Federal Writer's Project. In the 1940s she started her teaching career at Livingston College and at West Virginia State. By 1949 she was appointed professor of English at Jackson State College where she served for over thirty years. Walker is known primarily for her two books: For My People *(1942), a collection of poems that won a Yale literary award, and* Jubilee *(1966), a novel that won the Houghton Mifflin Literary Fellowship. In "On Being Female, Black, and Free,"" written for Janet Sternburg's impressive collection of essays,* The Writer on Her Work *(1981), Walker recalls how her special heritage as a black, Southern woman has shaped her life as a teacher and writer.*

Word Alert

abhorred	rejected vehemently; to shun, keep away from
adversity	a condition of suffering, destitution, or affliction; misfortune
avocation	hobby
biorhythms	intrinsically patterned cyclical biological functions or processes: breathing, sleeping, menstruation
Calvinistic	following the religious teachings of John Calvin which stress the omnipotence of God and the doctrine of predestination
Chisholm, Shirley	An American politician born in 1924, Chisholm was one of the first black women to serve in the U.S. Congress where she represented a district in Brooklyn, NY.
crucible	a severe trial or test
die	a small cube marked with one to six spots on each face; used in pairs in games of chance or gambling
die is cast	this expression means that once something is decided or done, it cannot be reversed
eke out	to earn with great effort or strain; to make something last by economizing

exigencies	pressing needs; urgent situations
foolhardiness	unwisely bold or venturesome; rash
fraught	filled or charged with
immutable	not capable of or susceptible to change
inimical	adverse to; hostile, unfriendly
integrity	firm adherence to a standard of values
insidious	spreading harmfully in a stealthy or subtle manner; subtle; having a gradual and cumulative effect
inviolate	not violated; pure
manifold	multiple, many kinds; having many features or forms
mundane	characterized by the practical and ordinary
mystical	having a spiritual meaning or reality
naive	lacking sophistication and worldliness; ingenuous
philosophical	based on wisdom and enlightenment
preeminent	superior to or notable above all others; having paramount rank
Protestant	a Christian belonging to a sect descending from those that seceded from the Church of Rome during the Reformation
racism	a belief that race is the primary determinant of human traits and capacities, and that racial differences produce an inherent superiority of a particular race
sonnet	a fixed 14-line verse form of Italian origin whose lines are typically 5-foot iambics rhyming according to a prescribed scheme; a poem written in this pattern
sordid	dirty, filthy, wretched, squalid, vile, mean
stigmas	marks or tokens of shame, disgrace, or reproach
tilting windmills	The term "tilting windmills" means dueling with something that exists only in the imagination. In the novel *Don Quixote* by Cervantes the main character, Quixote, charges with his lance on horseback what he believes to be a dragon. In fact, the dragon is actually a windmill.
tumult	uproar and confusion, commotion; a violent agitation of mind or feelings
vocation	an occupation

My birth certificate reads female, Negro, date of birth and place. Call 1
it fate or circumstance, this is my human condition. I have no wish to
change it from being female, black, and free. I like being a woman. I have
a proud, black heritage, and I have learned from the difficult exigencies of
life that freedom is a philosophical state of mind and existence. The mind
is the only place where I can exist and feel free. In my mind I am absolutely free.

My entire career of writing, teaching, lecturing, yes, and raising a 2
family is determined by these immutable facts of my human condition. As
a daughter, a sister, a sweetheart, a wife, a mother, and now a grandmother, my sex or gender is preeminent, important, and almost entirely
deterministic. Maybe my glands have something to do with my occupation as a creative person. About this, I am none too sure, but I think the
cycle of life has much to do with the creative impulse and the biorhythms
of life must certainly affect everything we do. . . .

It has always been my feeling that writing must come out of living, 3
and the writer is no more than his personality endures in the crucible of
his times. As a woman, I have come through the fires of hell because I am a
black woman, because I am poor, because I live in America, and because
I am determined to be both a creative artist and maintain my inner integrity and my instinctive need to be free. . . .

Despite severe illness and painful poverty, and despite jobs that al- 4
ways discriminated against me as a woman—never paying me equal money
for equal work, always threatening or replacing me with a man or men
who were neither as well educated nor experienced but just men—despite
all these examples of discrimination I have managed to work toward being
a self-fulfilling, re-creating, reproducing woman, raising a family, writing
poetry, cooking food, doing all the creative things I know how to do and
enjoy. But my problems have not been simple; they have been manifold.
Being female, black, and poor in America means I was born with three
strikes against me. I am considered at the bottom of the social class-caste
system in these United States, born low on the totem pole. If "a black man
has no rights that a white man is bound to respect," what about a black
woman? . . .

Racism is so extreme and so pervasive in our American society that no 5
black individual lives in an atmosphere of freedom. The world of physical
phenomena is dominated by fear and greed. It consists of pitting the

vicious and the avaricious against the naive, the hunted, the innocent, and the victimized. Power belongs to the strong, and the strong are BIG in more ways than one. No one is more victimized in this white male American society than the black female.

6   There are additional barriers for the black woman in publishing, in literary criticism, and in promotion of her literary wares. It is an insidious fact of racism that the most highly intellectualized, sensitized white person is not always perceptive about the average black mind and feeling, much less the creativity of any black genius. Racism forces white humanity to underestimate the intelligence, emotion, and creativity of black humanity. Very few white Americans are conscious of the myth about race that includes the racial stigmas of inferiority and superiority. They do not understand its true economic and political meaning and therefore fail to understand its social purpose. A black, female person's life as a writer is fraught with conflict, competitive drives, professional rivalries, even danger, and deep frustrations. Only when she escapes to a spiritual world can she find peace, quiet, and hope of freedom. To choose the life of a writer, a black female must arm herself with a fool's courage, foolhardiness, and serious purpose and dedication to the art of writing, strength of will and integrity, because the odds are always against her. The cards are stacked. Once the die is cast, however, there is no turning back.

7   In the first place, the world of imagination in which the writer must live is constantly being invaded by the enemy, the mundane world. Even as the worker in the fires of imagination finds that the world around her is inimical to intellectual activity, to the creative impulse, and to the kind of world in which she must daily exist and also thrive and produce, so, too, she discovers that she must meet that mundane world head-on every-day on its own terms. She must either conquer or be conquered.

8   A writer needs certain conditions in which to work and create art. She needs a piece of time; a peace of mind; a quiet place; and a private life.

9   Early in my life I discovered I had to earn my living and I would not be able to eke out the barest existence as a writer. Nobody writes while hungry, sick, tired, and worried. Maybe you can manage with one of these but not all four at one time. Keeping the wolf from the door has been my full-time job for more than forty years. Thirty-six of those years I have spent in the college classroom, and nobody writes to full capacity on a full-time teaching job. My life has been public, active, and busy to the point of constant turmoil, tumult, and trauma. Sometimes the only quiet

and private place where I could write a sonnet was in the bathroom, because that was the only room where the door could be locked and no one would intrude. I have written mostly at night in my adult life and especially since I have been married, because I was determined not to neglect any members of my family; so I cooked every meal daily, washed dishes and dirty clothes, and nursed sick babies.

I have struggled against dirt and disease as much as I have against sin, which, with my Protestant and Calvinistic background, was always to be abhorred. Every day I have lived, however, I have discovered that the value system with which I was raised is of no value in the society in which I must live. This clash of my ideal with the real, of my dream world with the practical, and the mystical inner life with the sordid and ugly world outside—this clash keeps me on a battlefield, at war, and struggling, even tilting at windmills. Always I am determined to overcome adversity, determined to win, determined to be me, myself at my best, always female, always black, and everlastingly free. I think this is always what the woman writer wants to be, herself, inviolate, and whole. Shirley Chisholm, who is also black and female, says she is unbossed and unbought. So am I, and I intend to remain that way. Nobody can tell me what to write because nobody owns me and nobody pulls my strings. I have not been writing to make money or earn my living. I have taught school as my vocation. Writing is my life, but it is an avocation nobody can buy. In this respect I believe I am a free agent, stupid perhaps, but *me* and still free. . . .

ACTIVE READING

The Active Reading exercise gives you an opportunity to reread the essay with a critical eye. By answering the questions that follow, you will extend and sharpen your understanding of the selection. This activity will help you become a more efficient reader and a more effective writer.

INTRODUCTORY PARAGRAPH (par. 1)

The author begins by giving us information from her birth certificate that defines her in terms of gender and race. By repeating and explaining the selection title, Ms. Walker provides a focus for the rest of the essay: her gender, her race, and her state of mind.

1. To what does the author attribute her human condition, her sex and race?

2. What word not listed on her birth certificate does the author use to define herself?

3. How does she feel about being female and black?

4. Sex and race are biological definitions which the author accepts as givens. What aspect of her existence does she choose for herself?

5. If the author says she is free only in her mind, how do you think she views her status as a black female?

DEVELOPMENT PARAGRAPH *(par. 2)*

6. The opening sentence serves as a transition linking the facts of her human condition to:

7. The focus of this paragraph is the author's:

   a. gender
   b. race
   c. age
   d. social class

8. What definition given does <u>not</u> define her in terms of gender?

   a. sister
   b. wife
   c. creative person
   d. grandmother

The author accepts that her sex has determined her various roles in life, and suspects that it may also have influenced her choice of occupation.

9. "The cycle of life has much to do with the creative impulse and the biorhythms of life must certainly affect everything we do." This is most likely a reference to:

   a. writing
   b. role playing
   c. reproducing
   d. child rearing

DEVELOPMENT PARAGRAPH *(par. 3)*

10. In this paragraph the author defines the writer as "no more than his personality endures in the crucible of his times." This definition says that writers write about:

    a. their fantasies
    b. their experiences
    c. their expectations
    d. their failures

11. What phrase does the author use to describe "the crucible" of her times?

Her experience results from who she is and what she wants. For the author, the crucible is a result of a conflict between how she is defined on the basis of external characteristics and how she defines herself, through her inner desires.

12. What external characteristics define who she is:

13. What are her inner desires?

14. Which sentence in this paragraph serves as the thesis statement for the essay?

The thesis statement of this essay not only defines the author's inner and outer selves, but also persuades us that internal desire can overcome external obstacles.

DEVELOPMENT PARAGRAPH *(par. 4)*

Here the author elaborates on the notion of a writer as shaped by the trials of his or her experiences. She offers examples of how this applies to her personally as a result of her being a poor, black female writer living in America.

15. Which of the following was <u>not</u> an obstacle the author had to overcome?

    a. sex discrimination
    b. painful poverty
    c. paid less than men for equal work
    d. poor literacy skills

16. Which of the following was <u>not</u> one of the author's accomplishments?

    a. raising a family
    b. writing poetry
    c. cooking food
    d. painting portraits

17. "But my problems have not been simple; they have been manifold."
Within the paragraph, this sentence serves as:

    a. an introduction
    b. an explanation
    c. a transition
    d. a conclusion

18. What does it mean to be female, black, and poor in America?

19. Where does the author believe poor, black females rank in the American social class system?

    a. at the top
    b. in the middle
    c. at the bottom
    d. none of the above

20. What can you infer is the order in the American social class system, from top to bottom?

The last sentence in the paragraph summarizes the position of black men and women in American society, and serves as a transition to paragraph five which discusses racism.

DEVELOPMENT PARAGRAPH *(par. 5)*

In this paragraph the author argues that racism is so extreme and pervasive in American society that no black individual lives in an atmosphere of freedom.

21. Racism inhibits freedom because people are judged by:

    a. their sex
    b. their religion
    c. their skin color
    d. their social status

The author states that in America the "vicious and the avaricious (are pitted) against the naive, the hunted, the innocent, and the victimized. Power belongs to the strong, and the strong are BIG in more ways than one."

22. To whom do you think the words *vicious, avaricious, strong,* and *BIG* refer?

    a. black males
    b. black females
    c. white males
    d. white females

23. Who does the author say is most victimized in this society?

DEVELOPMENT PARAGRAPH *(par. 6)*

Paragraph six continues the discussion of racism in America and the difficulty of being a black, female writer in this society.

24. What makes it more difficult for a black woman writer to gain recognition for her work?

25. What is it about racism that is insidious?

26. What myth about race does the author believe to be central to racism?

The author states that very few white Americans understand the true economic and political meaning of this myth, and therefore fail to understand its social purpose.

27. What might you infer is the meaning of the myth of racial inferiority/superiority?

    a. to justify the economic and political power of whites
    b. to redistribute wealth and power equitably
    c. to foster cooperation between blacks and whites
    d. all of the above

The economic purpose behind the myth of white superiority and black inferiority is to keep blacks as an impoverished underclass with no political power.

28. What might you infer is the social purpose of the myth of racial inferiority/superiority?

    a. to establish equality among the races
    b. to maintain racial segregation
    c. to eliminate class divisions
    d. to create an integrated society

Racism, sexism, and classism are encouraged by the belief that assumptions are facts. This is the basis of what is known in social psychology as a *non-conscious ideology*, a set of beliefs which are accepted implicitly, without awareness. The illusion of superiority allows people to think of themselves as better than others, not because they are smarter or more capable, but because they have been socialized to believe in this myth.

29. The author says her life as a writer is fraught with conflict, competitive drives, professional rivalries, even danger, and deep frustrations. While any writer might experience similar difficulties, what makes this author's life as a writer especially difficult?

30. According to the author how does a black, female writer find peace, quiet, and the hope of freedom?

31. To choose the life of a writer the black female must arm herself. Which of the following is <u>not</u> included in the author's list of "armor?"

    a. foolhardiness
    b. strength of will
    c. lack of purpose
    d. integrity

32. Why does the black, female writer need to arm herself in this way?

The last sentence of the paragraph speaks to the author's depth of commitment as a writer. Despite all the obstacles facing her, once the decision is made there is no turning back. She expresses this with an **idiom**, a phrase that has a meaning other than its grammatical or logical one.

33. What idiom does the author use to express that there is no turning back?

DEVELOPMENT PARAGRAPHS *(par. 7–8)*

34. Apart from the problems that race, sex, and poverty present, what does the author regard as the enemy of imagination?

35. What attitude does the author adopt toward this enemy in order to survive as a writer?

36. Which condition is <u>not</u> mentioned by the author as necessary in order to work and create art?

    a. a quiet place
    b. a private life
    c. peace of mind
    d. a large inheritance

DEVELOPMENT PARAGRAPH *(par. 9)*

In this paragraph the author discusses aspects of the mundane world that have interfered with her desire to be a writer. These included having a full-time job, being active in public life, and being married and raising a family.

37. Early in her life, the author discovered:

    a. she had to earn a living.
    b. she could not support herself as a writer.
    c. she could not write while hungry, sick, tired and worried.
    d. all of the above

38. The author says that her full-time job for forty years was "keeping the wolf from the door." This is an idiomatic expression that means:

    a. staying one step ahead of poverty.
    b. staying alert to danger.
    c. staying in one career.
    d. none of the above

39. Where did the author find a quiet and private place to write?

40. Why did she write mostly at night?

CONCLUDING PARAGRAPH *(par. 10)*

In this concluding paragraph the author summarizes her point of view by comparing the ideal with the real in her life.

41. The first sentence of this paragraph serves as a transition from the previous paragraph. The author says she has struggled against dirt and disease as much as she has against sin. Dirt and disease are a reference to what?

42. To what sins do you think the author may be referring?

43. The values with which she was raised are in conflict with:

44. This clash keeps her on a battlefield, at war and struggling. Which of the following phrases express this conflict?

    a. her ideal world with the real world
    b. her dream world with the practical
    c. her mystical inner life with the sordid, ugly world outside
    d. all of the above

45. "Always I am determined to overcome adversity, determined to win, determined to be me, myself at my best, always female, always black, and everlastingly free." In this statement the author's purpose is to:

    a. define herself.
    b. persuade her readers.
    c. support the thesis statement.
    d. all of the above

46. What does the author say the woman writer wants to be?

47. Like Shirley Chisholm the author defines herself as "unbossed and unbought." What does she mean by this?

48. How does she remain free to write what she wants?

49. The author uses transitional words and phrases to link ideas in this essay. List at least five.

50. The author's primary purpose in this selection is to:
    a. inform
    b. persuade
    c. entertain

The Active Reading exercise can be scored using the answer key and grading grid. Enter your grade in the progress chart.

The Guided Writing section that begins on the next page provides topics and plans for writing paragraphs and essays using definition. Select a topic and write an extended essay by following the writing plan that begins at the bottom of page 196.

GUIDED WRITING

This part of the chapter will help you apply what you have learned about writing paragraphs and essays using definition. Choose one of the topics listed below for each writing assignment that you do. If you want to write about something else, ask your instructor if the topic is appropriate for writing that uses definition. Follow the plan that applies to write your composition. Submit your completed composition to the instructor for evaluation. When you receive a grade for this work, enter it in the progress chart.

WRITING TOPICS

- **Etymology** is the history of a word or phrase shown by tracing its development since its earliest recorded occurrence in the language where it is found. Choose one of the following words or phrases and trace its derivation, as the author did for the word *junk*: achilles heel, auld lang syne, bagel, filibuster, free lance, gerrymander, grapevine, Halloween, paraphernalia, quiz, sundae, or turncoat.

- Define in your own terms the word *spirituality*.

- Write an autobiographical essay that defines you for the reader.

- Define one of the following concepts: charisma, despair, happiness, hate, jealousy, love, marriage, personality, racism, or prejudice.

- There are many words we use in English that are derived from other languages. Some examples are: bizarre, chutzpah, cliché, entrepreneur, machismo, pizzaz, taboo. Select one of these words or choose your own to define.

- Define one of the following in concrete terms: bicycle, human heart, parachute, roller coaster, typewriter, or waterslide.

PREWRITING: GENERATING IDEAS

Now that you have selected a topic, you will need to gather information and generate ideas before you begin to write. If you are writing about a personal experience you will probably rely on your memory, other people's input, and your own creativity. Other topics may require that you use reference works to collect this information for your composition.

If you are defining an object, use concrete terms such as shape, size, weight, texture, function, and action. In defining a person or an abstract concept, make your ideas tangible for the reader by using illustration, comparison and contrast, explanation, description, and narration. Create a detailed list of the characteristics or aspects that define your subject. Refer to this list as you follow the plan for writing a paragraph or essay using definition.

Guided Writing **195**

WRITING PLAN: THE PARAGRAPH

1. Decide the point of view of the narrator, first or third person. Write an introduction that gets the reader's attention and presents your point of view.

2. Set the tone for the paragraph, your attitude toward the subject. The tone might be serious or humorous, formal or informal.

3. Use the detailed list you have created to define your subject. Define objects in concrete terms. Make definitions of people or abstract concepts tangible by using illustration, comparison and contrast, explanation, description, and narration.

4. Write a conclusion to your paragraph that restates the topic and presents an overview, summarizes, or expresses an opinion.

5. To create unity in your writing, make sure that each sentence in the paragraph relates to the topic. Your writing will be coherent if ideas follow one another in a logical pattern and sentences flow smoothly from one to the other. Use transitions to link or connect ideas. The list of transitional words and phrases at the back of this book is for your use and reference when you write (see pages 259–264).

6. Use variety in your choice of words to maintain reader interest. Where appropriate, use figurative language to increase the impact of your words and to stimulate the reader's imagination. The most commonly used figures of speech are the simile, metaphor, personification, and hyperbole. Definitions of literary and rhetorical terms can be found in the Glossary on pages 265–270.

7. Create a title for your paragraph, a word or phrase that captures the reader's interest and tells what you are writing about.

8. Use the *Checklist for Revision* provided at the end of this section to help you review and revise your paragraph.

WRITING PLAN: SHORT AND EXTENDED ESSAYS

While short and extended essays are similar—both have introductory and concluding paragraphs—the extended essay has more development paragraphs. In the short essay, "Spirituality," the author examines several contemporary definitions and then offers one of his own. This essay makes use of illustration, description, explanation, and comparison and contrast. The author of the autobiographical essay "On Being Female, Black, and Free" looks at how others have defined her and how she defines herself. The author supports her thesis with narration, description, illustration, comparison and contrast, cause and effect, and explanation.

Introductory Paragraph(s)

1. Decide the narrator's point of view. Is the narrator of the essay involved in the action (first person), or an observer outside the action (third person)?

2. Begin with a strong statement, a question, or an illustration that focuses the reader's interest on the subject. Tell what the essay is about by introducing your topic and purpose. This is the thesis statement, the main idea to be supported throughout the essay.

3. Use your introductory paragraph(s) to set the tone for the essay, your attitude toward the subject. The tone might be serious or humorous, formal or informal.

4. An extended essay may contain more than one introductory paragraph.

Development Paragraph(s)

1. Development paragraphs can be used to define different aspects of your subject. Let the reader know the focus of each paragraph.

2. Use the list you have created to define your subject. If you are defining an object use concrete terms such as shape, size, weight, texture, function, and action. In defining people or abstract concepts make your ideas tangible by using illustration, comparison and contrast, explanation, description, and narration where appropriate.

3. If you are writing an extended essay, include more aspects of your subject in your definition. Make use of other strategies to reinforce your thesis.

4. All sentences in a paragraph should relate to the topic and to one another. All paragraphs in an essay should support the topic and follow some logical order. Use transitions to link ideas within paragraphs and to make connections between paragraphs. Refer to the list of transitional words and phrases on pages 259–264.

5. Use variety in your choice of words to maintain reader interest. Where appropriate, use figurative language to increase the impact of your words and to stimulate the reader's imagination. The most commonly used figures of speech are the simile, metaphor, personification, and hyperbole. Definitions of literary and rhetorical terms can be found in the Glossary on pages 265–270.

Concluding Paragraph(s)

1. Restate the thesis in some way for emphasis. Present an overview, summarize the major points, offer an opinion, or reach a conclusion that reinforces the point of your essay.

2. More than one paragraph may be used to conclude an extended essay.

3. The checklist below will help you to review and revise your essay.

note: The title of your essay should be a word or phrase that captures the reader's attention and tells what you are writing about. Create a title for your first draft and review it before making it final.

CHECKLIST FOR REVISION

1. My paragraph/essay has a first- or third-person point of view. My opening sentences appeal to the reader's interest, introduce my topic, and set the tone. If I am writing an essay, my thesis statement appears in the opening paragraph(s).

2. I use the detailed list I have created to define my subject. Objects are defined in concrete terms such as shape, size, weight, texture, function, and action. In defining people or abstract concepts, I make my ideas tangible by using illustration, comparison and contrast, explanation, description, and narration where appropriate.

3. The development paragraphs of my essay define different aspects of my subject. I let the reader know the focus of each paragraph.

4. In an extended essay, I use the development paragraphs to include more details and make use of other strategies to reinforce the thesis.

5. In concluding my paragraph or essay I present an overview, summarize, offer an opinion, or reach a conclusion that reinforces my point.

6. Sentences within each paragraph relate to the topic. Development paragraphs follow a logical order and support the point of the essay. I use transitions to link ideas within paragraphs and to make connections between paragraphs.

7. I use variety in my choice of words to maintain reader interest. Where appropriate, I use figurative language to increase the impact of my words and to stimulate the reader's imagination.

8. As I revise the form and content of my work, I correct errors in punctuation, capitalization, spelling, grammar, and usage.

9. The title of my paragraph or essay tells what I wrote about and captures the reader's interest.

Continue work in this chapter until you have finished all three Active Reading and Guided Writing Activities.

Chapter 9

CAUSE
AND
EFFECT

Cause and effect writing is a form of exposition that explains relationships and tells why something is the way it is. People have a need to understand the reasons underlying events and behavior. This need is so great that it leads some people to create myths or superstitions that serve as explanations. Other people try to discover and understand causes through the scientific method, a systematic investigation of the facts.

Whether writing about science or superstition, the use of cause and effect will help answer the question, "Why?" This writing strategy is used extensively in education, business, law, and politics. Writers of fiction, especially those who write mystery and detective stories, often use cause and effect to build suspense.

The most important purpose of cause and effect writing is to inform and explain. Informed people understand why things happen and may be in a better position to influence or control events. The goal of much writing about human behavior, the environment, natural resources, or the economy is to encourage people to take action. In this way, cause and effect writing can also serve as the basis of a persuasive argument.

Sometimes cause and effect analysis is speculative. In this approach the writer offers hypotheses and educated guesses about the factors causing certain events or what the consequences of certain actions may be. Newspaper and magazine writers often use this pattern, first choosing a topic of interest, like spring fever or extrasensory perception, and then speculating about why it occurs or what problems it causes. Such writing may be informative, entertaining, or both.

Before you begin to write your cause and effect essay, gather the information you will need. Your analysis could be based on personal experience, thoughtful reflection, or systematic research. Once you have listed possible causes and effects, the next step is to evaluate each item. Most likely, you will have listed more causes and effects than you can use. Include in your paper those explanations and outcomes which seem most relevant or convincing.

This chapter contains three reading selections, all of which use cause and effect as a writing strategy. The first is a paragraph, the second a short essay, and the third a longer piece. Each is followed by an Active Reading exercise that helps you to understand the form and content of the reading model. The Guided Writing section at the end of this chapter will help you to create three original pieces of writing using cause and effect.

Chapter Selections

The Santa Anna *by Joan Didion*

Japanese and American Workers: Two Casts of Mind *by William Ouchi*

The Plug-In Drug *by Marie Winn*

THE SANTA ANA
by Joan Didion

Joan Didion was born in Sacramento, California, in 1934 and educated at the University of California at Berkeley. She worked first as an associate feature editor for Vogue *and then later as a contributing editor for* Saturday Evening Post, National Review, *and* Esquire. *She is the author of three novels:* Run, River *(1963),* Play It As It Lays *(1970), and* A Book of Common Prayer *(1976). Didion is best known for a collection of essays that describes the psychological and cultural turmoil of the 1960s,* Slouching Towards Bethlehem *(1968). "The Santa Ana," an excerpt from this last book, tells us what happens when an ill wind blows.*

Word Alert

cantons the states or subdivisions of territory in Switzerland; a small territorial division of a country

Chandler, Raymond (1888–1959) Chandler was an American detective-story writer whose fiction is well plotted and brutally realistic. His novels feature Philip Marlowe, a tough yet honorable private detective with a brash sense of humor.

ions an atom or group of atoms that carry a positive or negative electric charge

leeward being in or facing the direction toward which the wind is blowing

malevolent having or showing ill will or spite; having an evil influence

mistral a strong, cold, dry northerly wind of southern France

mitigating extenuating, justifiable, excusable, forgivable

sirocco The sirocco is a hot, humid south or southeast wind of Italy, Sicily, and the Mediterranean islands, originating in the Sahara Desert of North Africa. It begins as a dry, dusty wind and becomes moist as it passes over the Mediterranean Sea.

"**O**n nights like that," Raymond Chandler once wrote about the Santa Ana, "every booze party ends in a fight. Meek little wives feel the edge of the carving knife and study their husbands' necks. Anything can happen." That was the kind of wind it was. I did not know then that there was any basis for the effect it had on all of us, but it turns out to be another of those cases in which science bears out folk wisdom. The Santa Ana, which is named for one of the canyons it rushes through, is a *foehn* wind, like the *foehn* of Austria and Switzerland and the *hamsin* of Israel. There are a number of persistent malevolent winds, perhaps the best known of which are the mistral of France and the Mediterranean sirocco, but a *foehn* wind has distinct characteristics: it occurs on the leeward slope of a mountain range and, although the air begins as a cold mass, it is warmed as it comes down the mountain and appears finally as a hot dry wind. Whenever and wherever a *foehn* blows, doctors hear about head-aches and nausea and allergies, about "nervousness," about "depression." In Los Angeles some teachers do not attempt to conduct formal classes during a Santa Ana, because the children become unmanageable. In Swit-zerland the suicide rate goes up during the *foehn*, and in the courts of some Swiss cantons the wind is considered a mitigating circumstance for crime. Surgeons are said to watch the wind, because blood does not clot normally during a *foehn*. A few years ago an Israeli physicist discovered that not only during such winds, but for the ten or twelve hours which precede them, the air carries an unusually high ratio of positive to negative ions. No one seems to know exactly why that should be; some talk about friction and others suggest solar disturbances. In any case the positive ions are there, and what an excess of positive ions does, in the simplest terms, is make people unhappy. One cannot get much more mechanistic than that.

ACTIVE READING

The Active Reading exercise gives you an opportunity to reread the paragraph with a critical eye. By answering the questions that follow, you will extend and sharpen your understanding of the selection. This activity will help you become a more efficient reader and a more effective writer.

This selection examines the effects of a certain kind of wind on human behavior. The paragraph begins by quoting detective-story writer Raymond Chandler who offers examples of how the Santa Ana affects people. A quotation is a good way to get the reader's attention.

1. This quote particularly effective at getting the reader's attention because:

    a. it is written by a famous author.
    b. it suggests unpredictable and violent behavior.
    c. it introduces the topic in a dramatic way.
    d. all of the above

2. What is the Santa Ana?

    a. a desert
    b. a state
    c. a mountain
    d. a wind

3. According to folk wisdom, the unpredictable behavior identified in the beginning of the paragraph was caused by:

4. According to the author, scientific evidence confirms this folk wisdom. Is this true or false?

5. The author defines the Santa Ana and offers examples of winds similar to it found in other parts of the world. How did the Santa Ana get its name?

6. The author identifies the Santa Ana as a *foehn* wind. What two other countries have this kind of wind?

    a. France and Italy
    b. England and Austria
    c. Switzerland and Austria
    d. Israel and Spain

7. The *foehn* wind is similar to all of the following kinds of malevolent winds except:

    a. monsoon
    b. mistral
    c. sirocco
    d. hamsin

8. Which of the following is characteristic of a *foehn* wind?

    a. occurs on the leeward slope of a mountain range
    b. air begins as a cold mass
    c. air is warmed as it comes down the mountain
    d. appears as a hot, dry wind
    e. all of the above

9. The author discusses the effects of *foehn* winds on people. Which of the following is <u>not</u> a physical symptom reported by doctors as associated with *foehn* winds?

   a. headaches
   b. nausea
   c. blurred vision
   d. allergies

10. Which of the following is <u>not</u> a psychological symptom reported by doctors as associated with *foehn* winds?

    a. schizophrenia
    b. nervousness
    c. depression
    d. both *b* and *c*

Below are some statements based on the ideas in the model paragraph. In each statement, one phrase is marked (*a*) and the other is marked (*b*). Identify each phrase as either the cause or effect part of the statement. Remember, the *cause* is the reason why and the *effect* is the result or outcome. Ask yourself, "What leads to what?"

11. (a) In Los Angeles some teachers do not attempt to conduct formal classes during a Santa Ana, (b) because the children become unmanageable.

12. (a) In Switzerland the suicide rate goes up (b) during the *foehn*.

13. (a) Because of the way the wind affects behavior, (b) the courts of some Swiss cantons consider the wind to be a mitigating circumstance for crime.

14. (a) Surgeons are said to watch the wind, (b) because blood does not clot normally during a *foehn*.

15. An Israeli physicist has provided a scientific explanation for the effects of *foehn* winds. He found that during such winds, and for ten or twelve hours preceding them, the air carries an unusually high ratio of:

    a. negative to positive ions
    b. positive to negative ions
    c. both *a* and *b*
    d. neither *a* or *b*

16. What might cause the air to carry an unusually high ratio of positive to negative ions?

    a. friction
    b. solar disturbances
    c. both *a* and *b*
    d. quarks

17. What effect does an excess of positive ions have on people?

18. The Santa Ana winds are found in what country?

19. The author uses transitional words and phrases to link ideas in this paragraph. List at least five.

20. The author's primary purpose in this selection is to:

    a. inform
    b. persuade
    c. entertain

The Active Reading exercise can be scored using the answer key and grading grid. Enter your grade in the progress chart.

GUIDED WRITING

The Guided Writing section at the end of this chapter (page 222) provides topics and plans for writing paragraphs and essays using cause and effect. Select a topic and write a paragraph by following the writing plan on page 223.

Continue work in this chapter until you have finished all three Active Reading and Guided Writing activities. Upon completion, you will have written three new compositions for your portfolio (one paragraph and two essays). Record grades in your progress chart and, if available, on the Academic Credit Statement in your *Writing Portfolio Organizer*.

JAPANESE AND AMERICAN WORKERS: TWO CASTS OF MIND

by William Ouchi

William Ouchi, born in Honolulu, Hawaii in 1943, was educated at Williams College, Stanford University, and the University of Chicago. He has taught business at several universities including Chicago, Stanford, and UCLA. Ouchi has worked for the National Opinion Research Center and as a business consultant for many of America's Fortune 500 companies. His research on the major corporations of Japan resulted in his best-selling book, Theory Z: How American Business Can Meet the Japanese Challenge *(1981). In "Japanese and American Workers: Two Casts of Mind," an important selection from* Theory Z, *Ouchi explains why the Japanese have been able to achieve greater productivity by emphasizing the spirit of cooperation, rather than the spirit of competition. In this excerpt from his book, Ouchi uses cause and effect to show how one thing leads to another. Differences in the geography of Japan and the United States have, of necessity, led to different ways of growing food. This, in turn, has affected the values and social organization of each country.*

Word Alert

arable	land that is suitable for cultivation
bottom line	an idiomatic expression that means the end result or outcome
feudal	The word refers to feudalism, a political and economic system in which the king owned all of the land. It had as its basis a strict division of social classes. Beneath the king were nobles, who in turn rented land to peasants and laborers for a fee. The feudal period in Japan lasted about 700 years and ended with the Meiji Restoration.
Hobbes, Thomas	Thomas Hobbes (1588–1679) was an English philosopher who presented his political philosophy in the *Leviathan*. He argued that man is by nature a selfishly individualistic animal at constant war with all other men. He says that in a natural state where there are no rules, people live lives which are "nasty, brutish, and short." Because of fear of violent death, men will create a state in which they surrender their natural rights to a monarch or a parliament.
kinship	relationship by blood or marriage between persons; relatives

Meiji Restoration	During this period, the power that had been held by the military in the person of the Shogun (the feudal lord) was returned to the Emperor. The Meiji Restoration was the chief event in the modern history of Japan for it signified the downfall of Japanese feudalism and the forging of a new and modern state. Emperor Meiji himself, who reigned from 1867 to 1912, had little political power but was a paramount symbol of the unity of Japan.
Plato	A Greek philosopher, Plato (427–347 B.C.) believed in reason, order, and truth. He thought that the philosopher, with an understanding of the Good, was the only one capable of ruling the just state. He believed that political liberty (individual freedom) was disorder and did not approve of it. One of Plato's main concerns was to establish an ideal form of government which he described in *The Republic*, the first political science text.
shinkansen	The *shinkansen*, also known as the bullet train, is a high-speed rail system in Japan where trains travel approximately 125 to 160 miles per hour.
Skinner, B.F.	An American psychologist, Skinner (1904–1990) was known as a proponent of Behaviorism. Skinner has argued that people's actions are the result of their genetic endowment, their personal history of reinforcement, and their culture. An individual, as a member of a group, profits from the social environment maintained by the group. To ensure a peaceful world, Skinner believed that we should arrange circumstances so that cooperation is rewarded, cheaters don't win, and aggressors don't stay in power.
staple	the sustaining or principal element; a commodity for which the demand is constant

The *shinkansen* or "bullet train" speeds across the rural areas of Japan 1
giving a quick view of cluster after cluster of farmhouses surrounded by
rice paddies. This particular pattern did not develop purely by chance, but
as a consequence of the technology peculiar to the growing of rice, the
staple of the Japanese diet. The growing of rice requires construction and
maintenance of an irrigation system, something that takes many hands to
build. More importantly, the planting and the harvesting of rice can only
be done efficiently with the cooperation of twenty or more people. The
"bottom line" is that a single family working alone cannot produce enough

rice to survive, but a dozen families working together can produce a surplus. Thus the Japanese have had to develop the capacity to work together in harmony, no matter what the forces of disagreement or social disintegration, in order to survive.

2   Japan is a nation built entirely on the tips of giant, suboceanic volcanoes. Little of the land is flat and suitable for agriculture. Terraced hillsides make use of every available square foot of arable land. Small homes built very close together further conserve the land. Japan also suffers from natural disasters such as earthquakes and hurricanes. Traditionally homes are made of light construction materials, so a house falling down during a disaster will not crush its occupants and also could be quickly and inexpensively rebuilt. During the feudal period until the Meiji Restoration of 1868, each feudal lord sought to restrain his subjects from moving from one village to the next for fear that a neighboring lord might amass enough peasants with which to produce a large agricultural surplus, hire an army and pose a threat. Apparently bridges were not commonly built across rivers and streams until the late nineteenth century, since bridges increased mobility between villages.

3   Taken all together, this characteristic style of living paints the picture of a nation of people who are homogeneous with respect to race, history, language, religion, and culture. For centuries and generations these people have lived in the same village next door to the same neighbors. Living in close proximity and in dwellings which gave very little privacy, the Japanese survived through their capacity to work together in harmony. In this situation, it was inevitable that the one most central social value which emerged, the one value without which the society could not continue, was that an individual does not matter.

4   To the Western soul this is a chilling picture of society. Subordinating individual tastes to the harmony of the group and knowing that individual needs can never take precedence over the interests of all is repellent to the Western citizen. But a frequent theme of Western philosophers and sociologists is that individual freedom exists only when people willingly subordinate their self-interests to the social interest. A society composed entirely of self-interested individuals is a society in which each person is at war with the other, a society which has no freedom. This issue, constantly at the heart of understanding society, comes up in every century, and in every society, whether the writer be Plato, Hobbes, or B.F. Skinner.

. . . In some ages, the kinship group, the central social institution, mediated between these opposing forces to preserve the balance in which freedom was realized; in other times the church or the government was most critical. Perhaps our present age puts the work organization as the central institution.

In order to complete the comparison of Japanese and American living situations, consider a flight over the United States. Looking out of the window high over the state of Kansas, we see a pattern of a single farmhouse surrounded by fields, followed by another single homestead surrounded by fields. In the early 1800s in the state of Kansas there were no automobiles. Your nearest neighbor was perhaps two miles distant; the winters were long, and the snow was deep. Inevitably, the central social values were self-reliance and independence. Those were the realities of that place and age that children had to learn to value.

5

ACTIVE READING

The Active Reading exercise gives you an opportunity to reread the essay with a critical eye. By answering the questions that follow, you will extend and sharpen your understanding of the selection. This activity will help you become a more efficient reader and a more effective writer.

INTRODUCTORY PARAGRAPH *(par. 1)*

1. The author introduces us to Japan by describing the view from the bullet train as it speeds across rural areas. What does one see from the train?

2. What caused this pattern of living to develop?

The remainder of the paragraph focuses on the way in which the growing of rice in Japan influenced the development of the social structure. Below are some statements based on the ideas in the model essay. In each, one phrase is marked (*a*) and the other is marked (*b*). Identify each phrase as either the cause or effect part of the statement. Remember, the *cause* is the reason why and the *effect* is the result or outcome. Ask yourself, "What leads to what?"

3. (a) In order to grow rice (b) many hands are needed to construct and maintain an irrigation system.

4. (a) The planting and harvesting of rice (b) can only be done efficiently with the cooperation of twenty or more people.

5. (a) A single family working alone (b) cannot produce enough rice to survive.

6. (a) A dozen families working together (b) can produce a surplus.

7. (a) The Japanese have had to develop the capacity to work together in harmony (b) in order to survive.

The author ends the first paragraph by drawing a conclusion as to why the Japanese have developed the capacity to work together in harmony. This sentence serves as a topic sentence for the paragraph and as a thesis statement for the essay.

DEVELOPMENT PARAGRAPH *(par. 2)*

The author explains how geography and weather have influenced agriculture and housing. He also discusses the relationship between agriculture and politics.

Below are some statements based on the ideas in this paragraph. In each statement, one phrase is marked (*a*) and the other is marked (*b*). Identify each phrase as either the cause or effect part of the statement. Remember, the *cause* is the reason why and the *effect* is the result or outcome.

8. (a) Little of the land is flat and suitable for agriculture (b) because Japan is built entirely on the tips of suboceanic volcanoes.

9. (a) Because little of the land is arable, (b) terraced hillsides make use of every available square foot.

10. (a) Small homes are built very close together (b) in order to further conserve land.

11. (a) Traditionally homes are built of light construction materials, (b) so a house falling down during a disaster will not crush its occupants and also (c) could be quickly and inexpensively rebuilt.

The feudal period in Japan lasted 700 years, from the 12th century until the downfall of the Shogun and return of the Emperor to the throne in 1868. Feudalism helped to shape the Japanese into a homogeneous society. Identify each phrase below as either the cause or effect part of the statement. Remember to ask yourself, "What leads to what?"

12. (a) Each feudal lord sought to restrain his subjects from moving from one village to the next (b) for fear a neighboring lord might amass enough peasants to form an army and pose a threat.

13. (a) Bridges were not built across rivers and streams until the late nineteenth century (b) since bridges increased mobility between villages.

DEVELOPMENT PARAGRAPH *(par. 3)*

The first sentence of this paragraph summarizes the previous paragraphs, and helps to explain the emergence of values which are central to Japanese society.

14. The Japanese people are homogenous with regard to all of the following except:

    a. race
    b. language
    c. social class
    d. religion

Identify each phrase below as either the cause or effect part of the statement. Remember to ask yourself, "What leads to what?"

15. (a) The Japanese, through their capacity to work together in harmony, (b) survived living in close proximity, in dwellings which gave very little privacy.

16. (a) Living in this situation, (b) it was inevitable that one central social value would emerge.

17. (a) The individual does not matter is a value that emerged (b) as a result of the Japanese need to to work together in harmony.

To this point the author offers reasons for the development of Japanese society and the values that have emerged. In the next two paragraphs the author compares Japan with Western society, specifically the United States. He uses the **divided** or **block** pattern to make this comparison; one subject, Japanese society, is discussed first and the other subject, Western society, next.

DEVELOPMENT PARAGRAPH *(par. 4)*

The topic of this paragraph is a basic issue confronting every society: how to preserve individual freedom without compromising the needs of the group.

18. Select a term or phrase that best completes the following analogy: Japan : group : : the West : _____

    a. group
    b. sociologists
    c. individual
    d. community

19. According to many Western philosophers and sociologists, individual freedom exists only when:

    a. the society is composed entirely of self-interested individuals.

    b. each person in the society is at war with the other.

    c. the social interest is subordinate to self-interest.

    d. self-interest is subordinate to the social interest.

Plato, Hobbes, and B. F. Skinner have each written about the relationship of the individual to society. Read statements A through D below, then answer questions 20–22. Refer to the Word Alert list on pages 204–205 to help you.

    A. Governments are formed because man is selfishly individualistic and constantly at war with other men.

    B. Political liberty is disorder and the philosopher is the only one capable of ruling a just state.

    C. Governments have the power to reward cooperation, punish cheaters, and make sure aggressors do not rule.

    D. The natural state of man is one of individual freedom, and it is government which corrupts and sets man against man.

20. Which statement above best expresses the view of Plato?

21. Which statement above best expresses the view of Hobbes?

22. Which statement above best expresses the view of B.F. Skinner?

23. The author believes that an important function of the central social institution in a society is to mediate between the opposing forces of self-interest and social interest to maintain freedom. In our present age, what institution does he believe serves this purpose?

    a. the kinship group

    b. the work organization

    c. the church

    d. the government

CONCLUDING PARAGRAPH *(par. 5)*

As a way of completing the comparison of Japanese and American living situations, the author looks at rural agriculture in the United States and the values that emerged from this way of living.

24. From his vantage point in an airplane, the author sees which of the following patterns?

a. a single farmhouse surrounded by fields

b. several farmhouses surrounding one large field

c. a single farmhouse surrounded by rice paddies

d. several farmhouses surrounding one rice paddy

25. What environmental factor contributed to the emergence of the social values of self-reliance and independence in the United States?

a. lack of transportation

b. great distance between neighbors

c. long winters and deep snows

d. all of the above

26. What value has emerged as most important for American society as compared to Japanese society?

a. cooperation

b. competition

c. interdependence

d. collectivism

27. Self-reliance and independence are characteristic of the _____, while harmony and cooperation apply only to the _____. Select the best answer to complete this sentence.

a. group, individual

b. group, group

c. individual, group

d. individual, individual

28. The author uses transitional words and phrases to link ideas in this essay. List at least five.

29. The author's primary purpose in this selection is to:

a. inform

b. persuade

c. entertain

The Active Reading exercise can be scored using the answer key and grading grid. Enter your grade in the progress chart.

GUIDED WRITING

The Guided Writing section at the end of this chapter (page 222) provides topics and plans for writing paragraphs and essays using cause and effect. Select a topic and write a short essay by following the writing plan that begins on page 224. Continue work in this chapter until you have finished all three Active Reading and Guided Writing activities.

THE PLUG-IN DRUG
by Marie Winn

Marie Winn was born in 1937 in Czechoslovakia, and was educated at Radcliffe and Columbia University. She is the author of ten books for children, as well as many articles for The New York Times Magazine *and* The Village Voice. *In her book* The Plug-In Drug: Television, Children and Family *(1977), Winn analyzes the effects on children of extensive television watching. In the selection excerpted here, the author argues that critics of television have focused on program content while ignoring the television experience itself.*

Word Alert

assuage	appease, relieve, quiet
bondage	captivity, a state of being bound, usually by compulsion; subjugation to a power, force, or influence
detrimental	causing harm or damage; injurious
epitomize	embodiment; to serve as an ideal example
gnawing	to plague; to afflict or trouble persistently
incessant	unceasing; continuous
irrelevant	not relating to the subject at hand; not relevant, inapplicable
overtly	clearly evident
perpetuate	to prolong the existence of; to cause to last indefinitely
repugnant	distasteful or obnoxious; repellent
shoddy	inferior, shabby; hastily or poorly done
subtly	so slight as to be difficult to detect or analyze; operating in a hidden and injurious way; insidious

1   Preschool children are the single largest television audience in America, spending a greater number of total hours and a greater proportion of their waking day watching television than any other age group. Even the most conservative estimates indicate that preschool children in America are spending more than a third of their waking hours watching television.

What are the effects upon the vulnerable and developing human organism of spending such a significant proportion of each day engaging in this particular experience? How does the television experience affect a child's language development, for instance? How does it influence his developing imagination, his creativity? How does the availability of television affect the ways parents bring up their children? Are new child-rearing strategies being adopted and old ones discarded because the television set is available to parents for relief? Is the child's perception of reality subtly altered by steady exposure to television unrealities? How does watching television for several hours each day affect the child's abilities to form human relationships? What happens to family life as a result of family members' involvement with television? . . . 2

Parents themselves, though often deeply troubled about television and its effects upon their children, center their concern on the subject matter of the programs their children watch, rather than on the television experience itself. Their content-centered approach is epitomized by the activities of an increasingly important parent-lobbyist organization, Action for Children's Television, known as ACT. This organization, formed by a group of Boston mothers, grew out of the common anxieties of the founding parents about television: their children were spending too many hours watching television, the mothers agreed, and the violence that seemed to dominate children's programs was appalling. Moreover, the incessant commercial interruptions were making their children crave a variety of shoddy toys and unwholesome foods. . . . 3

But is it the specific needs of *children* that are at stake when parents demand better programming? Surely the fact that young children watch so much television reflects the needs of *parents* to find a convenient source of amusement for their children and a moment of quiet for themselves. It seems, then, the need of parents to assuage their gnawing anxieties about the possible effects of hours of quiet, passive television watching underlies their desire to make those hours less overtly repugnant. 4

The needs of young children are quite different. The developing child needs opportunities to work out his basic family relationships, thereby coming to understand himself. The television experience only reduces these opportunities. 5

6   The child needs to develop a capacity for self-direction in order to liberate himself from dependency. The television experience helps to perpetuate dependency.

7   The child needs to acquire fundamental skills in communication—to learn to read, write, and express himself flexibly and clearly—in order to function as a social creature. The television experience does not further his verbal development because it does not require any verbal participation on his part, merely passive intake.

8   The child needs to discover his own strengths and weaknesses in order to find fulfillment as an adult in both work and play. Watching television does not lead him to such discoveries; indeed it only limits his involvement in those real-life activities that might offer his abilities a genuine testing ground.

9   The young child's need for fantasy is gratified far better by his own make-believe activities than by the adult-made fantasies he is offered on television.

10   The young child's need for intellectual stimulation is met infinitely better when he can learn by manipulating, touching, *doing*, than by merely watching passively.

11   And, finally, the television experience must be considered in relation to the child's need to develop family skills he will need in order to become a successful parent himself someday. These skills are a product of his present participation in family life, of his everyday experiences as a family member. There is every indication that television has a destructive effect upon family life, diminishing its richness and variety.

12   Thus it begins to appear that ACT and the concerned parents and educators who support it so hopefully may be misguided in their beliefs and efforts. The television experience is at best irrelevant and at worst detrimental to children's needs. Efforts to make television more attractive to parents and children by improving programming can only lead to the increased reliance of parents upon television as a baby-sitter, and the increased bondage of children to their television sets.

ACTIVE READING

The Active Reading exercise gives you an opportunity to reread the essay with a critical eye. By answering the questions that follow, you will extend and sharpen your understanding of the selection. This activity will help you become a more efficient reader and a more effective writer.

INTRODUCTORY PARAGRAPHS *(par. 1–2)*

1. The first paragraph of the essay states that preschool children are the single largest television audience in America. What two facts support this assertion?

2. Preschool children spend what proportion of their waking hours watching television?

   a. one-quarter
   b. one-third
   c. one-half
   d. three-quarters

3. The second paragraph begins with the thesis statement of the essay in the form of a question. What is the thesis statement?

The author poses questions about the causal relationship between the television experience and aspects of the child's development.

4. With regard to the child's development, which of the following is <u>not</u> a concern of the author?

   a. language development
   b. creativity
   c. physical development
   d. perception of reality
   e. ability to form human relationships

5. According to the author, what two aspects of adult life are affected by television?

   a. child-rearing strategies and family life
   b. language and physical development
   c. perception of reality and creativity
   d. imagination and brain development

DEVELOPMENT PARAGRAPH *(par. 3)*

This paragraph looks at parental concerns about children's television viewing habits, and actions that have been taken.

6. What is the focus of parental concern about children watching television?

7. Which of the following is <u>not</u> a concern of parents about children watching television?

    a. violence
    b. too many hours of watching television
    c. commercials and their effects
    d. the television experience itself

8. Focus on the subject matter of children's television programming led to the formation of what parent-lobbyist organization?

This group is also known by the **acronym** *ACT*. An acronym is a word formed from the initial letters of a name, like *WAC* for Women's Army Corps, or by combining the initial letters or parts of a series of words, like *radar*, which stands for **ra**dio **d**etecting **a**nd **r**anging.

DEVELOPMENT PARAGRAPH *(par. 4)*

This paragraph questions the motivation of parents who demand better programming for children's shows. Below are some statements based on the ideas in this paragraph. In each, one phrase is marked (*a*) and the other is marked (*b*). Identify each phrase as either the cause or effect part of the statement. Remember, the *cause* is the reason why and the *effect* is the result or outcome. Ask yourself, "What leads to what?"

9. (a) Surely the fact that young children watch so much television (b) reflects the needs of *parents* to find a convenient source of amusement for their children and a moment of quiet for themselves.

10. (a) ... the need of parents to assuage their gnawing anxieties about the possible effects of hours of quiet, passive television watching underlies (b) their desire to make those hours less overtly repugnant.

11. According to the author, whose need is met by better programming?

    a. the parent's
    b. the child's
    c. both the parent's and the child's
    d. neither the parent's nor the child's

DEVELOPMENT PARAGRAPHS *(par. 5–10)*

The author discusses what the young child needs and why, as well as the effects watching television has on meeting these needs. In the sentences below, identify each phrase as either the cause or effect part of the statement. Ask yourself, "What leads to what?"

12. (a) The developing child needs opportunities to work out his basic family relationships, (b) thereby coming to understand himself.

13. (a) The television experience only (b) reduces these opportunities.

14. (a) In order to liberate himself from dependency, (b) the child needs to develop a capacity for self-direction

15. (a) The television experience helps to (b) perpetuate dependency.

16. (a) The child needs to acquire fundamental skills in communication (b) in order to function as a social creature.

17. What communication skills does the child need to acquire?

    a. read
    b. write
    c. express himself clearly
    d. all of the above

18. (a) The television experience does not further his verbal development (b) because it does not require any verbal participation on his part, merely passive intake.

The widespread availability of television sets in the 1950s coincided with the beginning of a steady and continuing decline in reading and writing abilities. In a recent study, the National Assessment of Educational Progress found that school-age children watch television an average of three hours a day. The study also found that children's ability to read and write is poor at every level of school, from grade four through grade twelve.

19. The author would argue that this relationship is:

    a. coincidental
    b. correlational
    c. causal
    d. none of the above

In the sentences below, identify each phrase as either the cause or effect part of the statement. Remember to ask yourself, "What leads to what?"

20. (a) The child needs to discover his own strengths and weaknesses (b) in order to find fulfillment as an adult in both work and play.

21. (a) Watching television (b) does not lead him to such discoveries; (c) indeed it only limits his involvement in those real-life activities that might offer his abilities a genuine testing ground.

22. (a) The young child's need for fantasy (b) leads to inventive make-believe activities.

23. With what are the child's own make-believe activities compared?

24. (a) The young child's need for intellectual stimulation is met infinitely better (b) when he learns by manipulating, touching, *doing* . . .

25. With what are manipulating, touching, *doing* compared?

DEVELOPMENT PARAGRAPH *(par. 11)*

This paragraph looks at the effects of television on the child's development of family skills, and family life in general. In the sentences below, identify each phrase as either the cause or effect part of the statement. Ask yourself, "What leads to what?"

26. (a) The child needs to develop family skills (b) in order to be a successful parent himself someday.

27. (a) These skills are a product of (b) his present participation in family life, of his everyday experiences as a family member.

28. (a) Television (b) has a destructive effect on family life, diminishing its richness and variety.

The words "the child's needs" are repeated throughout the development paragraphs to emphasize the author's focus in this essay. **Repetition** is an essential unifying element in nearly all poetry and much prose. Sounds, syllables, words, phrases, stanzas, ideas, and allusions are repeated for emphasis.

CONCLUDING PARAGRAPH *(par. 12)*

In summary, the author talks about the efforts of ACT, the group of concerned parents who lobby for better children's television programs.

29. How does the author characterize the beliefs and efforts of this group and their supporters?

    a. irrelevant
    b. detrimental
    c. misguided
    d. helpful

30. How does the author characterize the effect of the television experience on children's needs?

    a. at best irrelevant
    b. at worst detrimental
    c. both a and b
    d. neither a nor b

The concluding sentence summarizes the author's view of efforts to improve television programming and their likely effects. In the sentence below, identify each phrase as either the cause or the effect part of the statement.

31. (a) Efforts to make television more attractive to parents and children by improving programming (b) can only lead to the increased reliance of parents upon television as a baby-sitter, (c) and the increased bondage of children to their television sets.

32. The author uses transitional words and phrases to link ideas in this essay. List at least five.

33. The author's primary purpose in this selection is to:

    a. inform
    b. persuade
    c. entertain

The Active Reading exercise can be scored using the answer key and grading grid. Enter your grade in the progress chart.

The Guided Writing section that begins on the next page provides topics and plans for writing paragraphs and essays using cause and effect. Select a topic and write an extended essay by following the writing plan that begins on page 224.

GUIDED WRITING

This part of the chapter will help you apply what you have learned about writing paragraphs and essays using cause and effect. Choose one of the topics listed below for each writing assignment that you do. If you want to write about something else, ask your instructor if the topic is appropriate for writing cause and effect. Follow the plan that applies to write your composition. Submit your completed composition to the instructor for evaluation. When you receive a grade for this work, enter it in the progress chart.

WRITING TOPICS

- Show how the more subtle events in nature affect people emotionally and behaviorally. Select and write about one of the following: the full moon, cold or hot weather, the day/night cycle, change of seasons, aurora borealis, lunar eclipse, solar eclipse, midnight sun, or an occurrence peculiar to the area in which you live.

- Choose a natural phenomena from those listed above and explain how and why it happens.

- William Ouchi's essay shows how Japan's homogeneity with respect to race, history, language, religion and culture makes a group strong. What strengths result from a diverse and pluralistic society?

- Feudalism is said to have helped shape the Japanese into a cooperative society. In what ways has capitalism helped to shape the United States into a competitive society?

- Examine the relationship between television viewing for young children and educational achievement in school. Use facts to support your thesis and to develop the topic.

- Family members may watch television as a way of avoiding communication with one another, or as a focus for sharing. How has television viewing affected the relationships in your household?

PREWRITING: GENERATING IDEAS

Now that you have selected a topic, you will need to gather information and generate ideas before you begin to write. If you are writing about a personal experience you will probably rely on your memory, other people's input, and your own creativity. Other topics may require that you use reference works to collect information for your composition.

When you use cause and effect, you are telling why something is the way it is. Make a list of causes and effects to help you explain how or why something happens. Show how one thing leads to another. Refer to this list as you follow the plan for writing a paragraph or essay using cause and effect.

WRITING PLAN: THE PARAGRAPH

1. Decide the point of view of the narrator, first or third person. Write an introduction that gets the reader's attention, and present your topic at the beginning of the paragraph.

2. Set the tone for the paragraph, your attitude toward the subject. The tone might be serious or humorous, formal or informal.

3. Use the list you have created to help you explain how or why something happens. Show how one thing leads to another. Use facts, description, definition, explanation, and examples where appropriate.

4. Write a conclusion to your paragraph that restates the topic and presents an overview, summarizes, or expresses an opinion.

5. To create unity in your writing, make sure that each sentence in the paragraph relates to the topic. Your writing will be coherent if ideas follow one another in a logical pattern and sentences flow smoothly from one to the other. Use transitions to link or connect ideas. The list of transitional words and phrases at the back of this book is for your use and reference when you write (see pages 259–264).

6. Use variety in your choice of words to maintain reader interest. Where appropriate, use figurative language to increase the impact of your words and to stimulate the reader's imagination. The most commonly used figures of speech are the simile, metaphor, personification, and hyperbole. Definitions of literary and rhetorical terms can be found in the Glossary on pages 265–270.

7. Create a title for your paragraph, a word or phrase that captures the reader's interest and tells what you are writing about.

8. Use the *Checklist for Revision* provided at the end of this section to help you review and revise your paragraph.

WRITING PLAN: SHORT AND EXTENDED ESSAYS

While short and extended essays are similar—both have introductory and concluding paragraphs—the extended essay has more development paragraphs. "Japanese and American Workers: Two Casts of Mind" looks at why certain social values emerged in each culture. The author uses comparison and contrast, explanation, and examples in this short essay. "The Plug-In Drug," an extended essay, discusses the effects of television viewing on young children. Here the author supports her thesis with explanation, illustration, and definition.

Introductory Paragraph(s)

1. Decide the narrator's point of view. Is the narrator of the essay involved in the action (first person), or an observer outside the action (third person)?
2. Begin with a strong statement, a question, or a quotation that focuses the reader's interest on the subject. Tell what the essay is about by introducing your topic and purpose. This is the thesis statement, the main idea to be supported throughout the essay.
3. Use your introductory paragraph(s) to set the tone for the essay, your attitude toward the subject. The tone might be serious or humorous, formal or informal.
4. State your plan for the development of this essay. An extended essay may contain more than one introductory paragraph.

Development Paragraph(s)

1. Each development paragraph can be used to examine a different aspect of your subject. Let the reader know your topic or focus for each new paragraph.
2. Use the list you have created to help you explain how or why something happens. Show how one thing leads to another. Use facts, description, definition, explanation, and illustration where appropriate.
3. If you are writing an extended essay, include more cause and effect relationships and make use of other strategies to reinforce your thesis.
4. All sentences in a paragraph should relate to the topic and to one another. All paragraphs in an essay should support the topic and follow some logical order. Use transitions to link ideas within paragraphs and to make connections between paragraphs. Refer to the list of transitional words and phrases on pages 259–264.

5. Use variety in your choice of words to maintain reader interest. Where appropriate, use figurative language to increase the impact of your words and to stimulate the reader's imagination. The most commonly used figures of speech are the simile, metaphor, personification, and hyperbole. Definitions of literary and rhetorical terms can be found in the Glossary on pages 265–270.

Concluding Paragraph(s)

1. Restate the thesis in some way for emphasis. Present an overview, summarize the major points, offer an opinion, or reach a conclusion that reinforces the point of your essay.
2. More than one paragraph may be used to conclude an extended essay.
3. The checklist below will help you to review and revise your essay.

note: The title of your essay should be a word or phrase that captures the reader's attention and tells what you are writing about. Create a title for your first draft and review it before making it final.

CHECKLIST FOR REVISION

1. My paragraph/essay has a first- or third-person point of view. My opening sentences appeal to the reader's interest, introduce my topic, and set the tone. If I am writing an essay, my thesis statement appears in the opening paragraph(s).
2. I use the list I have created to show causes and effects, how one event leads to another.
3. I use facts, description, definition, explanation, and illustration where appropriate. Each development paragraph in my essay explains a different cause and effect relationship.
4. In an extended essay, I use the development paragraphs to include more details that support the thesis.
5. In concluding my paragraph or essay I present an overview, summarize, offer an opinion, or reach a conclusion that reinforces my point.
6. Sentences within each paragraph relate to the topic. Development paragraphs follow a logical order and support the point of the essay. I use transitions to link ideas within paragraphs and to make connections between paragraphs.

7. I use variety in my choice of words to maintain reader interest. Where appropriate, I use figurative language to increase the impact of my words and to stimulate the reader's imagination.

8. As I revise the form and content of my work, I correct errors in punctuation, capitalization, spelling, grammar, and usage.

9. The title of my paragraph or essay tells what I wrote about and captures the reader's interest.

Continue work in this chapter until you have finished all three Active Reading and Guided Writing activities.

Chapter 10

PERSUASION
AND
ARGUMENT

Every day readers encounter persuasive and argumentative writing that tries to convince them to buy a product or service, to take an action, consider an idea, or accept an opinion. Writers explain and support their main idea, the thesis, with appeals to emotion and logic. The goal is always to convince you to see things their way.

Writing is classified as persuasion when it is highly emotional, uses biased language, offers opinions, and appeals to feelings and instincts. Writing is classified as argument when it is strictly rational, depends on facts and logical explanation, and appeals to intelligence. Advertising copy is mostly persuasive while scientific controversy is generally argumentative. When people write to convince others, they appeal to both emotion and reason. Persuasion and argument can be used to get people to commit themselves to a cause, to take action to change a situation, to change behavior and attitudes, to arouse sympathy and concern, or to provoke anger in order to win agreement.

There are three basic devices writers use when making an emotional appeal. The most common of these is the use of **connotative** language, emotionally charged words that produce positive or negative reactions in the reader. Words like *democracy, tyranny, heroic, cowardly* are connotative and so are words that appeal to the senses, such as *sour, creepy,* and *fiery.*

Figurative language, a second device, engages the reader's emotions and senses through the use of metaphors, similies, or allusions that draw comparisons and make associations for the reader. For example, when confronted with difficult choices, we say "It's like being between a rock and a hard place." This comparison, a simile, says there is no easy way out of the situation.

Writers also use **tone** as an emotional device to put readers in a frame of mind to accept a particular point of view. A friendly tone can be established by using the pronouns *I, you,* and *we.* By using conversational language and frequent references to personal experiences, writers can create a relaxed tone. Depending on the language you choose, you can convey an ironic tone, an authoritative tone, or whatever tone you want.

Rational or logical strategies appeal to reason and common sense through inductive or deductive argument. An inductive argument presents the facts first, then draws a conclusion based on the evidence. In contrast, a deductive argument starts with a generalization or a belief and applies it to a specific case. Logical arguments, both inductive and deductive, may also use cause and effect, comparison and contrast, examples and definition to convince you of a particular point of view. In order to be successful in making a rational appeal, you will need to present data and cite authorities.

This chapter contains three reading selections, all of which use persuasion and argument. The first is a paragraph, the second a short essay, and the third a longer piece. Each is followed by an Active Reading exercise that helps you to understand the form and content of the reading model. The Guided Writing section at the end of this chapter will help you to create three original pieces of writing using persuasion and argument.

Chapter Selections

Letter From Birmingham Jail *by Martin Luther King, Jr.*

Why Johnny Can't Write *by Norman Cousins*

A Nation At Risk *by David P. Gardner*

LETTER FROM BIRMINGHAM JAIL

by Martin Luther King, Jr.

Martin Luther King, Jr. (1929–1968) was born in Atlanta, Georgia, and educated at Morehouse College, Crozer Theological Seminary, and Boston University. An ordained Baptist minister, King founded the Southern Christian Leadership Conference in 1957, and established himself as America's most prominent spokesman for non-violent racial integration. In 1963 he was named Time magazine's Man of the Year, and in 1964 he was awarded the Nobel Prize for Peace. His assassination in 1968 in Memphis, Tennessee was an event that shocked the world. His works include Why We Can't Wait *(1964), and* Where Do We Go From Here: Chaos or Community? *(1967). King wrote the letter, which appears in* Why We Can't Wait, *while imprisoned for "parading without a permit." Directed at eight clergymen, a group of white moderates who feared violence in the Birmingham desegregation demonstrations, the letter received worldwide attention. In the excerpt below, King argues against "waiting" and offers painful examples of segregation in his own life, as well as in the lives of other black people.*

Word Alert

abyss   a bottomless pit; hell, a void

affluent   wealthy; having a generously sufficient and typically increasing supply of material possessions

concoct   invent, fabricate, contrive

humiliate   to lower the pride or dignity of

inferiority   a sense of inadequacy or a tendency to self-diminishment; of little value or merit

ominous   having a menacing or threatening aspect

segregation   the separation or isolation of a race, class, or ethnic group by enforced or voluntary residence in a restricted area, by barriers to social intercourse, by separate educational facilities, or by other discriminatory means

whim   arbitrary thought or impulse; a sudden or capricious idea or fancy

We have waited for more than 340 years for our constitutional and Godgiven rights. The nations of Asia and Africa are moving with jetlike speed toward gaining political independence, but we still creep at horse-and-buggy pace toward gaining a cup of coffee at a lunch counter. Perhaps it is easy for those who have never felt the stinging darts of segregation to say, "Wait." But when you have seen vicious mobs lynch your mothers and fathers at will and drown your sisters and brothers at whim; when you have seen hate-filled policemen curse, kick and even kill your black brothers and sisters; when you see the vast majority of your twenty million Negro brothers smothering in an airtight cage of poverty in the midst of an affluent society; when you suddenly find your tongue twisted and your speech stammering as you seek to explain to your six-year-old daughter why she can't go to the public amusement park that has just been advertised on television, and see tears welling up in her eyes when she is told that Funtown is closed to colored children, and see ominous clouds of inferiority beginning to form in her little mental sky, and see her beginning to distort her personality by developing an unconscious bitter-ness toward white people; when you have to concoct an answer for a five-year-old son who is asking: "Daddy, why do white people treat colored people so mean?"; when you take a cross-country drive and find it neces-sary to sleep night after night in the uncomfortable corners of your automobile because no motel will accept you; when you are humiliated day in and day out by nagging signs reading "white" and "colored"; when your first name becomes "nigger," your middle name becomes "boy" (however old you are) and your last name becomes "John," and your wife and mother are never given the respected title of "Mrs."; when you are harried by day and haunted by night by the fact that you are a Negro, living constantly at tiptoe stance, never quite knowing what to expect next, and are plagued with inner fears and outer resentments; when you are forever fighting a degenerating sense of "nobodiness"— then you will understand why we find it difficult to wait. There comes a time when the cup of endurance runs over and men are no longer willing to be plunged into the abyss of despair. I hope, sirs, you can understand our legitimate and unavoidable impatience.

ACTIVE READING

The Active Reading exercise gives you an opportunity to reread the paragraph with a critical eye. By answering the questions that follow, you will extend and sharpen your understanding of the selection. This activity will help you become a more efficient reader and a more effective writer.

1. The author gets our attention with a dramatic statement that refers to four centuries of American history. Who is he talking about when he uses the word *we*?

Almost four hundred years ago, in 1619, African slaves were first brought to Virginia by the British. Although slavery was later abolished by The Emancipation Proclamation of 1863, and by the thirteenth amendment to the Constitution, African Americans remained second class citizens. Through the use of laws that segregated the races, black people were prevented from participating fully in American society. The Civil Rights Movement of the 1950s encouraged non-violent, direct action forms of protest that challenged and eventually overturned these laws.

2. In the second sentence the author makes an analogy, a comparison, to further reinforce the point he is making. Complete the following analogy. Asia and Africa: United States : : jetlike speed: _____

The author challenges his audience by comparing black people, the victims of segregation, to those who have never felt "the stinging darts of segregation."

3. What feeling do you associate with stinging darts?

4. Why might it be easy for those people who have never experienced segregation to tell others to wait?

The development part of the paragraph is a response to those who would counsel patience and recommend waiting. The author uses numerous examples to illustrate the pain experienced by black people because of segregation. These "stinging darts" are physical and psychological in nature. The author's objective is to have the reader share the black person's experience, in order to understand why it is difficult to wait any longer.

5. Examples of physical attacks on Negroes include which of the following:
   a. lynching
   b. drowning
   c. kicking
   d. killing
   e. all of the above

6. Equally painful is the "airtight cage of poverty in the midst of an affluent society." What word does the author use to describe the Negro's experience of this situation?

7. The author presents examples of psychological pain that adults experience as a result of segregation. Which of the following is <u>not</u> part of this list?

    a. humiliated by signs reading "white" and "colored"
    b. harried by day and haunted by night because you are a Negro
    c. plagued with inner fears and outer resentments
    d. being called "boy" no matter how old you are
    e. unable to travel cross-country

8. The author presents examples of psychological pain that children experience as a result of segregation. These include which of the following?

    a. being told that "Funtown is closed to colored children"
    b. experiencing feelings of inferiority because of your skin color
    c. developing an unconscious bitterness toward white people
    d. being treated meanly by white people and not knowing why
    e. all of the above

9. The author summarizes his view of segregation by saying that it involves "forever fighting a degenerating sense of 'nobodiness.' " What would you infer to be the author's meaning for the word *nobodiness*?

    a. feeling unimportant and nonexistent
    b. feeling unhappy and humiliated
    c. feeling hopeless and helpless
    d. all of the above

The development is one long sentence, set off by semicolons, in which the author uses the word *when* repeatedly to emphasize why continuing to wait is not an option. While the use of repetition here is extremely powerful, the unusually long sentence deviates from conventional form. Here the author is using **poetic license**, liberties taken in deviating from conventional fact or form to achieve a desired effect.

The concluding sentences reinforce the point of the paragraph, that if his audience were to experience segregation first hand, they, too, would not want to wait any longer.

10. According to the author, what is it that Negroes can wait for no longer?

Metaphors use imagery and symbolism to make comparisons between seemingly unlike things. The author uses metaphors here to make his experience more vivid for the reader. Each metaphor in items 11–15 below presents obstacles faced by black people in our society. Match each metaphor with its outcome.

11. stinging darts of segregation
    a. inflict physical and psychological pain
    b. smothering those inside
    c. threatening to distort personality
    d. trapped with no hope of getting out
    e. tolerance and patience run out

12. airtight cage of poverty
    a. inflict physical and psychological pain
    b. smothering those inside
    c. threatening to distort personality
    d. trapped with no hope of getting out
    e. tolerance and patience run out

13. ominous clouds of inferiority
    a. inflict physical and psychological pain
    b. smothering those inside
    c. threatening to distort personality
    d. trapped with no hope of getting out
    e. tolerance and patience run out

14. abyss of despair
    a. inflict physical and psychological pain
    b. smothering those inside
    c. threatening to distort personality
    d. trapped with no hope of getting out
    e. tolerance and patience run out

15. cup of endurance runs over
    a. inflict physical and psychological pain
    b. smothering those inside
    c. threatening to distort personality
    d. trapped with no hope of getting out
    e. tolerance and patience run out

16. The author uses transitional words and phrases to link ideas in this paragraph. List at least five.

17. The author's primary purpose in this selection is to:

    a. inform

    b. persuade

    c. entertain

18. In his effort to convince us the author uses:

    a. logic (facts)

    b. emotion (opinions)

    c. both logic and emotion

    d. neither logic nor emotion

The Active Reading exercise can be scored using the answer key and grading grid. Enter your grade in the progress chart.

GUIDED WRITING

The Guided Writing section at the end of this chapter (page 253) provides topics and plans for writing persuasive paragraphs and essays. Select a topic and write a paragraph by following the writing plan that begins on page 254.

Continue work in this chapter until you have finished all three Active Reading and Guided Writing activities. Upon completion, you will have written three new compositions for your portfolio (one paragraph and two essays). Record grades in your progress chart and, if available, on the Academic Credit Statement in your *Writing Portfolio Organizer*.

WHY JOHNNY CAN'T WRITE

by *Norman Cousins*

Norman Cousins was born in Union Hill, New Jersey, in 1915 and educated at Teachers College, Columbia University. He started his career as a journalist for the New York Evening Post, *and soon after began his long and distinguished association with the* Saturday Review of Literature. *His many books include a collection of his own columns,* Writing for Love or Money *(1949); a collection of the writing of others,* Great American Essays *(1967); and commentaries on the central issues of our time,* Human Options *(1981). He wrote about his personal experiences with a near fatal disease, and about the causes of illness and the effects of "positive emotions" in two popular books:* The Celebration of Life *(1974) and* Anatomy of an Illness *(1979). In the essay presented here, Cousins, the social activist and critic, expresses his concern about deteriorating writing skills in this country. He argues persuasively that the fault of the "writing crisis" is due in large measure to the way writing is assessed by educators.*

Word Alert

conveyance	to impart or communicate by statement, suggestion, gesture, or appearance; transmit
demon	a persistently tormenting person, force, or passion
distinction	the quality or state of being worthy; excellence or eminence of performance, character, or reputation
glibness	showing little thought, preparation, or concern
heinous	grossly wicked or deserving strong condemnation; abominable
immaculately	free from blemish or stain; free from error or fault; impeccably clean, spotless
integrated	to make into a whole by bringing all parts together; to join with something else, unite
intricate	having many elaborately arranged elements; complex
murkiness	cloudy in mind, muddled; hard to understand, obscure
precede	to come before in time
reflective	careful consideration; meditative

<dl>
<dt>sanctioning</dt>
<dd>to make legitimate, authorize; giving authoritative approval or consent</dd>
<dt>status symbol</dt>
<dd>usually a material object representing something abstract of high relative position</dd>
<dt>valid</dt>
<dd>being at once relevant and meaningful; having a conclusion correctly derived from premises</dd>
</dl>

1   **O**ne of the first questions in the final examination of a California high-school English class asked the student to write a 500-word essay describing a character in a play by Shakespeare. Another question asked him to reconstruct a vivid conversation from a recent novel he had read. There were at least four other questions involving skill in English composition. All this was to be done in two hours.

2   An examination in a Midwest college asked the student to write a short essay on the subject: "The status symbols today are those other than money can buy." The paper was to be completed in an hour.

3   These tests reveal little except the unfortunate role of schools in fostering and sanctioning bad writing habits. If Johnny can't write, one of the reasons may be a conditioning based on speed rather than respect for the creative process. Speed is neither a valid test of nor a proper preparation for competence in writing. It makes for murkiness, glibness, disorganization. It takes the beauty out of the language. It rules out respect for the reflective thought that should precede expression. It runs counter to the word-by-word and line-by-line reworking that enables a piece to be finely knit. . . .

4   Speed is not the only demon. Neatness is often valued above style. A composition paper full of corrections and crossed-out lines may be far more valuable to the teacher in appraising a student's awareness of the preciousness of the right word or phrase than an immaculately typed essay. Writing is one subject in which the student ought to be encouraged to ramble around and even be messy, if need be, in search of his answers. Nor is there anything particularly heinous about the use of a dictionary during an English examination or even a test in spelling. Not everyone can spell, even with the most conscientious study; but everyone can develop the habit of using a good dictionary effectively and consistently.

It would be a mistake to blame it all on the English teacher. Poor 5
writing habits are developed in a wide range of courses. Homework
assignments aren't always integrated. It is not unusual for a child to be
given three overnight writing assignments, any one of which requires
several full days' work to be done properly. Moreover, the teacher doesn't
always have complete authority in the preparation of examinations, especially those of a year-end or state-wide nature. The root of the problem is
that not much thought has been given to the requirements of good writing.
The concept of expression as an intricate and highly demanding art has
never fully been accepted.

The area in which a poor education shows up first is in self-expression, 6
oral or written. It makes little difference how many university courses or
degrees a man may own. If he cannot use words to move an idea from one
point to another, his education is incomplete. Taking in a fact is only part
of the educational process. The ability to pass it along with reasonable
clarity and even distinction is another. The business of assembling the
right words, putting them down in proper sequence, enabling each one to
pull its full weight in the conveyance of meaning—these are the essentials.
A school is where these essentials should feel at home.

ACTIVE READING

The Active Reading exercise gives you an opportunity to reread the essay with a
critical eye. By answering the questions that follow, you will extend and sharpen
your understanding of the selection. This activity will help you become a more
efficient reader and a more effective writer.

INTRODUCTORY PARAGRAPHS (par. 1–2)

The author uses examples to illustrate what is typically required on exams in
composition. He helps us to see that what is required is extraordinary because
of the time limits imposed on the student.

1. A final exam in a high school English class asked the student to:

    a. write a 500-word essay describing a character in a play by
       Shakespeare.
    b. reconstruct a conversation from a novel.
    c. answer six questions involving skill in English composition.
    d. all of the above

2. The amount of time allowed to complete the final exam mentioned above was:

    a. one hour
    b. two hours
    c. three hours
    d. four hours

3. What opinion do you think the author has about the amount of time allotted to complete the exam?

    a. more than enough time
    b. not enough time
    c. just enough time
    d. none of the above

4. A question on a college exam asked students to write a short essay on the subject: "The status symbols today are those other than money can buy." This is a poor question because:

    a. the question is too broadly stated.
    b. it's difficult to write a specific answer to a vague question.
    c. the time allotted to answer the question is too short.
    d. all of the above

DEVELOPMENT PARAGRAPH *(par. 3)*

The author offers his opinion about these tests, saying that they foster and sanction bad writing habits. He also uses cause and effect to show the relationship between writing fast and writing competently. Identify each phrase as either a cause or an effect statement. Remember, the *cause* is the reason why and the *effect* is the result. Ask yourself, "What leads to what?"

5. (a) If Johnny can't write, (b) one of the reasons may be a conditioning based on speed . . .

6. (a) Conditioning based on speed (b) leads to little or no respect for the creative process.

7. (a) An emphasis on speed (b) does not adequately prepare the student to write competently.

8. (a) Tests for competency in writing that rely on speed (b) are not valid, i.e., these tests do not measure what they say they measure.

9. (a) The focus on speed in writing (b) leads to murkiness, glibness, and disorganization.

10. In assessing writing competency, which of the following is an effect of a focus on speed?

   a. Speed takes the beauty out of the language.
   b. Speed rules out respect for reflective thought.
   c. Speed runs counter to revision that enables a piece to be finely knit.
   d. all of the above

DEVELOPMENT PARAGRAPH *(par. 4)*

This paragraph focuses on the importance of revision as part of the writing process. **Revision** has two meanings. The dictionary definition of the word *revision* is "to amend or revamp, to prepare a new version of." Separated into its component parts, *re vision* means to *see again*. The author explains how an emphasis on neatness, as well as on speed, works against the writing process.

11. In appraising a student's writing, which does the author believe is most valuable?

   a. a composition paper full of corrections and crossed-out lines
   b. an immaculately typed essay
   c. no spelling errors
   d. student awareness of the right word or phrase

12. The author believes that the writing process should allow the student to:

   a. be messy
   b. ramble around
   c. search for answers
   d. all of the above

13. Which does the author believe to be more important, knowing how to spell or knowing how to use the dictionary?

DEVELOPMENT PARAGRAPH *(par. 5)*

In this paragraph the author attempts to explain the causes of students' poor writing habits.

14. Which of the following is a cause of poor writing habits?

   a. Writing assignments in different subject areas aren't coordinated; too many are given at one time.
   b. There is not enough time allotted to do writing assignments properly.
   c. Year-end or state-wide tests are poor ways of assessing writing.
   d. Teachers in many subject areas often lack understanding of what good writing requires.
   e. all of the above

In summary, the author says that the concept of expression as an intricate and highly demanding art has never fully been accepted. The focus has been on writing as a product rather than as a process.

CONCLUDING PARAGRAPH *(par. 6)*

The author concludes by expressing his opinion about the importance of writing in education.

15. The more courses and degrees you have, the better you will be at self-expression, oral or written. Is this statement true or false?

16. The mark of a well-educated person includes being able to:

    a. use words to move an idea from one point to another.
    b. pass facts along with reasonable clarity and even distinction.
    c. assemble the right words in the proper sequence.
    d. have each word be effective in the conveyance of meaning.
    e. all of the above

17. Who is Johnny?

    a. the author's son
    b. a high school student
    c. a college student
    d. a fictitious person who symbolizes any student

18. According to the author, where should the essentials of self-expression feel at home?

19. The author uses transitional words and phrases to link ideas in this essay. List at least five.

20. The author's primary purpose in this selection is to:

    a. inform
    b. persuade
    c. entertain

21. In his effort to convince us the author uses:

    a. logic (facts)
    b. emotion (opinions)
    c. both logic and emotion
    d. neither logic nor emotion

The Active Reading exercise can be scored using the answer key and grading grid. Enter your grade in the progress chart.

GUIDED WRITING

The Guided Writing section at the end of this chapter (page 253) provides topics and plans for writing persuasive paragraphs and essays. Select a topic and write a short essay by following the writing plan that begins on page 255. Continue work in this chapter until you have finished all three Active Reading and Guided Writing activities.

A NATION AT RISK

by David P. Gardner

David P. Gardner was born in Berkeley, California in 1933. He was educated at Brigham Young University and at the University of California, Berkeley. He served as Professor of Higher Education and in various administrative posts in the University of California. From 1973 to 1983 he served as President of the University of Utah, and since 1983 as President of the University of California. In 1981, Ronald Reagan appointed him to head a blue-ribbon commission, the U.S. Commission on Excellence in Education, to study and report on the condition of education in America. After eighteen months' work, this task force published a report entitled A Nation at Risk, *from which the following essay is excerpted.* A Nation at Risk *is a call to alarm. In powerful language, this report warns the American people about the worsening state of our educational system and outlines the drastic effects this decline may have unless fundamental reforms are initiated.*

Word Alert

attainment	achievement or accomplishment; to reach an end
depository	a place where something is deposited for safekeeping
dictum	a formal authorative pronouncement of a principle, proposition, or opinion
discretion	ability to make responsible decisions; freedom or power to act or judge on one's own
disenfranchised	to deprive an individual of a right of citizenship or of a privilege
global village	the concept of distant parts of the world connected by electronic means such as television, telephones, facsimile machines
idlers	those who pass time without working or avoiding work; individuals who are shiftless or lazy
malignant	showing great malevolence, evil; highly injurious, pernicious
mediocrity	the quality or state of being mediocre; average or moderate to low in quality

pluralism	a condition of society in which numerous distinct ethnic, religious, or cultural groups coexist within one nation
preeminence	outstanding; superior to all others
Sputnik	Sputnik was the first artificial satellite launched into orbit by the U.S.S.R. in October 1957. This spurred the dormant U.S. space program into action, leading to international competition popularly known as the "space race."
subsidies	financial assistance given by one person or government to another
undergirds	to gird, support, or strengthen from beneath
unilateral	involving or affecting only one side

Our Nation is at risk. Our once unchallenged preeminence in commerce, industry, science, and technological innovation is being overtaken by competitors throughout the world. This report is concerned with only one of the many causes and dimensions of the problem, but it is the one that undergirds American prosperity, security, and civility. We report to the American people that while we can take justifiable pride in what our schools and colleges have historically accomplished and contributed to the United States and the well-being of its people, the educational foundations of our society are presently being eroded by a rising tide of mediocrity that threatens our very future as a Nation and a people. What was unimaginable a generation ago has begun to occur—others are watching and surpassing our educational attainments.

If an unfriendly foreign power had attempted to impose on America the mediocre educational performance that exists today, we might well have viewed it as an act of war. As it stands, we have allowed this to happen to ourselves. We have even squandered the gains in student achievement made in the wake of the Sputnik challenge. Moreover, we have dismantled essential support systems which helped make those gains possible. We have, in effect, been committing an act of unthinking, unilateral educational disarmament.

Our society and its educational institutions seem to have lost sight of the basic purposes of schooling, and of the high expectations and disciplined effort needed to attain them. This report, the result of 18 months of study, seeks to generate reform of our educational system in fundamental ways to renew the Nation's commitment to schools and colleges of high quality throughout the length and breadth of our land. . . .

4   On the occasion of the Commission's first meeting President Reagan noted the central importance of education in American life when he said: "Certainly there are few areas of American life as important to our society, to our people, and to our families as our schools and colleges." This report, therefore, is as much an open letter to the American people as it is a report to the Secretary of Education. We are confident that the American people, properly informed, will do what is right for their children and for the generations to come.

5   History is not kind to idlers. The time is long past when America's destiny was assured simply by an abundance of natural resources and inexhaustible human enthusiasm, and by our relative isolation from the malignant problems of older civilizations. The world is indeed one global village. We live among determined, well-educated, and strongly moti-vated competitors. We compete with them for international standing and markets, not only with products but also with the ideas of our laboratories and neighborhood workshops. America's position in the world may once have been reasonably secure with only a few exceptionally well-trained men and women. It is no longer.

6   The risk is not only that the Japanese make automobiles more effi-ciently than Americans and have government subsidies for development and export. It is not just that the South Koreans recently built the world's most efficient steel mill, or that American machine tools, once the pride of the world, are being displaced by German products. It is also that these developments signify a redistribution of trained capability throughout the globe. Knowledge, learning, information, and skilled intelligence are the new raw materials of international commerce and are today spreading throughout the world as vigorously as miracle drugs, synthetic fertilizers, and blue jeans did earlier. If only to keep and improve on the slim competitive edge we still retain in world markets, we must dedicate our-selves to the reform of our educational system for the benefit of all—old and young alike, affluent and poor, majority and minority. Learning is the indispensible investment required for success in the "information age" we are entering.

7   Our concern, however, goes well beyond matters such as industry and commerce. It also includes the intellectual, moral, and spiritual strengths of our people which knit together the very fabric of our society. The people of the United States need to know that individuals in our society

who do not possess the levels of skill, literacy, and training essential to this new era will be effectively disenfranchised, not simply from the material rewards that accompany competent performance, but also from the chance to participate fully in our national life. A high level of shared education is essential to a free, democratic society and to the fostering of a common culture, especially in a country that prides itself on pluralism and individual freedom.

For our country to function, citizens must be able to reach some common understandings on complex issues, often on short notice and on the basis of conflicting or incomplete evidence. Education helps form these common understandings, a point Thomas Jefferson made long ago in his justly famous dictum: 8

> I know no safe depository of the ultimate powers of the society but the people themselves; and if we think them not enlightened enough to exercise their control with a wholesome discretion, the remedy is not to take it from them but to inform their discretion.

Part of what is at risk is the promise first made on this continent: All, regardless of race or class or economic status, are entitled to a fair chance and to the tools for developing their individual powers of mind and spirit to the utmost. This promise means that all children by virtue of their own efforts, competently guided, can hope to attain the mature and informed judgment needed to secure gainful employment and to manage their own lives, thereby serving not only their own interests but also the progress of society itself. 9

ACTIVE READING

The Active Reading exercise gives you an opportunity to reread the essay with a critical eye. By answering the questions that follow, you will extend and sharpen your understanding of the selection. This activity will help you become a more efficient reader and a more effective writer.

INTRODUCTORY PARAGRAPH *(par. 1)*

The author gets our attention in the first sentence by sounding an alarm, "Our Nation is at risk." The rest of the paragraph explains how and why our nation is at risk.

1. Which of the following best describes what is happening to our preeminence in commerce, industry, science, and technological innovation?

   a. it remains unchallenged
   b. it is being challenged worldwide
   c. it is being overtaken by competitors worldwide
   d. all of the above

2. The author's report identifies the problem as having:

   a. one cause
   b. two causes
   c. three causes
   d. many causes

3. What is the one factor that undergirds American prosperity, security, and civility?

4. According to the author, in what can the American people take justifiable pride?

5. The author offers his thesis, the point he will set out to prove in this essay. Which of the following best summarizes the author's thesis?

   a. Our preeminence in commerce and industry is being threatened.
   b. There are many causes and dimensions of the problem.
   c. Education is of minor importance to American prosperity and security.
   d. The erosion of our educational foundations threatens the future of our society.

6. What is happening now that was unimaginable a generation ago?

7. Select the best interpretation for the metaphor "a rising tide of mediocrity" as it is used in the selection.

   a. high waters threaten the future of our nation
   b. There is a growing number of inadequately educated students in our country.
   c. American prosperity, security, and civility are on the rise
   d. American schools and colleges can be lauded for present accomplishments

DEVELOPMENT PARAGRAPH *(par. 2)*

The author presents a hypothetical situation that illustrates what we have done to ourselves as a nation. He develops the paragraph with the use of cause and effect. Identify each phrase below as either the cause or effect part of the statement. Remember, the *cause* is the reason why and the *effect* is the result or outcome. Ask yourself, "What leads to what?"

8. (a) If an unfriendly power attempted to impose on America a mediocre educational system, (b) we might well view it as an act of war.

9. (a) As it stands, (b) we have allowed this to happen to ourselves.

10. (a) The Sputnik challenge (b) resulted in gains in student achievement.

The last time our nation was challenged to improve our educational system was in the Sputnik era. The Russians launched the first unmanned satellite to orbit the earth, prompting President Kennedy to act. He established a crash program to improve our scientific capability and put a man on the moon by the end of the 1960s.

11. (a) We have squandered gains in student achievement (b) by dismantling the essential support systems that made those gains possible.

12. (a) Through our actions (b) we have been committing an act of unthinking, unilateral educational disarmament.

Facts not included in the selection but presented in the Report illustrate the author's assertion that we have been committing unilateral educational disarmament. Since Sputnik was launched, the average achievement of high school students on most standardized tests has declined. The Scholastic Aptitude Tests (SAT) show a steady decline in average verbal and math scores from 1963 to the present. The College Board achievement tests reveal consistent declines in the sciences, mathematics, and English. Educational researcher Paul Hurd concluded that, "We are raising a new generation of Americans that is scientifically and technologically illiterate."

DEVELOPMENT PARAGRAPH *(par. 3)*

13. The author infers that our educational institutions have lost sight of three things. Which of the following is <u>not</u> part of this list?

   a. basic purposes of schooling
   b. high expectations
   c. educational disarmament
   d. disciplined effort

14. The Report:

   a. seeks to reform our educational system.
   b. proposes the need for further study of the problem.
   c. states that the situation will improve regardless of what we do.
   d. recommends reform of only certain elite schools.

DEVELOPMENT PARAGRAPH *(par. 4)*

15. At the Commission's first meeting, who noted the central importance of education in American life?

   a. President Kennedy
   b. President Reagan
   c. the Secretary of Education
   d. Thomas Jefferson

16. The author views the Report as an open letter to the American people. He expects the American people to:

   a. write letters to the Secretary of Education.
   b. ask to be properly informed the next time there is a problem.
   c. do the right thing for their children and for the generations to come.
   d. all of the above

DEVELOPMENT PARAGRAPH *(par. 5)*

In this part of the essay the author discusses the ways in which our lack of attention to education has created a risk for America.

17. In the past America's position in the world was assured by three conditions. Which of the following is <u>not</u> one of these conditions?

   a. abundance of natural resources
   b. inexhaustible human enthusiasm
   c. close knit family ties
   d. isolation from problems of older civilizations

18. According to the author, "The world is indeed one global village." How has this concept altered our once dominant position in the world?

    a. We now live among determined, well-educated, and strongly motivated competitors.
    b. We compete for international standing and markets for our products.
    c. Ideas coming from our laboratories and neighborhood workshops compete with ideas generated in other countries.
    d. all of the above

19. The author concludes that America's position in the world is:

    a. reasonably secure
    b. dependent on foreign competitors
    c. no longer secure
    d. dependent on natural resources

The first sentence of this paragraph says "History is not kind to idlers." Because we have not moved ahead we find ourselves falling behind. As a nation we have accomplished a great deal and expected this to carry us through. We are learning the hard way that past success does not insure future success.

DEVELOPMENT PARAGRAPH (par. 6)

This paragraph looks more directly at the nature of the risk to us from our competitors. The author compares America with its competitors in industries in which we were once preeminent.

20. By comparison to Americans, the Japanese:

    a. make automobiles more efficiently.
    b. are the largest producers of miracle drugs.
    c. built the world's most efficient steel mill.
    d. manufacture the best machine tools.

21. By comparison to Americans, the South Koreans:

    a. make automobiles more efficiently.
    b. are the largest producers of miracle drugs.
    c. built the world's most efficient steel mill.
    d. manufacture the best machine tools.

22. By comparison to Americans, the Germans:

   a. make automobiles more efficiently
   b. are the largest producers of miracle drugs.
   c. built the world's most efficient steel mill.
   d. manufacture the best machine tools.

These examples of industries in which the United States has been surpassed by its competitors illustrate a global trend toward redistribution of trained capability. It is here that the United States is at greatest risk.

23. According to the author, which of the following is <u>not</u> one of the new raw materials of international commerce.

   a. knowledge
   b. synthetic fertilizers
   c. information
   d. skilled intelligence

24. Which country would you infer has been responsible for the spread of miracle drugs, synthetic fertilizers, and blue jeans throughout the world?

   a. Japan
   b. South Korea
   c. Germany
   d. United States

The author makes a clear link between the need to reform our educational system and our ability to compete with the other nations of the world. In the sentences below, identify each phrase as either the cause or effect part of the statement. Remember to ask yourself, "What leads to what?"

25. (a) If only to keep and improve on the slim competitive edge we still retain in world markets, (b) we must dedicate ourselves to the reform of our educational system for the benefit of all.

26. Who will benefit from such an effort?

   a. old and young
   b. affluent and poor
   c. majority and minority
   d. all of the above

27. What indispensible investment is required for success in the "information age?"

    a. raw materials
    b. synthetic fertilizers
    c. learning
    d. machine tools

DEVELOPMENT PARAGRAPH *(par. 7)*

In a series of cause and effect statements the author stresses the importance of education above other matters, such as industry and commerce. In the sentences below, identify each phrase as either the cause or effect part of the statement.

28. (a) The intellectual, moral, and spiritual strengths of our people (b) knit together the very fabric of our society.

29. (a) . . . individuals in our society who do not possess the levels of skill, literacy, and training essential to this new era (b) will be effectively disenfranchised, (c) not simply from the material rewards that accompany competent performance, (d) but also from the chance to participate fully in our national life.

30. (a) A high level of shared education is essential (b) to a free, democratic society (c) and to the fostering of a common culture . . .

The author concludes the paragraph by referring to the United States as "a country that prides itself on pluralism and individual freedom." Among its major competitors, the United States is the most pluralistic society. The people of Germany, Japan, and South Korea are each relatively homogeneous with regard to language, religion, ethnicity, and culture. As a consequence the United States, more than other countries, needs a high level of shared education to bind a diverse people together.

DEVELOPMENT PARAGRAPH *(par. 8)*

In this paragraph the author expands on the idea of our country's need for education in order to reach common understandings. In the sentences below, identify each phrase as either the cause or effect part of the statement.

31. (a) For our country to function, (b) citizens must be able to reach some common understandings on complex issues . . .

32. (a) Education (b) helps form these common understandings.

Thomas Jefferson believed that the people themselves are the safest depository for the ultimate powers of society. In the sentence below, identify each phrase as either the cause or effect part of the statement.

33. (a) ". . . if we think them [the people] not enlightened enough to exercise their control with a wholesome discretion, (b) the remedy is not to take it [control] from them but to inform their discretion.

34. What does Jefferson mean by the phrase "inform their discretion?"

CONCLUDING PARAGRAPH *(par. 9)*

The author says, "Part of what is at risk is the promise first made on this continent." He is referring to the Declaration of Independence, written by Thomas Jefferson and adopted by the Continental Congress on July 4, 1776. It said, "We hold these truths to be self-evident, that all men are created equal, that they are endowed by their Creator with certain unalienable Rights, that among these are Life, Liberty, and the Pursuit of Happiness."

35. The author's thesis that we are a nation at risk is repeated in his concluding paragraph. Which of the following best restates the author's thesis in this essay?

    a. Some people need to be educated in order to make informed decisions.
    b. It is the promise of the Declaration of Independence that everybody will have equal opportunity.
    c. Our children need to be well educated in order to be gainfully employed and manage their own lives, thereby serving their own interests and the progress of society as well.
    d. Race, class, and economic status shall determine who will be able to develop their powers of mind and spirit.

36. If we do not provide a high level education for all, we risk losing:

    a. a free, democratic society.
    b. ability to manage our own lives.
    c. a high standard of living.
    d. all of the above

37. The author uses transitional words and phrases to link ideas in this essay. List at least five.

38. The author's primary purpose in this selection is to:

    a. inform

    b. persuade

    c. entertain

39. In his effort to convince us the author uses:

    a. logic (facts)

    b. emotion (opinions)

    c. both logic and emotion

    d. neither logic nor emotion

The Active Reading exercise can be scored using the answer key and grading grid. Enter your grade in the progress chart.

The Guided Writing section that begins on the next page provides topics and plans for writing persuasive paragraphs and essays. Select a topic and write an extended essay by following the writing plan that begins on page 255.

GUIDED WRITING

This part of the chapter will help you apply what you have learned about writing persuasive paragraphs and essays. Choose one of the topics listed below for each writing assignment that you do. If you want to write about something else, ask your instructor if the topic is appropriate for writing persuasion. Follow the plan that applies to write your composition. Submit your completed composition to the instructor for evaluation. When you receive a grade for this work, enter it in the progress chart.

WRITING TOPICS

- Martin Luther King was jailed for doing something he believed in, supporting the cause of civil rights in the United States. Have you ever confronted authority and been punished for doing what you believed was the right thing to do? Persuade the reader that your actions were fair, reasonable, and justified.

- Many "experts" have offered facts and opinions as to the reasons why Johnny can't write. Think about what has helped or hindered your learning how to write. Based on your experience, make recommendations to improve the situation for other students. Present convincing arguments.

- In this age of electronics in which people communicate via telephone, radio, television, computers, and FAX machines, it is not necessary to know how to write. Argue for or against this proposition.

- Many of our competitors in the international marketplace argue that we are falling behind because our society is too diverse. Others say that diversity and pluralism have helped to make our country successful. Present an argument in favor of one viewpoint or the other.

- There are other issues in the United States today that are highly controversial. Choose one from the following list and argue for or against the stated proposition:

    Our basic right to free speech should be protected, no matter how distasteful our statements.

    A woman's decision to have an abortion is hers alone and should not be subject to law.

    Because alcohol and tobacco are both hazardous to the health of the consumer, as well as to innocent bystanders, they should be reclassified as dangerous drugs and their sale banned.

People in many parts of the world are oppressed politically, economically, or both. As a beacon of freedom in the world, the United States should have an open door immigration policy.

The official language of the United States should be English, even though many citizens are literate only in another language.

PREWRITING: GENERATING IDEAS

Now that you have selected a topic, you will need to gather information and generate ideas before you begin to write. If you are writing about a personal experience you will probably rely on your memory, other people's input, and your own creativity. Other topics may require that you use reference works to collect this information for your composition.

To write persuasively you will need to offer reasons that appeal to logic, emotion, or both. If your appeal is to emotions, use strong words that produce a reaction in the reader. Use imagery such as similes and metaphors to make your appeals vivid. The tone you use can put the reader in a frame of mind to accept what you have to say. In making a rational appeal, present data and cite authorities. Make a list of the major points in your argument and gather information that supports each point. Include facts, opinions, examples, comparisons, quotations, and imagery. Refer to this list as you follow the plan for writing a persuasive paragraph or essay.

WRITING PLAN: THE PARAGRAPH

1. Decide the point of view of the narrator, first or third person. Write an introduction that gets the reader's attention and presents your point of view.

2. Set the tone for the paragraph, your attitude toward the subject. The tone might be serious or humorous, formal or informal.

3. Use your list of major points and the information you gathered to help you appeal to logic, emotion, or both. Convince the reader to see things your way by using facts, opinions, examples, comparisons, quotations, and imagery.

4. Write a conclusion to your paragraph that restates the topic and presents an overview, summarizes, or expresses an opinion.

5. To create unity in your writing, make sure that each sentence in the paragraph relates to the topic. Your writing will be coherent if ideas follow one another in a logical pattern and sentences flow smoothly from one to the other. Use transitions to link or connect ideas. The list of

transitional words and phrases at the back of this book is for your use and reference when you write (see pages 259-264).

6. Use variety in your choice of words to maintain reader interest. Where appropriate, use figurative language to increase the impact of your words and to stimulate the reader's imagination. The most commonly used figures of speech are the simile, metaphor, personification, and hyperbole. Definitions of literary and rhetorical terms can be found in the Glossary on pages 265-270.

7. Create a title for your paragraph, a word or phrase that captures the reader's interest and tells what you are writing about.

8. Use the *Checklist for Revision* provided at the end of this section to help you review and revise your paragraph

WRITING PLAN: SHORT AND EXTENDED ESSAYS

While short and extended essays are similar—both have introductory and concluding paragraphs—the extended essay has more development paragraphs. "Why Johnny Can't Write" convinces us that an emphasis on speed and neatness is part of the problem. The author uses examples, cause and effect, explanation, and definition in this short essay. "A Nation At Risk," an extended essay, persuades us that our children need to be well educated in order for our society to survive. Here the author supports his thesis with explanation, cause and effect, comparison and contrast, and examples.

Introductory Paragraph(s)

1. Decide the narrator's point of view. Is the narrator of the essay involved in the action (first person), or an observer outside the action (third person)?

2. Begin with a strong statement or a question that focuses the reader's interest on the subject. Tell what the essay is about by introducing your topic and purpose. This is the thesis statement, the main idea to be supported throughout the essay.

3. Use your introductory paragraph(s) to set the tone for the essay, your attitude toward the subject. The tone might be serious or humorous, formal or informal.

4. An extended essay may contain more than one introductory paragraph.

Development Paragraph(s)

1. Development paragraphs can be used to discuss each of the major points of, and reasons for, your argument. Let the reader know the focus of each paragraph.

2. Use your list of major points and the information you gathered to help you appeal to logic, emotion, or both. Convince the reader to see things your way by using facts, opinions, examples, comparisons, quotations, and imagery.

3. If you are writing an extended essay, you can present more points and provide more reasons in support of your argument. Make use of other strategies such as explanation, definition, cause and effect, comparison and contrast, and illustration to reinforce your thesis.

4. All sentences in a paragraph should relate to the topic and to one another. All paragraphs in an essay should support the topic and follow some logical order. Use transitions to link ideas within paragraphs and to make connections between paragraphs. Refer to the list of transitional words and phrases on pages 259–264.

5. Use variety in your choice of words to maintain reader interest. Where appropriate, use figurative language to increase the impact of your words and to stimulate the reader's imagination. The most commonly used figures of speech are the simile, metaphor, personification, and hyperbole. Definitions of literary and rhetorical terms can be found in the Glossary on pages 265-270.

Concluding Paragraph(s)

1. Be sure to restate the thesis in some way for emphasis. Present your opinion once again and reach a conclusion that reinforces the point of your essay.

2. More than one paragraph may be used to conclude an extended essay.

3. The checklist on the next page will help you to review and revise your essay.

note: The title of your essay should be a word or phrase that captures the reader's attention and tells what you are writing about. Create a title for your first draft and review it before making it final.

CHECKLIST FOR REVISION

1. My paragraph/essay has a first- or third-person point of view. My opening sentences appeal to the reader's interest, introduce my topic, and set the tone. If I am writing an essay, my thesis statement appears in the opening paragraph(s).

2. I use my list of major points and reasons to appeal to logic, emotion, or both. I try to convince the reader to see things my way by using facts, opinions, examples, comparisons, quotations, and imagery.

3. Each development paragraph in my essay presents a different point or reason in support of my argument. I let the reader know the focus of each paragraph.

4. My extended essay presents more points and provides more reasons in support of my argument. Where appropriate, I make use of other strategies such as explanation, definition, cause and effect, comparison and contrast, and illustration to reinforce my thesis.

5. In concluding my paragraph or essay, I restate the thesis for emphasis. I present my opinion once again and reach a conclusion that reinforces my point of view.

6. Sentences within each paragraph relate to the topic. Development paragraphs follow a logical order and support the point of the essay. I use transitions to link ideas within paragraphs and to make connections between paragraphs.

7. I use variety in my choice of words to maintain reader interest. Where appropriate, I use figurative language to increase the impact of my words and to stimulate the reader's imagination.

8. As I revise the form and content of my work, I correct errors in punctuation, capitalization, spelling, grammar, and usage.

9. The title of my paragraph or essay tells what I wrote about and captures the reader's interest.

Continue work in this chapter until you have finished all three Active Reading and Guided Writing activities.

TRANSITIONS

Transitional words and phrases can help you achieve coherence and unity in your writing. Use transitions to link ideas within paragraphs and to make connections between paragraphs. Connect your ideas with transitions in order to show time relationships, or place and position. You can also use transitions to express relationships between ideas, show comparison and contrast, or make summary statements and draw conclusions. You will find that some writing strategies make use of one kind of transition more than another. Transitions are grouped here according to the ways in which they function in writing.

TIME RELATIONSHIPS

after	first
after a while	following
after that	for a long time
afterwards	forever
always	fourth
as	from time to time
as soon as	immediately
at	in other times
at length	in retrospect
at the end	in some ages
at the same time	in the end
before	in the future
begin by	in the meantime
by the time	last
constantly	later
currently	long past
during	meanwhile
endlessly	next
early	next time
earlier	now
even now	now and again
even then	often
eventually	once
finally	only when

second
secondly
several years ago
slowly
someday
sometimes
soon
sooner
still
subsequently
suddenly

then
third
thirdly
this time
today
too often
until
usually
when
whenever
while

PLACE AND POSITION

above
across
adjacent
adjacent to
ahead
along
along the way
alongside
amid
amidst
among
around
at
at first
at the end
at the side
behind
below
beneath
beside
between
beyond
by
down

everywhere
far
finally
first
former
from
from aloft
here
horizontally
in
in front of
in the back
in the background
in the distance
in the first place
in the foreground
in the front of
in the midst of
inside
into
last
latter
near
nearby

next	secondarily
next to	there
on	third
one after another	through
opposite	throughout
out of	toward
outside	under
over	upon
parallel	vertically
primarily	where
second	within

RELATIONSHIPS BETWEEN IDEAS

about	at least
about this	because
according to	because of
accordingly	begin by
actually	begin with
all this	besides
along with	between
also	both
although	bring about
almost	but
and	by
another	certainly
apparently	contrary to
as	consequently
as a consequence	despite
as a result	differ
as an illustration	due to
as for	either . . . or
as if	equally
as it stands	especially
as it worked out	even
as long as	even as
as much as	even if
as though	even then
as well as	even though

except	like
except for	likely
except that	likely to
finally	likewise
for	mainly
for example	may be
for instance	maybe
for one thing	merely
for that reason	might well
for this reason	more important
from	more importantly
from time to time	moreover
further	most important
furthermore	most importantly
granted	most likely
have in common	namely
however	naturally
if	neither . . . nor
if need be	nevertheless
if only	no matter
important	no matter that
in addition	no matter what
in addition to	not only
in effect	not to mention
in fact	obviously
in order to	of
in some cases	of course
in spite of	on the basis of
in the same way	on the contrary
in this respect	on the other hand
in this situation	one of the reasons
in turn	only
indeed	only when
instead	or
instead of	other than
just	otherwise
just as	perhaps
lead to	probably

rather than
regardless of
same
seemingly
similar
similarly
simply
since
so
so that
specifically
such as
surely
the fact that
the reason for
the reverse
the same as
then
there comes a time
there is every indication that

thereby
therefore
though
thus
to be sure
too
too often
unless
unlike
usually
what's more
whereas
when
whether
whether or not
while
with
with respect to
yet

COMPARISON

alike
as
as well as
both
compared with
have in common
in comparison
in like manner
in the same way
less than
like

likewise
more than
none can compare with
not only
or
same
similar
similarly
the same as
too

CONTRAST

against
although
as opposed to

at the same time
but
contrary to

conversely
despite
differ
even though
except
except that
however
in contrast
in contrast to
in spite of
instead
instead of
much less
neither

nevertheless
nonetheless
nor
on the contrary
on the other hand
still
the reverse of
than
though
unless
unlike
whereas
while
yet

SUMMARY STATEMENTS AND DRAWING CONCLUSIONS

accordingly
all this and more
also
and if
as a result
as a result of
as for
as long as
because
because of
bring about
can only lead to
caused by
consequently
due to
due to this
evidently
finally
for of course
for this reason
hence
if

inevitably
in conclusion
in retrospect
in the simplest terms
in view of
it is evident
it seems
it turned out that
led to
not only . . . but also
on the basis of
perhaps
since
so
so that
summarily
taken all together
there is every indication that
there is every reason to conclude
thereby
therefore
thus

GLOSSARY

acronym   The word formed from the initial letters of a name, like *WAC* for Women's Army Corps, or by combining initial letters or parts of a series of words, like *radar* for **ra**dar **d**etecting **an**d **r**anging.

alliteration   The repetition of similar or identical sounds at the beginning of words is known as alliteration. It is used to create melody and establish mood. "The soft, soothing sounds of the sea" is an example of alliteration

allusion   A reference to some famous historical, literary, or cultural figure, event, or work that makes a comparison and gives us a new perspective on an idea. To say that someone has "the patience of Job" means that he is enduring hardships as did the biblical figure of that name. The allusion may be to myth, religion, or other aspect of ancient or modern culture.

alternating pattern   A method of comparison and contrast that involves a point-by-point examination of two subjects selected for discussion.

analogy   A form of comparison in which the writer explains one thing by showing its similarity to a different class of things.

anecdote   A very short humorous or entertaining incident, often based on personal experience.

block pattern   A method of comparison and contrast in which all information about the first subject is presented, followed by all information about the second subject.

cause and effect   Cause and effect writing is a form of exposition that explains relationships and tells why something is the way it is. The use of cause and effect helps to answer the question, "Why?" The cause is the reason why and the effect is the result or outcome.

characterization   A description of people in a written work that captures as vividly as possible their qualities. This may include physical appearance, actions, words, thoughts, and feelings.

classification   The chief purpose of a classification essay is to explain: to outline the various parts of a classification system or to define, analyze, and justify the system's organizing principle. Classification makes it easier to find things, as well as easier to understand, evaluate, and use them.

climax   The point of greatest excitement or intensity in a story.

comparison and contrast   In writing an essay using comparison and contrast, characteristics of two subjects are examined for the purpose of identifying their similarities and differences. In making comparisons we look for similarities between two or more things, people, places, or ideas; contrast involves finding differences.

composition	A term used for an essay or for any piece of writing that reveals a careful plan.
conflict	An external or internal problem or struggle of some kind. In a story there may be a single conflict or several related conflicts.
connotation	The implied, underlying, emotional meaning of a word, as opposed to its literal meaning.
definition	You can use definition to make clear the meaning of a word, an object, or an abstract concept. Definition helps to identify the special qualities of a person, place, animal, object, process, or concept, and distinguish it from others that are similar.
denotation	The literal or exact meaning of a word.
description	Description is used to create impressions that are vivid, real and lifelike for the reader. By appealing to the five senses the writer tells us how something looks, sounds, tastes, smells, and how it feels to the touch. These are five ways of describing a person, place, thing, idea, emotion, or event.
dialogue	Conversation between characters through which the author can establish the situation, develop characters, present actions and ideas, and express themes.
double entendre	A word or expression capable of two interpretations, one of which often has a risqué meaning.
essay	An essay is a composition with a thesis statement that states the main idea, reflects the author's purpose to inform, persuade, or entertain (amuse), and asserts a point of view. A good essay has a strong central theme and something important to say to the reader.
etymology	The history of a word or phrase shown by tracing its development since its earliest recorded occurrence in the language where it is found.
exaggeration	An overstatement or overemphasis, often with comic effect.
exposition	Writing that informs the reader by explaining facts and ideas so that they are easily understood. The subject of an explanation might be a person, place, thing, event, or idea. The key patterns of exposition are process analysis, comparison and contrast, classification, cause and effect, and definition.
fantasy	A form of fiction that deals with unreal or fantastic things.
figurative language	Words used outside of their literal or usual meanings. Figurative language is used to add beauty, increase vitality and impact, suggest associations and comparisons, and develop conciseness.

flashback	A narrative technique in which the writer begins the action in the present and moves to the past. This device can shed light on characters and events by providing background information.
foreshadowing	Clues or hints in a story about what is going to happen.
humor	An amusing or funny element which is warm and genial in tone.
hyperbole	A figure of speech using extravagant exaggeration to emphasize strong feeling and to create a satiric, comic, or sentimental effect. The word *hype*, derived from hyperbole, means to publicize extravagantly.
idiom	A phrase or expression that has a meaning other than its grammatical or logical one.
illustration	Effective writing in any form depends upon illustration, examples that provide details and facts. When you give an example, you offer specific information about a general category. Examples make writing vivid and illustrate the points you wish to make.
imagery	Words, phrases, and figures of speech that appeal to the five senses, and help a reader picture or imagine sensations and ideas.
inference	A reasonable conclusion drawn by the reader about the behavior of a character or the meaning of an event.
irony	A difference or contrast between appearance and reality. Writers use irony to reveal unpleasant or troublesome realities that exist in life, or to poke fun at human weaknesses and foolish attitudes. Irony is a common device in satire. There are three forms of irony: dramatic irony, irony of situation, and verbal irony.
irony, dramatic	When the reader or viewer is aware of something about which the character or characters involved know nothing.
irony of situation	A type of irony in which there is a contrast between what is expected and what actually happens.
irony, verbal	A contrast between what is said and what is actually meant.
jargon	Special words associated with a specific area of knowledge or profession. A form of jargon called *shop talk* is used in the workplace by members of the same trade or organization, but not by those outside the group.
literal meaning	Meaning based on actual fact, in contrast to figurative or symbolic meaning.
metaphor	A figure of speech that implies comparison between two fundamentally different things. The qualities of one are ascribed to the other; one thing is said to be the other. An **extended metaphor** continues throughout a stanza, paragraph, or entire work.

mood	The atmosphere and feeling that a writer creates in a work through the choice of setting, imagery, details, descriptions, and other evocative words.
narrator	The person who tells a story.
narration	Storytelling that makes a point and involves a sequence of related events leading to a conclusion. Narratives, both fiction and nonfiction, have the common elements of setting, plot, character, and point of view. What you tell about depends on your purpose, the meaning you are trying to convey.
paradox	A seemingly contradictory statement that, on closer examination, proves to be true or has elements of the truth. The term is also used for a person or situation that seems to incorporate two opposite elements. "Enough is too much!" is a paradox used by Benjamin Franklin as a caution against overeating or overindulgence of any sort.
paragraph	A paragraph is a group of related sentences that develop one main idea. The paragraph consists of a topic sentence, supporting details, and a concluding sentence. A good paragraph should be unified, coherent, and adequately developed.
personification	A figure of speech in which human characteristics are attributed to animals, objects, or abstract ideas.
persuasion	Writing is classified as persuasion when it is highly emotional, uses biased language, offers opinions, and appeals to feelings and instincts. Writing is classified as argument when it is strictly rational, depends on facts and logical explanation, and appeals to intelligence. When people write to convince others, they appeal to both emotion and reason.
plot	A series of related events that present and resolve a conflict. The usual pattern of plot is conflict, complications, climax, and conclusion.
poetic license	The liberty taken, especially by an artist or writer, in deviating from conventional fact or form to achieve a desired effect.
point of view	The relationship between the narrator of a story and the characters and action in it. The two most common points of view are first person and third person.
point of view, first person	The **first-person** narrator might offer a personal account of his or her own experiences, past or present, or may focus on what happens to other characters. This point of view uses the *I* vantage point, in which the narrator may be the main character or an observer.
point of view, third person	The **third-person** point of view refers to the vantage point of an outside observer who is the narrator of a story. This point of view may be objective, limited, or omniscient.

When the narrator records events without commentary or interpretation, the story is said to have an **objective** point of view. This is also known as the **dramatic** point of view.

The **limited third-person** point of view is a vantage point that centers on one character's thoughts, feelings, and actions.

The **omniscient third-person** point of view presents the narrator as an observer who knows all that the characters see, hear, think, and feel.

process analysis   Process analysis explains how something is done, how something works, or how something occurs. A process is a series of steps leading to a result. A process analysis essay presents each step individually, showing how each step is related to the others, and explains how the steps in the sequence get you from the beginning to the end of the process.

repetition   An essential unifying element in nearly all poetry and much prose. Sounds, syllables, words, phrases, stanzas, ideas, and allusions are repeated for emphasis.

resolution   The final part of a story that makes clear the outcome of the conflict.

sarcasm   A sneering, taunting, attitude in writing designed to hurt by ridiculing or criticizing.

satire   A technique that pokes fun at some weakness or vice in human nature or society. Satire can be gentle and lighthearted or bitter and savage. Exaggeration and irony are frequent devices of satire.

setting   The time, place, and circumstances of a narrative. The setting may serve as a background for characters and events, or help create the atmosphere from which the story evolves.

simile   A figure of speech involving a direct comparison between two unlike things, using words such as *like* or *as*.

slang   Language that uses racy and colorful expressions associated more often with speech than with writing.

style   The expression of the writer's personality and individuality through the choice of words, sentence structure, idea arrangement, tone, mood, and imagery.

symbol   Something concrete, such as an object, person, animal, place, or event that stands for or represents something abstract such as an idea, a quality, a concept, or a condition.

syntax   The order of words in a sentence and their relationship to each other. Good syntax requires correct grammar as well as effective sentence patterns, including unity, coherence, and emphasis.

theme The central idea in an essay is the theme, also known as the thesis. Everything in an essay should support the theme in one way or another.

thesis The main idea or point of an essay.

thesis statement A proposition that clearly conveys the writer's main idea to the reader. This statement appears early in the essay and should be introduced before other supporting ideas.

tone The writer's attitude toward his or her subject, also known as the "voice" given to an essay. Every writer can develop his or her own distinctive tone or voice. Tone is revealed by the author's word choice and arrangement of ideas, events, and descriptions.

total effect The central impression or impact a literary work has on its readers.

transitions Words and phrases used to connect ideas in order to show time, place and position, or relationships between ideas. They are also used to restate main ideas, draw conclusions, or show comparison and contrast.

About the Authors

Sandra Panman M.A., M.P.S., President of Active Learning Corporation, has taught high school and college writing for over thirty years. She is an author and educational consultant. Ms. Panman customizes and presents writing workshops for schools, organizations, and corporations.

Richard Panman Ph.D., Professor Emeritus of psychology, taught for thirty-three years at SUNY New Paltz and facilitated training programs in group dynamics and communication skills. The Panmans have worked together for thirty years as co-authors and workshop leaders.

What Educators Say About Active Learning Textbooks

"The Panmans produce excellent writing handbooks for all levels. Reading, thinking, and writing activities are designed for student success!"
> Dr. Robert Infelise, former Superintendent of Schools
> Carmel, CA

"After a few weeks of working on other materials, my students begged to get back to their Active Learning textbooks."
> Virginia Kelley, English Teacher
> Cartersville High School
> Cartersville, GA

"The books contain short, to-the-point lessons that are easy to read and teach valuable writing concepts."
> Janet Quaine, Special Education Consultant
> White Lake Junior High School
> Milford, MI

Writing Textbooks By Active Learning

- WRITING BASICS
- WRITING ESSENTIALS
- SHORT STORIES
- THE ACTIVE READER FOR WRITERS
- WRITING PORTFOLIO ORGANIZER

Active Learning Corporation

PO Box 254 • New Paltz NY 12561

Phone/ Fax: (845) 255-0844
Website: www.activelearningcorp.com
E-mail: info@activelearningcorp.com